Praise for *From In*

MW00467296

Those who have recently book that would give them a handle on the Bible most likely left the store frustrated, or bought a book that either put out propaganda or propagated diluted sentimentalism. In marked contrast, Edward W. H. Vick's book gives us a most welcome, rigorous, measured, illuminating tour of the concepts that must be considered if one is to understand what the Bible is. Here the Bible is not an abstraction floating in a vacuum. It is the church's book on the basis of two basic principles. It is the mediator of the reality of God, and functions in the church as the provider of meaning for the present. In *From Inspiration to Understanding* the reader finds engaging discussions of concepts like inspiration, revelation, authenticity, authority and others with both feet on the ground. In this process a long list of fallacies are shown to be what they are. Vick's presentation takes its clues from what the Bible actually contains, and builds its arguments according to the demands of serious theological reflection. I highly recommend this book to anyone who desires a better way of reading the Bible, no matter whether one is a believer, a non-believer, a lay person or a member of the clergy.

Herold Weiss, Ph.D., Professor Emeritus of New Testament, St. Mary's College, Notre Dame, IN

Seldom does one read so thoughtful, so disciplined and so scholarly an account of the need to rethink the basis for the authority of Scripture in the Christian church. Vick meets head-on most (if not all) of the difficult issues surrounding the traditional concept of "inspiration" as the foundation of Biblical supremacy for the community. While some may be discomfited by Vick's argument that the traditional understandings are inadequate for the modern church, every reader will greatly profit from taking seriously his urging that we ground biblical authority in the believing community itself. This work should be read by every lay and professional theologian.

James J. Londis, Ph.D., Chair, Department of Humanities, Kettering College

Professor Vick's approach to the Bible is informed, clear, and immensely helpful. If we view the Scriptures as the means by which God is revealed to the community of faith, he argues, we can account for the Bible's authority, without trying to "prove" it. And on this basis, we can appreciate the complex history and varied contents of the Bible, while avoiding the pitfalls that surround mistaken views of "biblical inspiration."

Richard Rice, Professor of Religion, Loma Linda University

Dr. Vick provides a thorough look at the inspiration of the Bible, giving the reader a better grasp at the way scripture should be interpreted. Most importantly, he rediscovers the scriptures to be fundamentally the Church's book, a book that is important only because of God's self-revelation to a people called Israel and Church. *From Inspiration to Understanding* is a helpful resource to any pastor or Bible study teacher interested in knowing what it means for the Bible to be the Word of God.

Rev. Geoffrey Lentz, First United Methodist Church, Pensacola, Florida

From Inspiration to Understanding

Reading the Bible Seriously and Faithfully

Edward W. H. Vick

Energion Publications

2011

Cover Design: Nick May

ISBN10: 1-893729-10-9
ISBN13: 978-1-893729-10-0
Library of Congress Control Number: 2011943673

Energion Publications
P. O. Box 841
Gonzalez, FL 32560

850-525-3916
www.energionpubs.com

Foreword

For the Christian the Bible has always held pride of place. But it has not always been easy to say just what feature or features constitute that position. Not least in our own time there have been many attempts to explain just what is the crucial function of the Bible in the experience of believer and of church. Often that place has been taken for granted, as if it needed no explanation. For many Christians whose devotional use of the Bible has become a part of their life no explanation is needed. But for other Christians in view of our developing understanding of history and of science and serious examination of the documents and their history, it has not always been clear how the uniqueness of the Bible is to be understood and presented. What is to be said about this complex book which will be acceptable both to the simple believer and worshipper and critical scholar? Can we achieve a consensus?

This book is an attempt to clarify the issues, by examining the proposals offered to explain that uniqueness. It is important to understand the notion of authority in a way appropriate to these unique documents that make up the Christian Scripture. The book also attempts to make clear that discussion of how the Bible is interpreted can be a very fruitful exercise.

Edward W. H. Vick

Table of Contents

SUMMARY OF CHAPTER I

APPROACHING THE BIBLE

Since there are different ways of approaching the Bible there are correspondingly different ways of understanding its significance. Only when we look at the ways the church actually uses the Bible can we understand from that practice what to say about its significance. It is a case of putting practice into theory, in this case into theology.

I

WAYS OF APPROACHING THE BIBLE

1 DIFFERENT WAYS: DEVOTIONAL, DOCTRINAL, ANALYTICAL, EXEGETICAL

There are many different ways of approaching the Bible. The Christian reader has his own particular interests in reading and in studying it.

(1) There is, first, the *devotional* use of Scripture. We read it to nurture our faith, to gain 'daily help' from it in the living of life. We relate what the helpful words say to our past memories and to our present experience. In doing this, we find that there are particular sections or passages of the book which make a particular impression and to which we constantly refer. We find that, approached as a book with a message from God to us in our particular situation, we can draw upon its varied resources and get a word of comfort or of courage, of reproof or of warning or whatever sort of word is appropriate for us in our particular circumstances. The words have direct relationship to the living of our life as they bear for us the appropriate word of God. We are not now concerned about a detailed analysis of the writings we read. We do not have to be. Read in this way, the Bible is a treasury of good things, waiting to be opened, explored and appropriated for the living of the life of faith.

What is here true for the individual is also true for the group. As the community comes together for worship, it looks for and gets encouragement as passages from the Bible are read, explained and applied to the experiences of the worshippers. Again, the words of Scripture become the occasion for the worshippers as a group to get comfort, correction, guidance and challenge — in short to hear the word of God, what God has to 'say' to them here and now. The words of Scripture live again in the midst of the church, and the believers are encouraged and strengthened in their faith and their activity. That such things happen is the experience and confession of multitudes of Christians.

(2) A second approach to the Bible we shall call the *doctrinal* approach. Every Christian community holds certain beliefs, and teaches particular doctrines. These teachings make that community different from others. Many Christian communities claim that their teachings are either directly taught in the Bible or are derived from the Bible. The claim is that there is a connection between the doctrine the church teaches and the words of the Bible. Often they will take the further step and claim that the teachings of the church have authority because the Bible, which is the source of those teachings, has authority. The authority of the Bible is, so to speak, transmitted to and represented in the doctrines. Or, it will be said that the teachings represent the church's understanding of Christian faith and life, both individual and in community, as the New Testament accounts represent the understanding of the first century with respect to its faith and its life.

(3) The third approach is the *analytical* approach. Here the questions we put to the text of the Bible are of an *historical and literary kind.* How did the writings come to have the present shape? How were they put together? How do they relate to the time when they were written? You ask who wrote the books and when they were written and want to find the appropriate evidence to give good answers to these questions. Further questions arise. How are the various writings related to one another? In particular you ask, as a Christian, How are the Old and the New Testament related? What constitutes the unity of the Bible? Such questions assume that we have appropriate methods to provide answers.

What you discover in using this approach will have an important bearing upon the first two approaches. How does the believer and the preacher get the encouraging message from the Bible? How does the church formulate its doctrines by reference to the Scripture? What of the claim concerning authority in these matters?

(4) A fourth approach to Scripture takes the text and seeks to render its meaning. This *exegetical* approach is distinct from the others. You must take account of it in giving a summary of the manner in which the Bible functions in the Christian community. Here it uses the text of Scripture as the basis for exposition. The meanings that result serve to maintain the distinctive life and understanding of the church and of the believer.

When you ask the question, 'What *did* the authors of Scripture mean by what they wrote?' you are asking an historical question. When you ask, 'What *do* the words of Scripture mean?' you are asking a different question. Some people would say that once you have found what the Bible meant, you have arrived at your goal. The Christian's job then is to understand and to display that meaning. Please notice that this is a *theory* about how the Bible is to be treated. Other Christians would disagree and say that the Bible is a living book and its interpretation gives us meaning for the present time, and that this is what is important. You will, on this viewpoint, have the complex task of saying both what Scripture *meant*, and also of searching for its present meaning, what it now *means*. The task of grappling with the actual text of Scripture is called *exegesis*. Its aim is to render the meaning, to clarify obscurities, to present the message of the text. It is the work of the commentator, the task of exposition. As such it must be distinguished from the work of explicit theological construction, which may also sometimes refer to the text of Scripture.

We have spoken above of the 'authors' of Scripture, rather than the 'writers,' although that is not entirely satisfactory. There is good reason for this. For the books of Scripture, or at least many of them, were not 'written' in the way a modern book is written. Indeed Bible books were often not written by their 'authors,' if by 'written' one means first, that the author actually put pen to paper and composed the product, engaging in the physical process of scribing his words as he proceeded. A secretary, an amanuensis, or a disciple, might be entrusted with the task of actually scribing the words. Second, the modern author is responsible for the production of all that he 'writes.' Then the author was often more like a collector, compiler or editor than like a 'writer,' in our modern sense, that is one who has himself produced and so is responsible for, all that gets written and published. Indeed sometimes a well-known name was deliberately associated with a particular book.

2 WAYS OF UNDERSTANDING THE SIGNIFICANCE OF THE BIBLE

To each of these approaches there corresponds an understanding of the significance, status and authority of the Bible.[1] What is the primary reason for the status the Bible has in the church?

The Bible is not primarily and characteristically a textbook of doctrines, nor a book of edification, that is to say of building up the teaching and the piety or the church. It is not primarily and characteristically an historical source. The reason that Protestant churches have given the Bible the place of primacy is not because it edifies, 'not because it builds up what is established but because it does the establishing.'[2] The Bible has occupied the place of primacy in the Protestant churches because it is indispensable for the very existence of the churches.

Once the church existed but Christian Scripture did not. This is of course the very earliest period of the church's existence. The church's one foundation is Jesus Christ. So we have the task of working out how the Protestant conviction of the primacy of Scripture, the 'indispensable' Scripture is related to the church's foundation. What is the relation between Jesus confessed as the Christ and the written Scripture confessing him and serving as the means for continuing faith and confession?

To each of the approaches we have outlined there are appropriate attitudes, appropriate questions and appropriate silences. Let us take them briefly, one by one.

When you read the Bible devotionally you are not questioning it. You simply make yourself available for whatever edification and help you can gain from it. Nor, when reading the Bible devotionally does the thought that it is infallible naturally occur to you, the reader. In the attitude of devotion, that is not the sort of thing that you would affirm or deny. When you read the Bible for devotional purposes you don't think of that.[3]

It is when you become aware of the disputes among churchmen and the ideas which they discuss, that you begin to ask questions about the status of Scripture. And it is of course true that some ideas and discussions can be very helpful. Others can seriously waste our time and divert our energies. One of these is prolonged discussion of the idea of infallibility.

If you are an intelligent reader of Scripture you will be bound to have questions about Scripture when you begin to think about what you read. You will ask the ordinary questions you ask about any ancient book. These are questions about style, composition, worldview and about the transmission and preservation of the text.

One of the most important and interesting questions is about the church's doctrinal use of Scripture.[4]

The word 'doctrine' has reference to what is taught in a particular community at a particular time. It is thus *recognised* teaching. How does such teaching come to be recognised? The answer is, quite simply, that certain people come to agree about it. Orthodox doctrine is doctrine agreed about by a group. The term 'theology' refers to the effort to understand the Christian faith and to express it discursively, that is to say, in words, concepts, systems of thought, arguments. Such faith can also be expressed in other ways, for example in liturgy, in art, in moral activity. The theologian serves the church by scrutinising the doctrine it professes to teach. Now our question is this: How is the acknowledged doctrine related to Scripture? How is the teaching derived from Scripture?

This is the question about the *relationship between the Bible and the doctrine*. How do you get from the Bible to the doctrine? What are the principles of interpretation which are used in the exposition of Scripture? What sort of frameworks are considered appropriate, and why?

There is no easy answer to this question, nor is there simply one answer to it. The different Christian churches derive their doctrine from Scripture in different ways. It is well that we are aware of this and ask how it is done. When we address the question: 'How is the particular doctrinal statement derived from the Scripture upon which it is based?' we shall discover that the answer to that question is complex.[5]

Let's reverse the familiar advice, 'Put your theory into practice!' and adopt the slogan, 'Put your practice into theory.' That will guide us in what follows. Let us see what the church actually does in respect of the Bible and insist that the account (the theory) it provides properly represents that practice. So we ask as our basic question, 'What does the church *do* with the Bible?'

3   PUTTING PRACTICE INTO THEORY

If you want to correct an erroneous theoretical explanation, you will have to show that the practice of the church is not adequately represented in the doctrine, and then propose an alternative construction of the doctrine.

Theology, in our case, as so often, is a four-fold activity. You describe the practice of the church. You test doctrine in relation to that practice. You qualify, correct or replace the doctrine when it fails to represent that practice. You propose doctrine which would lead to a revision of practice. Serious theology does not simply represent the practice of the church without questioning it. Should it understand the practice to be at fault, it will begin by describing what that practice is, and then proceed to make constructive suggestions for a different practice. In proceeding this way the theologian is being practical, and, if people understand, discuss and take heed, there will be positive and creative work within the community of faith. Such discussion will make a difference to the doctrine of the church on the one hand and to its practice on the other. But it is seriously misleading to speak as if there were a dichotomy between theory and practice. Practice influences our theory and just as, if not more important, our theory influences our practice. Hence the primary importance of theological discussion.

4 THE CHURCH'S ACTUAL PRACTICE IN USING THE BIBLE

What is the church's actual practice with regard to the use of the Bible? Are all portions of the Bible from beginning to end given the same attention in the public and private reading and upon the occasions where there is opportunity for exposition? Does the reading and exposition of certain books and passages assume greater significance than others? Are there passages and portions of the Bible which are never read at all and so play an insignificant part in the church's understanding? Are there other passages which are used over and over again in public worship, private reading and in exposition and in the construction of doctrine? What is the significance of these practices for an understanding of the Bible?

It is to such questions that we shall address ourselves as we discuss the issues of the interpretation and the authority of the Bible. By 'Bible' we mean *the whole* of the sixty-six books of the Old and New Testaments. This whole we call the 'canon.' These are the books the Christian church agreed upon. It agreed and agrees that it is right to set them apart from all other books. The church of today is one with the church of yesterday in so acting. It affirms the distinctiveness of *these* books. The church of today goes on endorsing the decision which was made long ago that these books, and these books only, should be separated out from all others and given a special place in the Church. They are, in some sense, primary. That is a tradition all Christians accept, one tradition upon which they agree. But it is a *tradition*. It is a tradition which most Christians go on accepting without asking about it, without asking why it should be so, and without asking who made the decisions that it should be so.

Now an interesting development has taken place in the last two hundred years in regard to the study of the Bible. Serious, dedicated, intensive and methodical study of the Bible has taken place and is taking place independent of the particular and partisan interests of any particular church. You can undertake study of Scripture without having the particular doctrinal concerns of a particular section of the Christian community in mind. Such biblical studies have developed in non-church related institutions and without the special interests of particular denominations. Many churches have gradually come to recognize that they must take the results and the methodologies of such studies seriously.

What this means is that there is a need to consider older positions, such as for example were proposed at the time of the Reformation. Gone is the time when a sarcastic cartoon, a cliché, or a label was enough to dismiss such analytic work on the Bible. Such work has in some form or other influenced all Christian churches. Gone is the time when it was enough to *assert* a non-historical interpretation of the Bible, to entrench behind a dogmatic position, and stop one's ears and hide one's eyes from the obvious progress which historical study of the Bible involved. Fortunately, we may now say, an analytic method of Bible study is now very widely accepted. Recognition and acceptance of this fact has meant renewed understanding of the Bible in our time. It is not to be thought abstract, 'clinical,' and remote from the concerns of the church. Nothing could be more misleading than such an unsympathetic prejudice.

So in our introductory chapter let us point again to the importance of *what the church actually does* with Scripture. We may here, as in other spheres of our experience, often learn more correctly what the attitude of the group is from what it actually does, from its actual practice, than from what it says, what it proposes as its formal belief or attitude. For example, statements of doctrine in some churches propose that the Bible is in all its parts the Word of God, and have a quite specific way of understanding that claim. That has appeared in official statements and is widely held as a formal belief. In actual practice the situation may be very different from what the formal doctrine would lead us to expect.

What then of the practice of the church in its actual attitude to and use of the books, chapters and verses of Scripture? Here are some pieces of evidence:

(1) The church makes selections from the Scriptures, giving greater importance to some passages than to others.

(2) It often employs Scripture to support and to endorse the doctrines it teaches.

(3) Certain of these doctrines come to have an importance above others. Hence the Scripture which 'supports' such central doctrine assumes special significance.

All Christians in fact do what Luther did. They do not all admit, as Luther did, what it is they are doing.

> . . . Luther, who mightily invoked the authority of Scripture to challenge that of Rome, yet who dismissed the Letter of James as an "epistle of straw," declared that the Word of God to Moses was not the Word to Luther, therefore not binding upon him . . . . A fundamentalist today may claim that no one should "tamper with God's Holy Word," yet he or she will by no means feel obliged to obey all the laws of the Old Testament.' 'As the New Testament advises us to 'test the spirits to see whether they are of God,' so I think we need to test the Scriptures. Indeed, I believe we already do this. As I have already pointed out, people pick and choose their levels of authority in the Bible, *yet we rarely confess that we are doing so.* It takes a Luther, a Sölle, and other bold people to say of a certain part of

the Bible, "I won't pay any attention to that," though this is what the rest of us are doing all the time. The New Testament writers, in their use of the Old, did the same.[6]

The process of selecting from Scripture what appeals to us and of neglecting the rest is made not only for the sake of building up a doctrinal system, but also in the public and private worship of the church. Some Christians make the discussion of faith central and so appeal to the writings of Paul. Others concern themselves primarily with the apocalyptic books. In such a case *Daniel* and *Revelation* become *effectively* more important than the Gospels for that community. For others contemplation of the life of Jesus is of first importance. Then the Gospels are of primary importance. If we ask: 'As a *matter of practice* what actually happens?' we must have regard for what the church does rather than what its formal teaching might lead us to think.

Since it is clear that use of the Bible is selective, we certainly must take that into account in developing a doctrine of the authority of Scripture. What this means is that in giving an account of the church's practice we shall point to two facts: first, the church claims that the Bible has unique authority; and second, in her practice and her use of Scripture some parts are more frequently referred to, some are built into a doctrinal scheme, others are passed over. The Bible, whose uniqueness the church acknowledges in her doctrine, is never uniformly treated as equally important in all its parts. If it were it could not support the doctrine of the uniqueness of Scripture.

5   TWO RIVAL VIEWS OF THE BIBLE: A DILEMMA?

So there is something of a dilemma between two rival views of the Bible.[7] Allowing for a certain latitude in the meaning of the term 'inspired,' we can for the present let the assertion stand that all Christians believe that the Bible is inspired. But the question, 'How is the Bible inspired?' gives rise to different answers. These answers stand in opposition to one another. One is the conservative view, the other the liberal-critical view. (We must not of course get stalled with names, but it is convenient to have some labels, to point to what may well be 'ideal types.') The conservative view stresses that the words are inspired, that the Holy Spirit is the author of the very words of Scripture. It teaches (in the judgment of one writer) 'a peculiarly materialistic conception of the inspiration of the Bible, identifying its truth with rigid exactness in matters of physical fact.'[8] The emphasis here is on the inerrancy of the Bible. Since God spoke through the writings, they are guaranteed to be free of all error. This is the view not only of the conservative Protestant. It is also the officially stated view of the Roman Catholic Church. The writers rendered with infallible truth all that God commanded. The Bible is unassailable, for its truth is God's truth. Hence all of its statements are true.[9]

The other view recognizes as of primary importance that the writers of the Bible lived at particular times and in particular places, that since they were human they were conditioned by the understanding of their time. They lived in particular circumstances, under specifiable historical conditions, which provided the milieu, the context in which they worked, thought and spoke. That context can be studied historically. Light is shed on the words they wrote by an historical analysis of the contexts and procedures which influenced them.

The Jewish and Christian faiths are historical. The events which give meaning to faith were historical events. The Exodus, the rise of the prophets, the coming of Jesus, the setting down in writing of the messages of important spokesmen, the compilation, preservation and interpretation of such writings — all these are historical events. That means that they can be studied historically.

One of the great events of recent times is the development of the historical method. It has revolutionized our outlook. We now know so much more than people two centuries ago could know about the composition of the Bible, the history of Israel, of the early Christian movement and of the relationship of the writings of the Bible to that history. This has been the result of a dedicated, painstaking and continuing application of the historical method to the Bible. We now carefully consider what we may call the humanity of the persons we study, the social conditions of the time in which they lived and the nature of the experience of individual and group. We put questions to the Bible and carefully analyse its text and content, according to well-established literary and historical principles.

The fact that the Bible has a special and irreplaceable authority in the Christian church is not in question when the historical, analytical, critical approach is used. In fact the historical studies of the last two centuries have made it possible to answer questions which the traditional view either did not consider (and which it should have considered), or which it considered inappropriate. Such historical studies have enabled us to find answers to problems of interpretation we had not hitherto been capable of solving.

This can be disturbing. When we question older positions we have to consider anew what we mean by the authority of the Bible. But the labours of such dedicated scholars are labours of love, seeking for truth and understanding, often the labours of sincere Christians.

The contrast between these two approaches can be put in various ways. An unquestioning acceptance of the text of the Bible is set over against a dedicated effort to establish the text that we are best able to achieve, even if this means the raising and the consideration of critical questions.

Some doctrines of the Bible's authority so emphasise the divine that they minimise, even overlook, the humanity, the historicity, of the 'writers' of the Bible. The writers of the biblical books were human beings with limitations of understanding and experience. Of course, some had extraordinary gifts and perception.

The belief that there is a *direct* divine source of all that is written in Scripture contrasts with the principle that the place to start is where and when the human writer lived and see life as far as is possible in the light of the history we are able to reconstruct. This means dealing first with the text, and *then* framing a theory of inspiration, of revelation, of canon.

Emphasise the non-historical, the supra-natural in sharp contrast to the historical, the divine rather than the human and you then think of the person as the supernaturally inspired spokesperson for the divine. Their native abilities are in abeyance as the divine spirit takes over. But why set divine authority in contrast to, even in opposition to, the human character of the biblical writings? Why claim that where God acts the human diminishes to the vanishing point? The principle of incarnation, that the divine reveals himself through the human, sets itself against such an extreme view.

Can one reasonably affirm the divine authority of Scripture and at the same time recognize the genuine humanity of its writers? Can Christians believe the Bible to have unique religious authority and at the same time accept the genuine humanity and historicity of the writings? Is there a way of affirming that the Scriptures are both the word of God *and* the word of men? It would seem that the Christian, holding the fundamental principle of incarnation, that God operates through the human, should be striving for a position which can do full justice to both sides of what, expressed in an exaggerated form, leads to paradox. The heavenly treasure is contained in earthen vessels. Recognise the humanity and historicity of the 'writer' and he is then the discerning and perceptive human being speaking out of his understanding and discernment at a particular time and to a specific situation. To give a theological expression to this principle in relation to the Bible, to affirm that the human is a suitable vehicle for the divine: — that would seem to be the task.

In what follows we shall seek to present a carefully studied account of the Bible which will try to do justice to both of these interests: an interest in the divine authority and in the genuine humanity of the writers. We shall not 'plead' for either, but move forward in the belief that in trying to account for both we can arrive at a balanced and reasonable Christian account of the Bible.

We shall not shirk the real problems, but in every case we shall try first to see clearly what the facts are. We must not turn aside from the facts of the matter, but give them their due weight as we try to provide a theological account of the Scriptures. No theology is worthy if it finds it inconvenient to pass over salient facts. In our exposition we shall find ourselves constantly coming back to the facts of the matter.

CHAPTER I NOTES

[1]Martin Kähler in *The So-called Historical Jesus*, develops this threefold rubric.

[2]*Ibid.*, p. 130.

[3]'Whether the writers of the New Testament are infallible or not is a question which rarely occurs to me. Somehow when they tell me a truth, I come to know it for myself; the truth is mine and not merely theirs.' R. W. Dale, quoted in Albert Peel, 'The Bible and the People,' in C. W. Dugmore, *The Interpretation of the Bible*, p. 72. ff.

[4]See the suggestions based on case studies of contemporary theologians in David H. Kelsey, *The Uses of Scripture in Recent Theology.*

[5]See below: chapters IX to XI address some problems involved in interpreting the text of Scripture.

[6]Tom Driver, *Christ in a Changing World*, pp. 86, 94.

[7]A. G. Hebert, *The Authority of the Old Testament*. London: Faber and Faber, 1947. pp. 23-42.

[8]*Ibid.*, p. 25.

[9]See below: Chapter V. 7,8, where we discuss the concepts of inerrancy and infallibility.

Summary of Chapter II

Canon

It is by looking back at the story of how the books came to be accepted and used that we can understand why there are just sixty-six in the canon of Scripture. It was a gradual process both in the case of the Old Testament and of the New. Some of the books were read more widely and valued more highly than others. By producing a list of accepted books, the church arrived at a unity about them, which has been accepted ever since. But there is a distinction between a formal canon and the canon in use, even if the church holds to the principle of *sola scriptura*.

II
CANON

1 SIXTY-SIX BOOKS

'In the Bible there are sixty-six books, Genesis to Revelation.'
This statement expresses the fact in its most obvious sense that
there is wide diversity between the various component writings
that make up the whole Bible. It expresses the fact that there are a
great number of writings coming from different times, different
places, different persons, written in different styles and with
different purposes in mind.

'In the Bible there are two books: the Old Testament and the
New Testament.' expresses the fact that there were separate
collections of literature, one of thirty-nine and the other of twenty-
seven pieces. One is called 'old,' and the other is called 'new.' This
expresses their difference. It also expresses the fact that they were
considered to have sufficient unity for both to go by the same
name, the name of 'testament'!

'The Bible is one book, the Holy Scriptures.' We speak of the
unity of these diversified materials. We think of these sixty-six, and
these two, books as in some sense one. We must not take this unity
for granted.

Why are there in this collection sixty-six books, no more and
no less? Why did the Old Testament get put alongside the New
Testament? Why is it in this case, as in no other religion, that

Christians have taken over *as a whole* the book of another religion, a book moreover which is very considerably longer than their own distinctive writings? Why did those who read the Old Testament alongside the New Testament call it the '*Old* Testament'? The Hebrews called it the Tanach or 'The Law, the Prophets and the Writings.' It was thus itself the putting together of three books, each of which had its own story. Why did they put these three books together? Why did they, as the later Christians did, then treat them as one book?

Further questions arise. What has the recognition of the books as special, unique, got to do with their being put together, used and preserved? How did they, whoever *they* were, come to recognize just this number of books? Why does the contemporary Christian accept their decision about which were the books to put in and which to leave out of the collection?

Most Christians never even raise the question. They find a trimly bound book, sometimes printed on India paper and edged with gold, with the title 'The Holy Bible,' and they take for granted that it has unique authority for their faith and for their church, and are not the least bit concerned that this collection of writings has had a history. But the collection as it is now is not the same as the collection it has been at other times and in other places. Sometimes there have been more than sixty-six and sometimes effectively rather less.

2   THE IMPORTANCE OF THE STORY OF THE BIBLE

It is essential then that we look back. The reason is that unless we look back at their history we shall not be able to understand, let alone answer, the question, 'Why does the Christian community take these particular books to be distinctive?' An adequate doctrine of the Bible must give careful consideration to the story of the book. 'The history of the canon can and must be the foundation on which any modern doctrine of Scripture shall be built.'[1] When we examine that history, we find that decisions which make a difference to the books considered were taken at specific times and with good reason. 'For some who first discover as adults that the canon has not always been as we now have it, but came about via a long and complex history, serious questions about its inspiration and authority may arise.'[2]

Christians took over the Jewish Scriptures *as a* whole. The Bible, a set of documents, came from a time span of at least a thousand years. That is a very, very long time. The Old Testament represents traditions which go back even further than that. It is an extremely varied collection of many kinds of literature. So it is fitting that we address ourselves to two questions: first, how did this collection of writings come to be written and put together i.e. become a whole; and second, how did this collection of writings come to be acknowledged and accepted as 'sacred' writings? Other writings did not. Why these? Why were some taken and others left?

The first important point is that the books circulated and were given a standing in the community. In the case of the Old Testament it was the Jewish community. Members of that community read them and chose them from among others. The standing they had in the community derived from the experience and the judgment of that community, as it read and used them. These writings *gained* an authority which other books did not. In due course they achieved a status. They became sacred books.

It is interesting that the term 'scripture,' which etymologically simply means 'writing,' has itself come to acquire a special meaning, namely writings which have particular value for religions, and so 'holy' writings, writings set aside from ordinary use, writings which 'defile the hands.' Such holy writings are distinguished from others by being set aside, considered as having a special status and repeatedly used within the religious community.

3 THE OLD TESTAMENT

The process by which the books of the Old Testament came to have authority was a gradual one. It was complete roughly by the beginning of the Christian era. The books of the Old Testament are divided into three groups: the *Torah*, or Law, the *Nebi'im* or Prophets and the *Kethubim*, or Writings. The Prophets are divided into two and called the Former Prophets and the Latter Prophets. The Former Prophets include the history books.

The Law includes narratives of ancient Israel and codes of law. The whole is divided into five parts and thus comes to be known as the Pentateuch. This collection is the core of the Old Testament. It was the first to become recognized as sacred literature by the Jews. It was promulgated by Ezra and was the foundation of the Jewish community after the Exile (which ended 538 BC). It thereafter had a special status in Jewish life.

The Prophets, the second section, includes writings separated by several centuries. Later prophets quote earlier ones. The writings representing the earlier prophets were in circulation before the later prophets wrote. By about 200 B.C., a body of writings other than the Law was in circulation. However, we must stress, this does not mean that such a body of writings is fixed and settled, either as to its text or as to its extent. Obviously such a book-collection is incomplete until the last book to be written is included. If this is Zechariah, or a part of it, that will be about 135 B.C.

The *Writings*, the third section, is a collection of different kinds of literature. It began with a small group of writings which grew as time passed. It includes the 'wisdom literature' namely Proverbs, Ecclesiastes and Job. There is poetry, the Psalms, the hymn book of the second temple. Psalms came to be significant because of its being used in worship. So the *Writings* established themselves as having special importance through the use to which they were put, long before the Christian era.

This does not mean that the boundary between the scriptural and non-scriptural books was clearly, formally and decisively drawn. It is *usage* that provides the basis for more formal recognition. The fact is that collections of writings, which include other books than these, the *Law*, the *Prophets* and the *Writings*, were being used in Jewish communities, for example by the Essenes and at Alexandria.

If the Jews were not clear as to the extent and the limits of their canonical literature, how could Christians be clear about it? The debate continued long into the Christian era.[3]

Meanwhile the Greek culture and language sponsored by the successors of Alexander the Great (who died 323 B.C.) had spread throughout the empire. The international language was Greek, a language used in ordinary human affairs. It was called *koine* (common) Greek. The Jews who lived in the cosmopolitan centres in the Empire understood Greek and used it. They lost the ability to speak Aramaic. To make the Jewish Scriptures available to this population, a group of scholars translated the Hebrew Scripture into the Greek language. Ptolemy II (285 - 246 B.C.) sponsored them. The result was the Septuagint, sometimes known by the symbol LXX, the Latin term for 'seventy'. The atmosphere in Alexandria where it was produced was liberal and it may well be that a longer canon was accepted there than elsewhere. There was uncertainty regarding the extent of the canon.

Jerusalem fell in A.D. 70. Jewish leaders felt it imperative to settle the question of the limits of the canon and so to put an end to uncertainty about it. Meanwhile Christian writings were in circulation, and apocalyptic writings were becoming very popular indeed. The so-called Council of Jamnia in A.D. 90 limited the Old Testament canon to the non-Greek books, which they believed were in existence before prophecy had ceased. It ceased, they thought, in the period after the Exile. Since the *Law* and the *Prophets* had already been decided, it was a question of fixing the limits of the *Writings*. The criterion was that the book be in harmony with the Torah.[4]

Jews who became Christians brought the Septuagint, the Greek version of their Scriptures, with them. Paul knew it well and quoted from it. Gentiles, who accepted the Christian faith, found the Old Testament already in an authoritative position. They accepted its authority and assumed its inspiration. They all knew that Jesus quoted the Old Testament. They knew also that Christian preachers held it in esteem, using it in teaching, counselling and proclamation.

The church thus readily accepted the Old Testament into its life and witness without question. They believed that God had inspired these writings. This understanding of inspiration was in due course applied to the Christian writings themselves. However when the New Testament refers to 'Scripture' or to 'inspiration,' it has in mind some book or books of the Old Testament.

What was the underlying reason why the canon as a whole, that is to say a certain body of books, was accepted by Christians? To this question there is an historical and a theological answer. Christians achieved community as they read their experiences in the light of the ideas and experiences of the Hebrew community. The new community of Christians thought of itself as in continuity with the older community, the Hebrew people. With the coming of Jesus and of faith in him, something decisive had happened, and now for the first time the language of the Old Testament was applied to Jesus. Christians saw him as the fulfilment of Old Testament hopes. Some of the New Testament writings were written with the Jew particularly in mind, for example *Matthew* and sections of Romans. 'Christ' was itself a key term.

Christians inherited the idea of a holy book. The New Testament books were produced in the context of a community which accepted the Old Testament as a holy book. So the New Testament speaks of 'scripture.' The New Testament refers to the *book* with the words, 'It is written.' The New Testament writers see the events which are their central concern as fulfilling what that book, the Old Testament, had said. That is not, of course, a sufficient ground for putting the two collections of books together and treating them as one, as a unity. They could have emerged as two independent collections. Or, since the events of the New Testament were treated as fulfilments of the Old Testament prophecies, the New Testament could have superseded the Old. What was the point of retaining the Old? Why did they not say that the prophecy has been rendered redundant by its fulfilment and dispense with it? Why take the two together as one complete whole? The New Testament believers and writers thought of themselves as part of the ongoing history. They believed their history to be in continuity with the events in the history of the Hebrew people. The God who had acted in that history had now acted in the new event, the event of Jesus Christ. So the earlier history could now be understood in relation to the faith in Jesus Christ which was the unifying feature of the new community. Christians took the Hebrew past as their own past. They found a 'fit' between themselves and that Hebrew past, with its developing belief in God.

Once Christians expressed this continuity by adopting the book of the Jews as their own they had to undertake the task of interpreting the Old Testament in a suitable way. For there was much there. Could it, in all of its diversity, be christianised?[5]

For the writers whose works appear in our New Testament, the only book which could be called 'Scripture' was the Old 'Testament.' This was their only written source of authority. By the end of the first century there were collections of Jesus' sayings.[6] The epistles of Paul were known and so were the Synoptic Gospels. II Peter is probably the latest book of our New Testament, a pseudonymous book as all the evidence indicates. It informs us that Paul's writings are being misinterpreted and perverted. This means that they have begun to be taken as Scripture. The crucial passage reads: 'There are some things in them (that is the Pauline letters) hard to understand, which the ignorant and unstable twist to their own destruction, as they do the other Scriptures.'[7] What then are these 'other Scriptures'?

The Scriptures being accepted are the Old Testament. Then there are the letters of Paul, to which II Peter makes direct reference in this passage.[8] The fact that II Peter speaks of these in the plural means that there are many which he knows, including some of the later ones. II Peter alludes to the Gospel of Mark, in the reference to the transfiguration.[9] So he knows and probably recognizes the Gospels as Scripture. If II Peter is typical, we have a good idea of the situation at the beginning of the second century.

To sum it up then: By around A.D. 100 Christians have accepted Old Testament books, Paul's letters, and Gospels.

4   THE WORD 'CANON'

Now, a brief comment about the word *canon*. This word, *kanon* in Greek, had a variety of meanings, and was rather loosely used in early times. It meant a carpenter's measure or rule, or (like a row of numbers on a measure) a list. A canon was an ideal standard, something which served as a norm. So canonical people or books were those whose names were found on a list. A collection of writings is called a 'canon,' for example at Alexandria, because it sets a standard and can serve as a model.

The term *canon,* when used of 'Scripture,' has three distinct meanings. All of them point to a collection of writings taken to have authority, to be unique. The word *canon* can be used of the books first, as they set the standard; secondly, as they conform to a standard; and thirdly, as they are found on a list.

Canonical books are recognized books. Recognition involves decision. Somebody at a particular place and time recognized such books. Somebody eventually drew up a list and, in so doing, expressed a judgment about the books on it and those not on it. To produce such a selection required a principle of selection. It takes time, a considerable amount of time, several centuries, for such a selection to be completed.

5   THE NEW TESTAMENT

We can trace the stages in this process. First the books are written and that process, in regard to the New Testament, takes us to the second century. Then the books circulate in the churches. This involves somebody copying them by hand, and taking them from one place to another, storing them carefully, at a time when Christianity was not a recognized religion and its meetings for worship were illegal. The next stage is that some people in different places, say Antioch, Jerusalem, Alexandria, make a collection of the books and arrange them in an order which other churches throughout the Empire recognize. So a *general* recognition began to grow that there was a collection of books, some of them written by apostles, or by people associated with apostles and others of them *thought* to have been written by such people. These books helped the growing church to become stable in its beliefs in face of challenges. Gradually and with good reason it dawned on the leaders of the churches that it would be helpful to have the collection clearly defined. Lists of accepted books were produced and the different churches largely agreed. That list of books corresponds to the books which now appear in our Bibles. The compilation of a list of books which corresponds to our New Testament takes us into the fourth century.

The process is called canonization. To produce such a canon involves that those who make the selection know many books other than the books they finally recognize. Most contemporary Christians do not know of, let alone have read, other books than the books which came to be canonical. So they are not in a position to make a judgment about them and about the propriety of the selection. If one is not acquainted with the books not included how does one know that they were wisely excluded?

The alternative is simply to accept the decision of the church in the long ago past on these matters. Whether one realizes it or not that is what one is doing if one simply takes the Bible for granted.

Consider the following most interesting statement by Eusebius who wrote about AD 325.

> Now the writings which bear the name of Peter, of which I recognize only one epistle as genuine and acknowledged by the elders of olden time, are so many; while the fourteen epistles of Paul are manifest and clear (as regards their genuineness). Nevertheless it is not right to be ignorant that some have rejected the Epistle to the Hebrews, saying that it is disputed by the church of the Romans as not being Paul's.[10]

Eusebius knew many writings that bore the name of Peter. But, drawing on the judgment of the elders, that is to say, sources from the second and third centuries, he recognized only one writing as genuine which bore the name of Peter. It was not sufficient that the book be attributed to an apostle. But, it counted against it, if it could not be, as in the case of the book of Hebrews. Eusebius knew a lot of other books and made his judgment about the worthiness of what we call the first epistle of Peter on the basis of that knowledge, and on the basis of the attitude of former church teachers. It is clear that he has rejected II Peter, a book which appears in our New Testament. There were other writers who also found II Peter not to be genuine.

To put some books in means to leave others out. Why were the twenty-seven put in and the other dozens left out? Who decided that? Was it a good choice? Do we want to endorse that decision? If we do not, what difference does it make? There was no shortage of books. Many were left aside. Others did not survive. By the middle of the second century there were many writings. As well as the twenty-seven books which Christians are familiar with from their New Testament there were such books as the two Epistles of Clement, the Didache, or The Teaching of the Twelve Apostles, the Shepherd of Hermas, Letters of Ignatius, the Epistle of Barnabas, Polycarp, various Gospels and Apocalypses, the Wisdom of Solomon.

Already there were different assessments of all these books. Not all churches agreed as to what were and were not acceptable books, as to which ones were written and which ones were not written by apostles or by someone closely associated with an apostle. From early lists we know that there were several disputed books, books whose standing as Scripture was questioned. These were Hebrews, James, II Peter, II and III John, Jude and Revelation.[11] These books were included in later lists, but in assessing their position, we should not overlook the fact of earlier judgments about them. From the beginning the church was aware that some of the books it would later endorse were less important, and less widely accepted than were others, less important in particular than the Gospels and the letters of Paul.

It was not until judgments and lists began to appear that it could not agree with, that the church made an effort to secure uniformity.

The heretic Marcion produced a list of books which led the church to give attention to the matter. By the end of the fourth century the church came to agree, almost unanimously, on the twenty-seven books which form our New Testament.[12] That decision and that list was handed down and was accepted thereafter as right. The limits of the Christian Bible had (it seemed) been finally decided upon. After the list had appeared in the Festal Letter of Athanasius in A.D. 376 there is no serious question as to which books constituted the New Testament.

It is important to observe that while councils made such pronouncements, it was not the pronouncements that established the authority of the books. The books were not authoritative because they were included on a list, because a council or two, or an archbishop or two, or a pope or two, pronounced them so. They were included on the list *because they had already won recognition.* The fact that a list is made does not confer status on the books. It constitutes a formal recognition that the books have performed and are performing a most important function in the church. It gives formal recognition to a state of affairs in the church. These books were the books the communities were reading and were finding helpful in promoting their life and mission, worship and proclamation. The church *in her practice* had already settled the question. The pronouncements of the synods and the lists drawn up endorsed and expressed the implications of that practice.

Christians pronounced on the limits of the Canon for three particular reasons:

(1)   to exclude heretical books, such as those of the Gnostics, whose teachings ran counter to the teachings of Christianity.

(2)   because an unsatisfactory list of writings had appeared. This was Marcion's canon. Marcion separated the God of the Old Testament (whom he rejected) from the God of Jesus. He 'mutilated' Luke and dismembered the letters of Paul,[13] so as to make them agree with his teaching. These two reasons are historical ones.

(3) Underlying them is the theological conviction that for a collection of books to have authority, you have to be quite clear which books are to be included. The limits of that collection must be clearly fixed.

When the books are taken as doctrinal sources, as providing the resources for true teaching, it is obviously necessary to know precisely which books are to be taken in this way, and which other writings are not. If we are going to get authoritative guidance for both practice and teaching, we have to know which are reliable books to give such guidance, and which are not. A decision is appropriate, provided such guidance is sought for. Agreement in the Christian community that certain teachings, for example about faith, about Jesus, about the resurrection of believers, are true, goes along with an agreement about those books that teach correctly. So the ideas of heresy and of unacceptable writings develop together in the formative period of the church's growth. So do the ideas of orthodoxy and of canon.

But what do we mean when we say that the church used, endorsed and then formally recognized particular writings?

We should not take for granted the idea that Scripture is holy. Christopher Evans raises the question sharply. He asks, 'Is Holy Scripture Christian?'[14] The fact is that the books of the New Testament came to be *regarded* as holy Scripture. How did they? Various explanations have been offered.

(1) The writings came to have authority because of their contents.
(2) The writings came to have authority because they were written by authors who were recognised as having authority, by apostles.
(3) The writings come to have authority because they are included on a list which is considered authoritative, that is to say canonical.

A writing comes to have influence as it is read widely and accepted as helpful and edifying for the growing and struggling

Christian community. Because it actually built up the communities the writing would, by that very fact, have approved itself. It would have shown its worth, its merit. It would then be accepted as authoritative, because it had shown and was showing its value in its effectiveness. It exhibited its 'authority' by its effects. It thus ensured its place in the actual life of the church. This is what some writers mean when they say that it is 'self-authenticating.' It is not necessary to appeal from the writings and their effect in edifying the church to some other, external, criterion, for example: to who wrote them, or to whether they appear on a list which is officially accepted. It is enough that they nurture the faith of the community.

The books at first held their place because of their effect upon the groups of believers who read them. Paul's writings were effective. They built up the piety and unity, doctrinal and practical, of the congregations to which they were addressed, and of the wider church in due course. This is what, I take it, Evans means when he says that the books made 'profound religious sense.' That was at the beginning. 'It is, however, the case that the criterion of self-authentication is speedily overtaken by that of authorship, and the writings are then on their way to becoming canonical on other grounds.'[15] Evans prefers such self-authentication to the appeal to apostolicity, finding that the evidence does not permit us to establish the 'authority' of the books on the ground of their being traceable either directly or indirectly to an apostle as their source. He regards such apostolicity as a fiction, a fabrication.

6   THE CANON AND THE QUESTION OF INSPIRATION

Christians inherited a doctrine of inspiration from the Jews. The doctrine of inspiration was later made into a very elaborate scheme and led to no little confusion. One thing is noteworthy. The term itself is not in evidence in the earliest judgments of the church about Scripture. Only much later did it become in some circles *the* standard, *the* orthodox way of speaking of the authority of the Bible. But from the beginning it was not so. And with good reason. You can, as did the early church, affirm the primary importance of Scripture without elaborating a theory of inspiration.

Would it be true to say that the books considered canonical had qualities which the doctrine of inspiration was later to emphasize? Are we able to say: because *we* recognize the books are inspired, we endorse *their* decision? But the fact is that it is just as difficult to determine whether a book is inspired as it is to say whether it is canonical We have already seen that the word 'canonical' has at least three meanings, namely (1) functioning in the community in a special way; (2) apostolic, that is traceable to an apostle or a close associate of one; and (3) being included on a list.

We shall discover that the term *inspiration* is also ambiguous and that we can give no simple answer to questions we have here raised. We do not simplify the problem by introducing a theory of inspiration to establish canonicity.

One procedure would be to accept the decision about the canon and *starting there* proceed to discuss inspiration. Or, one might start rather earlier, look at the practice of the church, consider the books available and ask whether, for whatever reasons, the books they chose were wisely chosen. One might then relate the reasons for accepting the books to the discussion of inspiration.

To conclude this section:

(1) We cannot determine whether a book is canonical by finding out whether that book is inspired.

(2) We cannot infer from how the book got written whether or not it has authority in the community. These are two different questions and we must not confuse them.

(3) We cannot, without further ado, i.e. without further thought and investigation, simply accept the claim that the book or the writer is inspired or has authority, even if the book makes the claim for itself.

(4) We must appeal to facts external to the writing to determine whether that writing has authority.

(5) It is not sufficient to appeal to the fact that a book is included in a list of accepted books. Canonicity, in that

sense, does not establish authority. We must ask whether we can agree with the reasons why the list was set up in the first instance in the way it was, and whether it has continuing relevance.

(6) We must inquire whether the list they made of acceptable books still has contemporary relevance. To do that we shall set the books in the context in which they are used. For that is where the issue of their inspiration and their authority is properly discussed. We may not find these terms to be the most satisfactory.

To establish the status of a book we must consider the community in which the book is read and accepted, both its past — Who made the decision and why? — and the present — Who confirms the decision once made, and how? Does present attitude agree with past decision? Is there reason to reconsider, to reaffirm, or to revise older decisions once made? Answer these questions and then we may come to a reasonable view of the matter.

We conclude that the question of canonicity is the question of the book's use and influence in the community. That is determined by empirical considerations, e.g. by asking, Does it have an influence which is unique? Books which have current influence have authority. Thus the question becomes central. *What influence does the book have in the Christian community?* Answer that and you have a dynamic rather than a formal answer to the question of Scripture. We must put practice into theory and then test the theory. We are then ready to address one further question: What *sort* of authority do such writings have?

7 A Paradox

The contemporary church has inherited both the books and the decisions about which books are to be taken as primary and which as secondary. It inherits the decision and affirms it. But it does not examine all the books. It affirms the books it reads, and those it finds have been accepted. But it may not be aware of what other books there were, and are, to choose from. It does not say to itself something like: 'Here are the books produced during the first two Christian centuries. Let us examine them, and choose the ones we consider appropriate and profitable to set aside for special use in the church. Something similar, *mutatis mutandis*, might be said about the Hebrew books.

We should ask: Why does a particular church community not do that? We can obtain and examine all these writings without difficulty. But most Christians have never read any of them. Why are we content to *inherit* and endorse a decision we did not make about which are the right books when we have not considered such books as, for example, actually were included in only some of the lists which were drawn up? Why do we continue to retain some books which were seriously questioned and whose place in the canon, i.e. on the list, was contested? Is it strictly honest to endorse such books as we are somewhat familiar with and exclude other books we have never read? Are we really prepared to leave that decision to someone else, without giving ourselves convincing reasons for endorsing that decision?

Of course Christians are influenced by decisions of the past in the way in which we use the writings. That *these* writings are handed down to us as those chosen by some historical decision means that we do not, and will not, read other important writings, or consider them in the same way as we consider these.

So Christians continue to use certain books and not others. That is the important fact, however it has been influenced by decisions of the past.

This means that most Christians, most of the time, simply endorse the tradition. They simply accept what has been handed down to them from the past. Even those who most enthusiastically affirm the principle of 'the Bible and the Bible only' depend upon the tradition about the canon so that they can identify what the limits of the Bible are. This is usually done without much concern or criticism. As a result we have a strange paradox: to affirm both 'The Bible and the Bible only,' *and* to affirm as well the *traditional* identification of the Bible, limiting it to those books which the tradition has affirmed. It is particularly ironical that most Protestants assert that the Bible stands alone, while relying upon tradition to identify which are the books which constitute the Bible, tradition which existed long before the divide between Protestant and Catholic took place.

So when the church acknowledges Scripture is this anything other than a *formal* recognition of sixty-six books?

The fact is that the *effective* canon is not identical with the sixty-six books which the church formally defines as its official canon. The church does not use all portions of the canon consistently. 'The church' refers to the congregation, the churchman, the preacher, the theologian, the individual believer. Each of these is a particular entity. By 'use' we refer to doctrinal definition, proclamation, devotional reading, liturgical practice and have in mind the distinctions we made at the very beginning of this book.

It is essential that we now make a clear distinction. It is that between books formally and traditionally defined as canonical and books or portions of books actually, repeatedly and consistently used in the various activities of the church. The effective canon of the church consists of those books and parts of books the church actually uses. These are a limited selection and are drawn from the whole which the church formally calls its canon. The official canon is the list of accepted books. Some will be used frequently, some seldom, some not at all. The 'canon' sets the outer limit. Within that limit there is selection. This means that there are inner limits. In the performance of its varied activities the church appeals to *certain* portions of the writings whose outer limits are defined by the official canon. The books whose limits are formally defined and the books actually used repeatedly and consistently are not identical.

We might use technical language to make this important distinction.[16] The community might say, We are not bound to an historical decision, a contingent decision about the canon, for the manner in which we use these books. The church identifies herself by specifying which books she uses. That means that the definition of the canon is made by, and at the same time is an identification of, the church itself. The church identifies itself by specifying as canonical those writings it uses in its varied activities.

A further observation is important. We have in what precedes been speaking of the canonical books as formally defined, in contrast to books or portions of books actually used regularly and seriously. But, of course, books outside of the formally defined canon can, and often do, exercise as much or even greater influence on Christian understanding, worship and practice than writings from the canon of Scripture. What writing is *effectively authoritative* within the church will be assessed in proportion to the influence it exercises and the acknowledgment it receives. The writings of a teacher, a charismatic figure, a churchman, a theologian may, in a given community, have more effective influence than whole sections of the formal canon. That is an important fact of church life which the Protestant must take into account in understanding what the principle of *sola scriptura* can mean. The activity of the Holy Spirit, so the church claims, manifests itself in many ways in the church. Some of them may not be directly related to the actual words of formally canonical Scripture.

It looks as though the Protestant principle of *sola scriptura* might be compromised on two levels:

(1) because of an acceptance of a definition of the limits of Scripture handed down by tradition, i.e. of an endorsement of the traditional pronouncements about the canon; and

(2) because a non-Scriptural office or person or tradition may, in any given community, wield more effective influence and be referred to more consistently than the writings of the canonical Scripture, whole portions of which may be quietly left aside.

So a doctrine of Scripture cannot be isolated from the life and practice of the community which uses Scripture. Otherwise the doctrine becomes formal and the church's claim concerning Scripture does not then correspond to its actual practice.

8 THEOLOGICAL SIGNIFICANCE OF THESE CONSIDERATIONS

We conclude this chapter with a brief suggestion about the theological significance of these considerations.

(1) That the books of Scripture have a history means that human elements play an essential part from the very beginning and throughout the whole process of the book's production. It is necessary to say this only because (at times) there has been a misleading emphasis in the opposite direction, to play down, even to suppress, any reference to the human. We may then have to insist that the books are human productions because so much emphasis has often been laid on the divine.

(2) It is then a matter of saying how to speak well of God's revelation in and through the books whose history we can trace. Christians affirm that these are the books through which God reveals himself, as they recount how God revealed himself in the past. This book is the written Word of God because of its intrinsic relationship with God's revelation to the church.

(3) Authority means influence. These books have influence of a particular kind. Christians accept them for having had and for continuing to have such influence. We must then, in giving a theological account of Scripture in relation to the life of the church, carefully state what this influence is. This will require clear, unprejudiced thinking.

(4) The context for discussion of the Bible is where the Bible is spoken of as Holy Scripture, where it is received as having a special status, where, if it happens, God reveals

himself. The authority of the Bible is not a property which inheres in it and which can be demonstrated, for example by showing that it is inspired, but rather connotes a relation in which divine and human elements both play an important role. Hence our insistence that we observe what actually happens with regard to the Bible in the practice of the church.

We cannot do justice to the status of the Bible without dealing with the community, the church, in which the Bible is used, and in which judgments about the Bible are made and passed on, sometimes formally and sometimes informally. Only by speaking in relational terms shall we be able to do justice to the problem of the authority of the Bible.

CHAPTER II NOTES

[1]Donald E. Gowan, *Bridge Between the Testaments,* p. 334.

[2]*Ibid.* p. 331.

[3]The Reformers decided that the so-called apocryphal books were to be read but not to be held as having authority. The Roman Catholic church at the Council of Trent (AD 1545 - 1563) decided that the apocryphal books were to be included, since they had been long used in worship. So a difference arose among Christians.

[4]B. W. Anderson comments: 'These principles may strike us as being rather arbitrary. It would certainly not have detracted from Jewish Scripture, if for instance some reason had been found to substitute the *Wisdom of Ben Sire* or some of the psalms from the Qumran community for the *Song of Songs* or *Esther.* We must remember, however, that the question of the authority of most of the writings now found in the Hebrew Bible had been answered before the Academy of Jamnia, especially in the worship practice of the community. Those writings were preserved and used devotionally which spoke authoritatively to the community of faith.' B. W. Anderson, *op. cit.,* pp. 536-537.

[5]It leads us into complex problems of interpretation. See below, chapters X and XI.

[6]The evidence for this is presented in Robert M. Grant, *The Interpretation of the Bible.* Chapters III and IV.

[7]II Peter 3:15,16.

[8]*Ibid.*

[9]II Peter 1:17-18.

[10]Eusebius, *Ecclesiastical History,* III. 3. 4-5.

[11]Evidence for this is readily available. See J. Stevenson, *A New Eusebius.* pp. 144-146, 337-340.

[12]Our list of twenty-seven books appears in the proceedings of the synod of Laodicea (AD. 363) and again in the proceedings of the synod of Carthage (AD. 397). A council held in Rome in AD 382 under Damasus agreed.

[13]This is the language of Irenaeus. Cf. J. Stevenson, *op. cit.,* pp. 97-98.

[14]Christopher Evans, *Is 'Holy Scripture' Christian? and Other Questions.*

[15]*Ibid.*, p. 24.

[16]D. H. Kelsey, *The Uses of Scripture in Recent Theology.* pp. 105, 117. The *theological* judgment that precisely these writings are canonical is an analytic rather than a contingent judgment. For historical judgments are contingent and uncertain. (Footnote 16).

SUMMARY OF CHAPTER III

AUTHORITY

There is an important distinction between investing books with authority, and recognizing them as having authority. In the latter case, the book commends itself for what it does, for the function it has in the life of the Christian community. It thus has an *intrinsic* authority, whoever its author was. The Bible has historical priority in its connection with the Christ-event. The apostolicity of the New Testament books, for example, means their effectiveness in the church and their historical position as primary witness to the Christ-event. Authority and recognition of authority are correlative. Here it is not a matter of demonstration.

III

AUTHORITY: INFLUENCE AND ACCEPTANCE

1 STAGES IN THE FORMATION OF THE CANON

Christians call their Scriptures the 'Holy Bible'. They also speak of God as holy, the 'holy one', and claim that holiness is a special attribute of God. They also claim that if creatures are holy, they are holy because they derive their holiness from God's holiness. Whatever is holy has derived what holiness it has from its source in God. We are then to be warned at the outset, for good theological reasons, against the idea of a book which has an intrinsic holiness, that is a holiness in and of itself and independent of God. We shall be expounding the idea of a 'dynamic' authority. We shall relate Scripture to what goes on in the church and in the world. In this case the term 'authority' connotes something dynamic and not static. It connotes not a property but a relationship. It is, in brief, a relational term.

The point at issue here is whether the church is the primary authority which invests these books with authority, or whether the Scriptures have the capacity to evoke a recognition of their own uniqueness. These books came to be recognized as Scripture and others did not. To say that they came to be recognized is not the same as saying that they came to be invested with authority. To *invest* the books with authority would mean to impose on them something which they did not possess before being so invested. It would entail that there was some already accepted authority in the community that could impose authority on these writings. That is not the sort of authority appropriate in the case of the Bible. Authority is not a property to be conveyed. These writings do not need authentication from without.

The important issue can be brought out by contrasting the very different meanings of the following two sentences:

> The Bible is now to be recognized because it has been invested with authority
>
> The authority which the Bible has has now been recognized.

The Church did draw up a list of books. By so doing it included some and excluded many. What was happening? Was the Church giving to, i.e. bestowing on these books a status which they did not already have? Or, was it recognizing a status they in fact already had? Even if one were to answer that the Church at a point (say in the fourth century) invested books with an authority they did not previously have, we would still have to ask how this came about and why it was done. Who approved the books and for what reasons? For what purposes were such books approved? Was the move an authentic one? If so how can it be authenticated? That pushes the question one stage further back. Before the books were formally declared, by being included on a list, to be 'Scripture,' to have authority, someone had already recognized them and approved them. What was the basis of such recognition and approval? The answer that the books gain authority for the reason that they are included on a list will not do. To get on the list they have already been recognized and approved.

The idea of a canon and of canonical authority is quite different from the idea of the authentication of the writings on the basis of what they themselves contain. To call a book or a set of books canonical is to *invest* them with authority. A book is not invested with a spiritual or a religious authority because it appears on a list of approved books. 'Why are they approved and what for?' That is the question which leads us to examine the facts of the case.

We might distinguish three stages in the formation of a canon of Scripture. First, the writings establish themselves on the score of their contents. Second, they establish themselves as authoritative on the score of their *authors*. Third, they are authoritative because they belong to an *authoritative list*. 'Authoritative' now means 'canonical,' and 'canonical' means 'belonging to the canon.' First, that is to say, a book commends itself, and holds its place because it makes profound religious sense, as in the case of the writings of Paul. This Evans calls 'self-authentication,' and sees it as the primary and decisive criterion. What that particular term means and whether it is satisfactory we shall have to inquire. At all events, to consider this as a criterion we must focus on the book itself and find the reason for its having authority by considering its content and its influence. Its authority is in itself and not in something else asserted of it or imposed upon it. The writing speaks for itself. The community responds to these writings, finding satisfaction in them and getting guidance from them. The community recognises them for the help they had provided and were providing. 'These are the writings that build us up and give us guidance we can understand and act upon.' That is sufficient reason for saying they have a special status. This is the way the community speaks about the writings after they have spoken for themselves. They have a special status because they perform a special function.

The Bible does not become something that it was not. It gets recognised for what it is. There are analogies. A great scientist does not become a great scientist only when he is recognised as such. He is then simply acknowledged for what he already is. It is not like the conferring of an academic degree. You were not a Doctor of Philosophy. But now you are. But you would not have been if the university had not conferred the degree upon you. With the Bible it is not like that. Rather the Bible is recognised for what it is.

However this criterion of 'self-authentication' of the writings gets replaced. It is 'speedily overtaken by that of authorship, and the writings are then on their way to becoming canonical on other grounds.'[1] The idea is that these writings are canonical because they can be traced to particular authors. The authors have a special position of authority. So the writings which can be traced to these authoritative figures come to have authority. The writings are recognized as having authority because they were written by authors whose authority was already established, that is to say, recognized. If the writing of a book can be traced to some such authoritative figure then it has authority. If it cannot be traced to such an authoritative figure then it does not have authority. The authority of the apostle is original and primary. The authority of the Bible is thus a derived authority.

The process of tracing a book to a particular figure is an historical exercise. So, the authority of the New Testament book depends upon the success of an historical exercise. The process by which such a book came to be written was a complex one. It involved a telling and retelling by word of mouth, the activity of amanuenses who transcribe the verbal message, and of scribes who copy it, of the editor who puts it all together. Our historical evidence is debatable in many cases.

Let us consider a particular possibility, using the first category, 'self-authentication,' in a somewhat modified form, and relate it to the second, 'authorship.' Suppose there is a book widely read in the churches, valued because it edifies the congregation and helps the individual in understanding and living the Christian faith, but whose author is not known beyond doubt. Should it, or should it not, be accepted as Scripture? The problem of being able to identity the author might become more difficult as time passed. Origen in an interesting comment on the epistle to the Hebrews said 'But who wrote the epistle, in truth God knows.'[2] That was in the third century.

So apostolicity is a problem. This term assumes one can identify an apostle as the author of the book. Or, if an apostle is not himself the author of the book, at least an apostle was the *source* of the material of the book, or that the author was the disciple of an apostle. So Mark is a disciple of Peter and Luke a follower of Paul. On this account of the matter their books get included because they are connected with an apostle, not because of their intrinsic worth, nor because of their function in the churches.

This argument makes the important assumption, which again throws us into the midst of historical debate, that in the early church the figure of apostle was clearly distinguished, and so well recognized as to set aside the person from all others. It is a good question, whether even in the first century this accurately represents the real historical situation.

Another point concerns the meaning of the term 'authentic.' A book is authentic if, when it claims to have a particular author, it does in fact have that author. Obviously, a writing can *claim* to come from one author and not do so. In fact what was often done in ancient times was to write pseudonymously, that is, to write a book and associate it with someone else, well known. In that way, the real author hoped that the renown of the figure whose name attached to the book would guarantee it a wider and more favourable response than it would otherwise get, would guarantee it a kind of authority from the outset. That was a widespread practice at the time when the New Testament writings were being produced. So we call a writing 'authentic' if the author who claims to write it was the one who actually wrote it. It is one of the tasks of historical assessment to make judgments about the authenticity of particular books. But suppose we cannot be sure?[3] Are we then going to stick by this criterion of apostolicity and follow out the logical consequences of so doing? That would mean that in every case acknowledgment of the authority of a book would depend upon a historical judgment about its author rather than experience of its influence in the Christian community. That would mean that it would be the historian who established its authority. But that is surely quite misguided.

Whether it is important to be able to identify the author of any New Testament book, and connect him with an apostle will depend primarily on whether we deem the figure of the apostle to be the key figure. If the apostle did not and cannot be shown to have such 'precise and central position' of authority, then our appeal to apostolicity in order to authorize the sacred books will not be convincing.[4]

At stake here are very important issues concerning the New Testament. What are the right questions to ask? What is the church (and what goes with it) for, or what is it from? Is the question about the Bible's authority a functional question or an historical question? We can put the problem somewhat differently. Is the New Testament authorized by its connection with apostles, people who held an office recognized to be authoritative? If so, what sort of thing is it that needs such authorization? If the writings are the sort of thing that they must be authorized then they are secondary. What authorizes is primary. Is it not an historical fantasy to invest the apostles with such original, primary, underived authority? After all, their immediate connection was with Jesus himself. This gives them historical primacy over every other source. Indeed apostolicity in this sense constitutes the church, and all secondary sources of authority must demonstrate their roots in the apostolic age.

The third stage in the process was the drawing up or a list of the books considered to have authority. A list separates those that are included from the rest which are not. Those included are recognized books and they continue to be recognized. *Now* the word 'canonical' means 'on the approved list,' and 'having authority for the reason that it is on the list.' A canonical book on this view derives its unique status and authority by reason of its inclusion on the list.

The alternative to this is that those who draw up the list *recognize* the authority the book already has. The drawing up of the list is evidence of their recognizing the authority which the book has, for whatever reason it has that authority. It displays that recognition and makes it formal. In this case two things follow. First, the canon can only be provisional. Second, that reasons must be given why each individual book was included on the list. On such an explanation, inclusion on a list does *not* confer authority on the book. It recognizes an authority which the book already has. But how it has come to be that it already has such authority needs to be further explained. How has it come to have that authority which the list formally recognizes and states?

2 INTRINSIC, EXTRINSIC, INSTRUMENTAL

Let us distinguish between *intrinsic* authority and *extrinsic* authority. If someone whose authority I accept tells me to accept the authority of a book (assuming this all makes sense), then I shall accept it. I accept the book's authority because I accept that person's authority. So, some authority says to me, 'These are the books whose authority you are to accept.' And I duly follow. In such case, the book gets invested with an authority extrinsic to it. I may know very little about the book itself. I then have implicit, but not explicit, faith in the proposition that the Bible has authority. My acceptance is not based on what I know about the book or about the belief, because I have carefully and critically assessed it, found reasons for my attitude to it. My acceptance is second-hand. I accept it as such because I acknowledge the right of a third party to direct me to accept it. I accept that the Bible has authority because I accept the right of the church to direct me in this matter. But then I would need to have been already convinced of the right of the church so to direct me. That the Bible has authority has in such a case become a dogma.

Extrinsic authority means authority bestowed from another, given from outside. Intrinsic authority means an authority which comes either through or from the book itself. Think of the Bible as *instrumental*. If these books are the instruments, by means of which a certain purpose is fulfilled, if the Bible is the only means necessary for a certain event to happen, to produce a particular condition, and that event and condition comes about, then it has an authority no other books have. If I am involved in the event the Bible produces, included in the purpose it fulfils, then I can speak directly, rather than on someone else's recommendation, of the function the Bible has performed. If I am a member of the community which the Bible has been instrumental in producing, and my participation in that community is an intelligent and involved participation, and I am aware of the function of the Bible in that continuing process, then I can speak of the role (and thence of the authority) of the Bible. I can do so out of my own knowledge and experience, and not at second-hand. I can testify that this book has an 'authority' no other book has, since it has produced an effect which no other book has. I can say this, whoever the authors of the particular books in the Bible were, and whether the books are on a list or not. If they are on the list, then I can understand why they have been put there. Since the uniqueness of the Bible is in what it does, we must, in accounting for this, give primacy of place to *the function* of the Bible. Questions about authorship and official lists are secondary.

What we are saying about these writings is that they have been the instrument for their own recognition. They were not 'authorized'. They were recognized. The Christian community recognized that as Scripture was expounded, faith was nurtured, and the community was built up in the faith. They saw that *that was enough* to set these writings apart from all others. They continue to do so. So there is both an historical and a contemporary argument for setting these writings apart from all others. What they did in the past, they go on doing now. 'These are writings which have accompanied the Christian movement; they are the best we have and they have proved themselves.'[5]

The term 'self-authenticating' is not the happiest one. It means not requiring support from something or someone external to itself. To be self-authenticating means that it authenticates itself *to someone*, the individual and the community for whom it has been effective. The kind of authority the book will have will depend on whether that effect is considered primarily in relation to the community's life and piety, or primarily in relation to the community's doctrine. What the church values will show itself in its doctrine of Scripture.

The term 'authenticate' means (1) to show that an item is genuine i.e. has its origin in the person it claims to be its author or producer. To establish this connection is an historical task. A play is authentic Shakespeare if Shakespeare wrote it. A painting is authentic Vermeer if Vermeer painted it.

To show that a writing is authentic, in the historical sense i.e. coming from its purported source, one appeals to the available and relevant historical evidence. We have a similar case with a work of art. Whether this painting is genuine Vermeer or not is settled by examining the evidence. But an examination of the evidence may lead to a false conclusion. However whether the historical judgment is true of false, it makes no difference to the aesthetic value of the work.

Pursue the analogy for a moment. If a work of art is beautiful and evokes a positive aesthetic response, comparable to that of an original and authentic production then, *aesthetically,* it does not matter who painted it. It is beautiful and it evokes response. That it is not 'original' in the sense of 'attributable to the author/artist' does not matter. Originality value is often relic value. Such value has nothing to do with aesthetic judgment.

The term 'authenticate' also means (2) 'shows itself by the response it evokes to be a worthy work of art, a worthy artefact.' Such a work authenticates itself by evoking an aesthetic response. Such evocation does not depend upon the historical authenticity of the work. Such aesthetic value, and so such authenticity, is independent of historical knowledge. Authenticity in sense (1), with its opposite, forgery, fake, is historical. Authenticity, in sense (2), as (in the case of art) aesthetic value is not historical.

Now we turn to Scripture. The concept of authenticity as referring to the authorship of a book is an historical concept. The concept of authenticity as referring to the religious authority of the Bible is not historical. The authority, as for example, applied to the Bible, is independent of the historical evidence relating to the author of the book. That is authenticated by historical research. The other (so to speak) authenticates itself by what it does, i.e. in its functioning in the life of the community and in evoking appropriate responses. That this is so is the justification for using the notion of 'self-authentication.' It has reference to the influence the book has in the community in which it is recognised. Whoever produced the book, the book has influence of the appropriate kind in the community of faith.

The community of Christians, and the individual Christian, appeal to experience, and see the Bible as the instrument of the experience to which they appeal. They testify and then reason on the basis of this book, these words and this experience. Hence for the Protestant the claim s*ola scriptura*, 'the Bible and the Bible only,' points to the position of primacy Scripture has in the life of the church.

Catholics also recognise that the Scripture has a primary function for the church. They formulate statements about that primary function differently from Protestants, setting it beside what they consider to be other primary functions for the church, in addition to that of the Bible. For the Catholic the Bible is one primary authority. The living tradition of the church is another.

We can now put our point in historical terms. When Christians testify to their present experience, they claim that the Bible has mediated to them the revelation of God and as such an instrument is an irreplaceable means of that revelation. By means of this book they have come to know his love, his demand, his forgiveness, his call, his succour. The claim about these writings from the very beginning is the claim that they are a part of the total event of God's revelation through Jesus Christ, that they are instruments creative of Christian faith and of the Christian community. There was a point in history when Christian faith had its beginning. It is because of this event and of the connection of the Christian writings with this event that these books have an irreplaceable position in the church.

Historically, these books are those which came out of the total event in which God revealed himself in Jesus Christ and established the Christian community upon the grounds of faith in the person and work of Jesus Christ. It is these particular books and not others, these books we now call the New Testament, which have this particular historical status.

The New Testament books have a certain historical primacy. They are the historical deposit of the movement of the first century of our era, which included the life and death of Jesus and the coming into being of the Christian church. These documents are unique in that they have survived from this crucial and formative period. Thus they cannot be replaced by later documents, important and even primary as such other documents may be. The historical primacy these documents, our New Testament, have, ensure their irreplaceability as mediating to us our knowledge of that Christian movement whose faith in Jesus Christ we have come to share. They bear witness to that faith. We, in our turn, bear witness to what they bore witness to. Something literary remains of their witness. These are our primary documents reporting it, recording it.

The Old Testament writings participated in this formative event, the Christ-event. They provided the ideas, the means for interpreting what happened. They make it possible for Christians to regard Jesus Christ as the fulfilment of human and Hebrew history. They provide the background for the events which had recently taken place when the New Testament began to be written.

The New Testament writings are historically irreplaceable. They are the bridge from Jesus to the church. In this sense we may speak of their apostolicity. The apostles were those who first publicly proclaimed their faith in Jesus Christ, and interpreted his life and death from the viewpoint of their faith in him. They were the first leaders in the church and assumed the task of public witnessing. The term 'apostolicity' connotes their distinctive features, their priority as preachers of the Christian gospel. They provide the link with the earliest Christian faith and with the historical Jesus. So the term has sometimes been applied to the books of the New Testament.

Apostolicity does not mean that because a book is written by an apostle its special status is guaranteed. Conversely, it does not mean that we must demonstrate that a book is written by an apostle before we accept its authority. The specific identity of the author is relatively unimportant. The books are the instruments of God's saving revelation in Jesus Christ without the author being specifically identified. To identify an author is an historical task, and the continuing faith of the church does not depend upon our success or failure at establishing such historical facts. *Whoever wrote it, the book does what it does.* That is the important thing. It does now and it did from the beginning mediate the reality of God. This is recognized in church doctrine by attributing the effectiveness of the proclamation of Scripture to the activity of the Holy Spirit. The Bible has authority if and when God mediates himself through it. Should one then wish to speak of the apostolicity of the New Testament books one can certainly do so. The term 'apostle' is reserved for those who were the first to announce the good news about Jesus. The books share with the men who were apostles that they are the primary historical witnesses to the resurrection, to faith in Jesus Christ. In the one case such primary historical witnesses were human beings. In the other case they are writings. In both cases they have an irreplaceable historical position. They are the first, and in that sense the primary, witnesses of the Gospel of Jesus Christ and its meaning. These books continue to be the means, as they were from the time of their writing, for understanding and for experiencing the Christian faith. As in the case of the human apostle, the book is what it is because of what it does and because of what it has done. It is its effectiveness and its historical position that constitutes its apostolicity.

3   INTERPRETATION AND TRADITION

It is clear that we need an appropriate concept of authority when we speak of the 'authority of the Bible.' We shall discuss the meaning of the word to some purpose as we discover how it is used by those who acknowledge that authority. The community of faith recognizes the Bible. We must give due consideration to the implications of that recognition.

The Bible has always held a unique position in the church. So also has the interpreter, the teacher, the charismatic leader. The Bible 'speaks' only as someone interprets it, and, in turn, only as someone understands it.

The Bible is a text. That means that it has fixed foci: so many books, so many chapters. It is a set of writings arranged in an order. The words are there, once written by hand, now printed. Whether in some translation or another, or in the original languages, the Bible is a text. As a text it is fixed and static. There are the scrolls, the original pages. There is the book bound between two covers, now sitting on the shelf, now open on the desk, now closed on the table. In what sense can we speak, then, of the authority of the Bible? How can we say that the Bible is the living and challenging word of God, when the Bible is a book of silent words, ink-marks on paper? The Bible has no authority simply by being there, whoever 'wrote' it and whatever the circumstances of its 'writing.'

Does the Bible have authority only when someone in the community interprets and expounds it? In that case does not the teacher, the interpreter, wield the authority by virtue of his ability to interpret the text, which text would otherwise be a dead letter? Is not the authority then within the church which engages in the activity, and exercises control over the process of interpreting the Bible? Does not the church draw limits, give guidance and impose sanctions concerning what the Bible means and how it is to be interpreted? Indeed, is it not the case that the church produced the Bible, that the church decided which books it would accept as Scripture and which books it would reject? Is the authority then not rather of the church than of the Bible? If so we decide the question about authority discerning the church's attitude to the Bible.

Moreover, interpretations of what the Bible means, when endorsed and agreed upon, are passed on from one generation to the next so that an accepted meaning becomes widely recognized within a particular community. That meaning then has become a tradition. The tradition then provides guidance in indicating what

Scripture means, what is the right and proper interpretation of Scripture. The particular tradition guides the reader by providing him with the questions and the concepts with which to read and interpret the Bible. This church, that church, any church says: 'This is how we read the Bible,' and then refers you to its teachings, which it claims are the teachings of the Bible or are related to the Bible. When we come to inquire about the meaning of Scripture we are offered a particular tradition of understanding. So the authority lies in the tradition. It does not matter whether the tradition has its source in a council, in a creed, in the words of a reformer, or in the deliverances of a charismatic. If tradition is the means by which we understand Scripture, then the tradition has the real and primary authority. A particular church accepts a distinctive method of interpretation and produces a doctrinal system. Its reading of the Bible will reflect that doctrinal tradition. The authority then lies in the doctrinal system.

Appeal to the authority of Scripture may not, under analysis, turn out to be what it appears to be.

4   THE CONCEPT OF AUTHORITY

The term 'authority' refers to a relationship. It is a relational term. The term, like 'revelation,' points to a two-term relationship. Someone or something has authority over or for someone else. Someone reveals himself to someone else. Someone acknowledges the authority of another. Someone understands what is revealed.

The institution or the person that has authority has power over another. It has the capacity to influence that other, and it sometimes in fact has done so and does so. The authority may be charismatic or official. Authority may be the effect of the charm or persuasiveness of a person. It may be due to the social pressure of wide acceptance of power as legitimate. It is difficult not to be influenced by a widely recognized authority. We may accept it simply because there is no alternative. We are persuaded by the orator. We bow to pressures we cannot escape. Pressures and sanctions, or simply the threat of pressures and sanctions, can persuade us to act in one way rather than in another. The forces at work around us lead us to the acceptable behaviour. In this sense the term 'authority' refers to the effective influence which a person, a book, a custom, a belief, an institution has over people.

The term 'authority' is also used of the experts, the persons who know what they are talking about and who, because of this, deserve our respect when speaking. A person who does something competently may also be regarded as an authority when it is a matter of discussing how to do what he can do.

To have authority is to have influence. Someone influences because he is a friend and we are trying to please him, or perhaps because he is an expert and we acknowledge the right he has to be respected. 'Authority,' 'competence,' and 'recognition' are thus all very closely related concepts.[6]

They are closely related when we attempt to analyse the Bible's authority. Here it is clear that the *effective authority* of the Bible is identical with the *influence* it exerts. It is also clear that an appropriate response on the part of the reader is necessary. One can acknowledge authority when one has experienced the influence of the writing in a particular way.

Authority is *acknowledged* power. When people recognize that a person, an institution, a class has the right to exercise power, authority is in evidence. 'Power' means the capacity to influence another, to get one's purpose fulfilled, one's ideas accepted and acted upon, to get one's will done. Power can be exercised without being recognized as right and proper. Such power may lead someone to perform exactly the same act as the exercise of legitimate power might produce. If someone flourishes a revolver in my face, that will certainly provide me with an incentive to co-operate with the person flourishing it. But there are also legitimate ways of relieving me of — say — my money. I may recognize the structured power of bureaucratic authority and permit the taxman to claim some of my money. On this definition, 'authority' means both the exercise of power and the recognition of it as legitimate.

Indeed, recognition is the defining element. This is the important element in our present considerations. Authority means recognition. Authority 'is exercised only over those who voluntarily accept it' (Juvenal).[7]

How and why do we come to acknowledge an authority? Does such an acknowledgment commit us to an automatic and uncritical acceptance of our authority's pronouncements and demands whatever they are? What reasons can we give for our initial acceptance? Can a critical acceptance of authority lead to an uncritical following of its demands?

(1) One reason for recognition of an authority is *belief in the rightness of established customs and traditions*. We are taught that we should adopt beliefs and behaviour patterns, and we never question them. They teach us, they train us, before we are able to reason. Later we may find reasons for believing what they have trained us to believe, and doing what they have taught us to do. They socialize us into a tradition of values, beliefs and behaviour, and having accepted that tradition we may never question its validity. We have our authorities handed to us. It is precisely because we have received them in this way, without engaging in a serious process of rational justification, that we feel greatly threatened when we are confronted with alternatives. Do we entrench or do we explore? Shall we give consideration to the criticisms or shall we dismiss them without further ado?

(2) Max Weber[8] recognizes another form of authority which he calls *charismatic* authority. An exceptional leader, endowed with outstanding persuasive qualities, gets a following. Such qualities as he manifests are seen as if supernatural, or superhuman. They set the leader apart from ordinary mortals, and make belief, loyalty, devotion and obedience easy and natural.

(3) But we do not need to be impressed by such outstanding personalities to accept our beliefs on authority. Most of

what we believe comes from other people's testimony. We have not ourselves been in a position to test all the claims we accept. Nor ever shall. We are usually not inclined to test them. We simply accept them. Such acceptance works and we live together constructively. It was Bishop Butler who said that 'probability is the guide to life'. We must act on the evidence we have. We can't prove everything. In fact, we cannot prove much. We have to take things on trust. Our trust is shown to be reasonable in that when we act on probabilities that things go right and not wrong. Many things we simply accept. We couldn't get along if we didn't.

(4) But human beings, even the most exceptional of human beings, and even human beings under the influence of the divine, are fallible, limited and. suggestible. Suppose there were a human being who was infallible and at the same time was limited. Such a logical possibility is very relevant to the subject under discussion. We can think of an infallibility which extends to some matters and not to others, just as we think of an authority in some areas and not in others. I mean, It is conceivable that someone be infallible about some things but not about others. We can distinguish between total and partial infallibility. 'He's never wrong when he's talking about such-and-such' could be inferred from 'He's never been known to be wrong when he has talked about such-and-such.' If we keep within the limits we could accept his authority.

But if we began asking him questions beyond the limits within which he is infallible, that person would be of little help, indeed might even be misleading, if not irrelevant. That would certainly be the case if he were not infallible and we took him to be so, and it was important for us that he be right.

(5) Authorities sometimes conflict. Which, if any of them, are you going to accept? When authorities conflict you

have to decide between them. You can start with a high-sounding claim, 'The Bible says so and so.' And so it does. But one authority says that the Bible means this, and another says the Bible means that, and yet another says the Bible means something else when the Bible says so and so. When the authority, in this case the Bible, gives rise to such divergence in interpretation the individual will have to choose between the secondary authorities. I'll choose my secondary authority, and repose my confidence there. But that only slides the issue along the corridor where I'll meet it again. For why should I repose such confidence in that secondary authority rather than in another one? I have not settled, only shelved, the question of authority. This problem is acute when there is a conflict between interpretations, when for example contradictory doctrinal conclusions are constructed and presented as the biblical teaching.. Of course, a passage may be set in different contexts and speak to different situations without providing the problem of conflict.

(6) Religious believers sometimes combine authoritarianism with scepticism.[9] They will sometimes say, 'The authority is so sacred that we must not question it.' Neither must we try to establish it, give reasons for it. It does not permit, nor require, proof nor even support.' Such authoritarianism has its particular psychological appeal and that is the main reason why it persists. The intellectually timid or indolent are sometimes quite happy to let others do their thinking for them and believe what they are told to believe. They ask 'What do we believe?' and then demand, 'Please tell me.' rather than seeking the truth for themselves. They enjoy conforming and the freedom from responsibility such conformity brings. Such a person 'may be more comfortable, for the search after wisdom often brings sorrow and disillusionment. . . . Better to raise one's eyes to the sky and seek humbly for

the truth, even though the search result in failure and unhappiness, than to give our beliefs into the keeping of another.'[10]

The sinister counterpart to such conformity is a belief in the virtue of conformity. That may lead to the opposition and persecution of those who quest for truth by those who are certain that they have found it. The will to dominate requires the will to conform. One psychological type supplements the other.

The appeal to the sacredness of the text of Scripture is one example of this type of conformity, of this type of submission. One must not question a sacred text. But questions arise. Once admit the sacredness of the text and one is then free from the responsibility of answering questions that inevitably arise in relation to that text. It may then happen that the purported sacredness of the text gets projected on to the interpreter so that the interpretation is itself put beyond question.

It is the initial step which must be questioned, the initial acceptance of the authority, in this case the text of Scripture, as untouchable, as beyond question. What if any is the rational ground for taking this decisive step in the first place? Or is it irrational? At what point does one refuse to give reasons for one's belief?

5   THE EFFECTS OF THE BIBLE

It is as the Bible is effective within the church that the church is in a position to acknowledge its authority. It is when God has made his presence known within the church that the church is in a position to confess his present reality. As God's presence becomes known through the instrumentality of the Bible, the church confesses the authority of the Bible. This means that the 'question' of the Bible's 'authority' is a question about an answer which has already been found.

It is when the individual acknowledges the Bible as the means of God's word, the avenue through which he 'speaks' to the individual and to the church as a community, as something which has become real to one in one's experience, that one can recognize the authority of the Bible. It is then a real and living thing. If the question of its authority comes up one then knows what the appropriate answer is. The Bible has exerted influence, has produced certain effects. You acknowledge that it has done so and agree that it has authority. This authority cannot be imposed upon you. You assent to it, agree that it is this way. In your acknowledgment you recognize something which comes to you. You do not constitute the Bible authoritative because and when you recognize it to have authority.

The authority of the Bible is '*acceptable* in the sense that, while independent of the person upon whom it imposes itself, it secures the assent of that person.'[11] The person does not assent because some authority insists that the Bible must be believed. The believer should not be irrational. The believer acknowledges the Bible because it has become the instrument through which God has made himself known, whatever other instruments or agents may have been involved in the process. The Bible is a constant factor in the complex process which results in the Christian confession of faith. The term 'assent' therefore is rather misleading.

6 ACCEPTANCE, RECOGNITION

The believer responds, makes a judgment. He is aware of and responsible for what he hears and experiences of the word of God. In saying this we avoid one-sidedness. The Bible is not an external authority imposed on the believer by another external authority. If it can be and sometimes is, the believer himself being a willing accessory in the process, that is to misunderstand. It is to avoid this, while not reducing the word of God, or the testimony of the Spirit, to the believer's or the church's experience, we must hold firmly to two complementary assertions when we speak of the authority of the Bible:

(1) Its authority is not constituted authoritative by our acceptance and recognition of it.

(2) Our recognition of it is essential to its having authority. The recognition or acknowledgment of this authority takes place when the Bible has had and continues to have the effect upon the believer, of evoking and nurturing Christian faith. In the words of C. H Dodd,

> a book is as external as a church, or rather it is much more so. The act of faith which accepts the authority of the Bible is as purely individual a judgment as that which accepts the authority of the church. What is the ground of it? . . . . Really — may we not say? — he believes the Bible to be authoritative because of the effect it produces upon his own mind and spirit. In this as for all his beliefs he must accept personal responsibility.[12]

The acceptance of the authority of the Bible, associated with and dependent as it is upon confession of faith in God, is a reasonable and responsible act.

7 TESTIMONY NOT PROOF

Authority resides in the truth alone, in the mind and will of God. The Bible possesses authority in religion as it mediates the truth, as the 'Word of God.' The truth is not given in an external, self-subsistent form. In dealing with the question of biblical authority we must consider the response of the subject. 'Granted that religious authority somehow resides in the Bible, how does it become authoritative *for me*?'[13] The answer to this question is not to be found in thinking of the Bible as a repository of doctrine, waiting to be excavated. 'The most important thing we find in the Bible is not "doctrine" but something that helps us in a new attitude to God and to life.'[14] If we treat the Bible as a source of information, whether doctrinal information or historical information, we are missing the point. The traditional theory valued the Bible 'as giving authoritative information, in the form of dogma, upon matters known only by special revelation.'[15] The critical method treated it as a source of historical information. In both cases there is a failure to understand the real character of the Bible. The authority of the Bible is not in its being a source of doctrine, but rather and 'primarily in inducing in us a religious attitude and outlook,'[16] not in providing static and unchanging dogma, but in including us within 'a tradition of life and experience.'[17] That means that we are caught up in a progressing movement, in which (as the New Testament says) the Spirit of God is leading us into a developing and forward-looking experience. It is in performing this activity that the authority of Scripture consists.

The Christian believer's claim is that the religious authority of the Bible is known when God makes himself known. Such authority is known in the experience of the believer. The Bible is the instrument through which believers receive the word of God. 'The Scriptures are holy because they are the vehicle through which the Gospel is communicated to us . . . . Hence there is no outside standard by which we can measure the adequacy of the biblical communication.'[18] This unique authority can be witnessed to but it cannot be proved. It is a matter of testimony and not of proof.

8   RELIGIOUS AND FACTUAL AUTHORITY

The religious value and authority of the Bible does not depend on its reliability as a different kind of authority, namely its historical and factual trustworthiness. It is not my purpose at all to re-engage in the battles fought and fought again in the nineteenth century over this issue. I shall survey and draw lessons from some of that debate later.[19] If we learn a lesson from history it will be that we must fight our own battles and not simply replay old ones, even if in some contexts it seems we are very much doing the latter, or observing others doing the latter.

Statements in the Bible frequently have reference to historical, geographical and other factual states of affair. Such statements may be confirmed where there is appropriate evidence. We can check such biblical statements by examining the relevant evidence.

The cosmological *assumptions* of the Bible are a quite different matter from its factual claims. By 'cosmological assumptions' we mean what they took for granted about how the universe is structured, how it operates, how the bodies that make it up and the events which take place within it are related to one another, about whether there is something more than the natural world to be accounted for and, if there is, how the supernatural world is related to the natural. The Bible is an ancient book and its writers operated with pre-scientific assumptions. It is pre-Einsteinian, pre-Newtonian, pre-Copernican. This means that *they* had a different kind of understanding, a different mode of thinking from ours. We understand Newton and know he is a watershed in the history of human development. We may not well understand Einstein, but we well know that we live in a quite different world from the ancients when it comes to our understanding the universe. The words 'nature,' 'universe,' *as we use them* were unknown to the ancients. There is a great divide between us. It is the advent and long success of scientific method that has brought about this change.

What they have to say about God and the world and his relation to the world and history they say in *their* idiom. They were well able to say what they had to say in the form and within the thought-patterns within which they operated. It did not stand in the way of their communicating what they had to communicate, which were their convictions about what God was doing in the world, what they understood God to have done and what he would yet do.

Christian believers, who live in a different world from them and who try to understand them, have to make allowance for the important fact that their world was very different from ours. We want to understand their message, and we want to let God speak through their words. We also want to put the message about the God of whom they speak in our words, to relate the message about him to our problems. So we must *interpret* their message, understand their expression. We may do so because we experience through their words the revealing activity of the same God who revealed himself to them. To say this is to claim that we find the unity of the Bible in its witness to the revealing activity of God.

The Christian's task is to make that clear and to find in the present time the means to speak intelligibly about the activity of God within the world.

Science resulted from the discovery of scientific method. Ancient peoples did not know what scientists of the seventeenth, eighteenth and later centuries discovered. Ancient writers did not know the scientific method. For example, the Bible writers did not know about the circulation of the blood, the constitution of the universe, the movements of the planets, and the diurnal motion of the earth as it makes its annual circuit around the sun. Their astronomy was geocentric.

What does it matter that they thought very differently about the way things are than we do, that they did not have the idea of nature which we have? How could they? For us the eighteenth century is history. But not for them! They could not, and therefore did not, think of nature in Newtonian terms, let alone in post-Einsteinian terms as we do. There is a distance between them and us. The temporal gap is also a cultural gap. We think of a universal order of nature with each event linked to every other in a chain of cause and effect. Our science does not speak of God nor of divine or supernatural activity as cause in any sense whatever, neither in physics, nor in psychology, nor in economics. We explain nature and history in secular terms. So our horizon is very different from their horizon.

9 MUST?

Christians sometimes speak of the Bible as the 'word of God.' 'To believe the Bible' means then to accept it as the means through which God 'speaks.' By using this analogy from human speech as communication, they convey the idea that God communicates with the human person through the reading and exposition of the words of Scripture. To have Christian faith is the product of this revelation of God through Scripture.

But this does not entail belief in the literal accuracy of all the statements of Scripture.

To decide whether the Bible is the 'word of God' requires a different sort of approach than to decide whether its statements are true or false. If the Bible has proved to be the vehicle through which readers and hearers have come to have faith, the means through which that faith is strengthened, then there would be sufficient ground for a special claim about the Bible. But the Bible will have a quite different kind of 'authority' in this case from that which it would have purportedly in the case where someone says, 'I will demonstrate why you have to believe the Bible,' and then try to establish its factual accuracy. Or even, as one sometimes hears, 'The factual claims of the Bible must be true, and therefore we can, in principle, show them to be true, as a necessary condition for accepting it as having authority.' That is a most extreme position indeed!

No one can say *in advance* that every claim the Bible makes is true. You cannot reasonably believe an historical claim, unless and until you have evidence to establish that claim. You may be pre-disposed to believe it. You may hope that it will prove to be true. But it would be unreasonable to say that it *must* be true. Historical judgments are not necessary. They are contingent. That means that you cannot say in advance of having considered the evidence that claims will be true, or that they must be true. You have to test the claims and find out whether they are. You have to check the evidence and decide whether the historical (or other factual) claim is probably true. We cannot say *a priori*, before examining the evidence what the outcome of the investigation will be. Whether you wish it to be true or are predisposed to believe it true is neither here nor there. You can only reasonably believe a factual claim for which there is evidence that makes it probable. You must examine the particular case and follow the rules of evidence. You may then be able to decide whether the claim, explicit or implied, is probably true or probably false. The evidence may lead you to conclude that it is highly probable that it is true, or false. The probability may be such that you have good reason for being certain that your judgment is correct.

This is correct procedure *in principle*. That means that it applies in whatever context claims are made and so in considering the historical and other factual claims of the Bible. The Bible does not have a special status when it is a question of deciding whether its factual claims are true. It would be irrational to claim in advance of a reasonable consideration of the appropriate evidence that its claims must be believed. If that is accepted, and if a person says he is quite prepared to be irrational there can be no further discussion. For that person will believe what he wants and feel no obligation to give reasons for his belief. It is impossible to hold intelligent discourse with such a person.

One writer claims that the New Testament commands our unconditional obedience. He speaks of the 'authoritative preaching and teaching of (the) apostles.' Since Paul is an apostle his writing 'therefore demands obedience.'[20] But what does that mean? It just will not do to speak so vaguely about 'the New Testament' or 'the Bible.' Does the writer mean, 'Broadly and vaguely, the New Testament commands our unconditional obedience,' or does he mean that every command, exhortation or directive, wherever found and on whatever theme, commands our unconditional obedience? Speaking broadly and vaguely conveys little or no meaning. We cannot obey or believe broadly and vaguely. Our unconditional obedience is quite specific. Is every command or directive of an apostle's teaching to be obeyed? Are women to remain silent in our churches?[21] Are we to practice celibacy?[22] Must we maintain rules and procedures regarding hygiene such as Jesus commended?[23] Should one Christian never ever file a law suit against another?[24] Is there to be no separation after marriage?[25] And so on! Are Christians to take these demands as absolute and unconditional? The obvious fact is that they do not do so. So since they do not do so, that practice needs to be put into theory. They need to say how it is that they approach the Bible so as not to do what in many instances it says should be done.

The words of the New Testament were written in particular contexts and addressed to quite specific situations. Those contexts and situations have passed and the advice and direction given to them may well be no longer relevant. However, there may be an important principle behind the particular directives. But that principle will have to be discerned. It will require a sympathetic interpretation of the text to show what that principle is. Does the Christian, if disagreeing when the interpretation is presented, reject the authority of the text? If you derive the principle from the specific instances dealt with in the text, is it the text or is it your interpretation which has authority?

The Bible does not lack authority because it is not verse by verse 'immediately employable.' For example, How does one apply the principle of love to difficult and complex personal and social situations? Where there is disagreement about ethical questions, one can hardly settle the matter from the text of Scripture when parties appeal to the same text but draw different meanings from it, different directives for action.

The following warning is appropriate here. 'Authority is often confused with immediate applicability. It is then thought that every word and command in Scripture is forthwith obligatory for faith and conduct . . . The Bible is not authoritative because it is verse by verse immediately employable.'[26]

It is not an uncommon procedure to assert the authority of the Bible on inadequate grounds and then to demand unconditional belief or unconditional obedience. Take the following as examples of this logic:

> 'The New Testament is clothed with his supreme authority and commands our unconditional obe-dience.'[27]

> 'The most basic and fundamental of all claims made on behalf of the Bible, and that which it makes for itself, is that it is true. This means that whatever statements it makes on whatever subject are all true. The Bible is a book of truth not lies, of integrity not falsehood. The reason the Bible claims to be true is because what it contains comes to man from God. Holy and good men

wrote the Bible, but what they wrote was not their own ideas or wisdom. They wrote what God gave them to write. What they committed to writing was the Word of God expressed in human language.'[28]

We should now consider two questions. What is entailed in demanding belief and obedience in the name of an authoritative writing? Does the demand for obedience rest upon the demand for belief?

10 RECAPITULATORY STATEMENT

(1) Christians find themselves recognizing the authority of the Christian community with which they are connected.

(2) The Christian community appeals to the Bible, as authority. At the same time it presents its teachings for acceptance as authoritative for the member.

(3) By pronouncing that the Bible has authority, whether for doctrine, organisation, practice, the community is making a judgment about the Bible.

(4) The community demands that such judgments, usually indeed a whole series of judgments, often in great detail, about the Bible be endorsed by the members of the community.

(5) The believer's acknowledgment means that he lets himself come under the influence of both the Bible *and* the 'authority' which interprets the Bible to him.

(6) It is then his responsibility to assure himself that he is doing so for the right reasons. If he gives the right reasons he may be reasonably sure that he has not misconstrued the Bible, that his attitude to it is reasonable.

(7) The authority of the Bible is not identical with its immediate applicability. The meaning of the biblical passages is arrived at through interpretation.

CHAPTER III NOTES

[1]C. Evans, *op. cit.*, p. 24

[2]Reported in Eusebius, HE, VI, 25, 11-14 Cf. Stephenson, *A New Eusebius*, p. 223.

[3]Adam Fox, *Meet the Greek Testament*, pp. 16-17. 'I am not sure if John in all the five cases where his name indicates an author is the same John, nor whether he is John the son of Zebedee one of the Twelve, nor another John, the aged divine of Ephesus, or a young disciple of the Lord outside the circle of the Twelve. I am not sure if Matthew whose name is connected with the first Gospel is the same as Levi, called from the receipt of custom to be one of the twelve (*Mark* 2:14). I do not know who wrote the Epistle to the Hebrews or the Second Epistle of Peter. I do, however, know a great deal about Paul and Luke and I feel fairly certain that between them they wrote about half the New Testament.'

[4]Evans, *op. cit.*, pp. 25-27.

[5]*Ibid.*, p. 25.

[6]Cf. Article, *Authority* in Paul Edwards (editor), *The Encyclopaedia of Philosophy*, Vol. 1, p. 216. 'A person may fall in with another's suggestions, however, not precisely because he feels that he has a duty to obey, but because the other person is an *authority*, meaning that he is believed to possess expert knowledge and therefore the right to be listened to because he knows what he is talking about. This is the borderline case between authority and influence. The authority of the expert . . . involves the notion of someone qualified to speak. It presupposes standards by which expertise is assessed and recognized, for example, degrees or professional reputation. Evidence of this kind serve (sic) as reasons why laymen should take the expert's word without understanding his reasons, even without asking for them.'

[7]Quoted in P. Edwards, *op. cit.*, p. 215.

[8]Cf. the excerpt in *Sociological Perspectives*, Edited by Kenneth Thompson and Jeremy Tunstall, pp. 67-79.

[9]Cf. W.P. Montague, *The Ways of Knowing*, pp. 39-53.

[10]*Ibid.* p.49.

[11]J.K.S. Reid, *The Authority of the Bible*, p. 235.
[12]C.H. Dodd, *The Authority of the Bible*, pp. 25-26.
[13]*Ibid.*, p. 265 (italics in original).
[14]*Ibid.*, p. 268.
[15]*Ibid.*, p. 270.
[16]*Ibid.*, p. 271.
[17]*Ibid.*, p.273.
[18]John Baillie, *The Idea of Revelation in Recent Thought*, p. 117.
[19]See below, chapter VI.
[20]J. Nowal Geldenhuys, 'Authority and the Bible' in Carl F.H. Henry (editor), *Revelation and the Bible.*, p. 384.
[21]I Corinthians 14:34-35.
[22]I Cointhians 7:1, 38.
[23]John 9: 6.
[24]I Corinthians 6: 1-9.
[25]I Cointhians 7:10, 11.
[26]J.K.S. Reid, *op. cit.*, pp. 235-236.
[27]Geldenhuys, *Ibid.*
[28]Patrick Boyle, 'Evidence for the Book', *Focus*, p. 10.

SUMMARY OF CHAPTER IV

AUTHORITY: A SERIES OF MISTAKES

There are wrong reasons for taking the Bible to be authoritative. We now examine ten such reasons.

IV

AUTHORITY: A SERIES OF MISTAKES

1 WRONG REASONS FOR TAKING THE BIBLE TO BE AUTHORITATIVE

The right and proper ground for accepting and believing the Bible to be authoritative is that it has been the instrument of God's continuing revelation of Jesus Christ to the believer, and to the believing community. We may put it in the past tense. This is what has happened in the past. So it is over and done with. That is already a mistake. A more adequate account of the matter is that the experience of God's revelation through the Scripture confirms its authority. It is not something we then establish and for which we give grounds or provide justifying explanations. In some cases category mistakes occur when we give bad reasons. In others they occur when we give *any* reasons, if by giving reasons we think we can provide a demonstration. It is not a question of proving but rather one of witness. It is not a matter of demonstration but rather of pointing. Reason is explanatory not demonstrative.

2 TEN CATEGORY MISTAKES

The following are reasons sometimes given for accepting the Bible's authority. The Bible has authority

(1) because the Bible claims to have authority,

(2) because Jesus claimed that the Scriptures have authority,

(3) because the church teaches that the Scriptures have authority,

(4) because what the Bible says can be shown to be true, when it makes reference to matters of fact,

(5) because we can demonstrate that when the Bible makes predictions those predictions have come true,

(6) because the apostles had authority, their writings have unique authority. They, in turn, acknowledged that the Old Testament writings had authority. The Old Testament writings therefore have authority. So the writings of both the Old Testament and New Testament have authority.

(7) because the miracles of the Bible have their source in God, so the Bible is shown to be authoritative as having its source in God,

(8) because the writers of the Bible were inspired,

(9) because the Bible is a book written by spiritual experts,

(10) because the requirements of a doctrinal system demand the authority of the Bible.

None of these reasons individually or taken all together provide adequate grounds to establish the kind of authority which the Bible distinctively has. You could give all of these reasons and not have established the unique status which the Bible has. Indeed, you can go one step further and say that the sort of authority which the Bible has is not established, and cannot be established, by giving reasons, by providing arguments. The error is not that you've not given the right reasons alone. It is that you cannot give reasons in this way at all. You cannot *establish* the authority of the Bible by providing reasons. You can however, reasonably give an account of the authority of the Bible. That is what this whole book is attempting to do. There is no question of providing a logical demonstration of this kind of authority. But one can give good reasons once the kind of authority which the Bible may have has been experienced. We can avoid certain category mistakes when giving an account of the authority of the Bible.

A category mistake occurs when we apply ideas appropriate in one sphere of discourse, to another subject matter or area of discourse, where they are not appropriate. We may apply ideas and perspectives analogically across spheres of discourse, but their appropriateness cannot be taken for granted. For the fact is that some ideas are meaningful only within their original context. Any attempt to transfer them from one framework to another is hopeless since they are incommensurable between frameworks.[1]

A category mistake occurs when ideas are wrongly used, put in a context where they do not belong. Such mistakes are made by people who do not know how to wield concepts in the right way. So puzzles arise, due to 'inability to use certain items of the English vocabulary.'[2] So for example you cannot say that the typical student has just passed his exams with honours, or that the average housewife is at this moment doing her shopping. 'Typical students' and 'average housewives' don't do anything. It is a mistake to speak of them as if they did. It shows a misunderstanding of language to make them subjects of a sentence in the same way as you would 'students' and 'housewives.' They feature in statistical tables not in kitchens and classrooms.

You are talking to a visitor to your country, say America. He says that he has travelled widely and has now seen Washington, New York, North Carolina and San Francisco. He's seen Yellowstone National Park, and been to Nashville. He then says, 'But now I would like to see America.' You would then very quickly assure him that he has already seen America, since America is not something else besides these places. To think that it is would be to make a category mistake as some tourists do when visiting Oxford. They see colleges, the Bodleian Library, and the Ashmolean Museum, and then ask, 'But where is the University?' Since the University is not something else in addition to what they have already seen, the answer is, 'You have seen it already.' To think that America or the University of Oxford was something in addition to those places and institutions is to commit a category mistake.

What then is the category mistake in reference to the authority of the Bible? The believer reads the Bible. It helps him. It gives him new understanding. Primarily it mediates for him the reality of God, his demands, his love, his succour, the reality of Jesus Christ. The category mistake is to think of the authority of the Bible as something else, something other, something in addition to this. In a word it is even misleading to say that.

The ten reasons given above, whatever truth they contain, represent category mistakes in reference to the authority of the Bible. We take them up briefly, one by one.

(1) In order to achieve a certain 'objectivity' one may appeal to the 'Bible's own testimony to itself,' as if by so doing one had bracketed out of consideration the party which is asserting this self-claim of the Bible. There is nothing so subjective as such 'objectivity.' It is a category mistake to assert the authority of the Bible in isolation from the person or group making the assertion. Someone says, 'The Bible has authority and is to be believed and obeyed.' We have to take into account the someone who is saying this. That someone wants you to accept their claim. They want you to overlook that fact that they, a subject, are presenting their own interpretation and assertion.

It is a case of an authoritarian statement about authority. 'I have authority to say that the Bible has authority.' Why should anyone accept someone else's claim that the Bible (or any book or set of books) has authority, and is to be interpreted, believed and obeyed in a certain way?

Two possibilities are open. First, you can accept the claim that the Bible has authority because you have come to know the influence of the Bible for yourself. Second, you can accept their authority on other grounds when they make such statements. But you then have two problems rather than one. You have to settle the problem of why you should accept (a) their authority and (b) the authority of the Bible. As we have seen earlier, you have to have grounds for accepting someone as an authority before you may reasonably accept their statements or recommendations as authoritative. So if you accept the authority of the Bible (and along with this an interpretation of what the Bible teaches) on the grounds that some other authority proposes that you do so, the authority of the Bible is thus made secondary and derivative. The question is whether or not for the Christian the authority of the Bible is like that.

(2) The argument that the Scripture is authoritative because Jesus quoted it is a very important one in the traditional theology. When 'being authoritative' is taken to involve inerrancy, the argument takes the form: Jesus spoke of David (or of Daniel) as the source of a particular statement. Therefore David (or Daniel) was the author of that statement quoted. Even to question is a sign of failing to trust him, to make him untrustworthy on all matters.

It is a bizarre argument. It confuses Jesus as Saviour with Jesus as source of historical information. It is a serious category mistake.[3] It assumes that only if Jesus were always correct in every statement he made could he be reasonably believed in as Saviour. This position, be it noted, assumes that our reports about Jesus are also accurate. So it in fact assumes the very thing it sets out to demonstrate, that the Gospels, (and by a long extension from this 'other books of The Bible'), have authority. It assumes, that is to say, that as historical sources the Gospels inerrantly report Jesus' inerrant sayings about the writings and content of the writings of the Old Testament. It makes the spiritual, religious, authority of Jesus to depend upon what is historically probable or improbable. Lessing had long ago pointed out that truths of religion (he spoke of 'absolute truths') could not be made to depend upon contingent historical facts.

(3) The church teaches that the Scriptures have authority. But consider the denial of this, i.e. that the Scriptures do not have authority because the church teaches that they do. The church teaches that the Scriptures have authority not because it can confer an authority upon them, but because it has acknowledged the authority of God as mediated through these writings. The church teaches that the Bible has authority because the Bible has had

authority for the church. There can be no isolation of the Bible from what it does in and for the Christian community. The authority of the Bible is wrongly understood if one is led to think that one can accept it at second-hand. The authority of the Bible follows participation and involvement.

Of course an onlooker can examine the empirical evidence and make a report and say: the church accepts the Bible as authoritative. So it is a fact that such-and-such a community recognizes the Bible as authority. But such a sociological or historical statement does not involve the one making it in acknowledging the authority observed. But it is only in such acknowledgment that the unique status of the Bible is properly understood.

It is thus another category mistake to appeal to the church as the source and ground of the authority of the Bible. But the fact is that Christians sometimes argue in this way. In doing so they have confused their acknowledgment of the right of the church to interpret the Bible and their acknowledgment of the church's interpretations with the authority of the Bible itself.

(4) We establish the authority of the Bible as an historical document as we establish the authority of any other historical source. The value of its historical statements is assessed by historical methods. In this respect the Bible is to be treated like any other historical document. What the historian demonstrates, if it were to turn out that way, is that the Bible a propos the historical propositions under investigation, is a reliable historical authority.

The question then is, What is the relation between the Bible as an historical source, and the Bible as the vehicle of the communication of the Gospel? The primary purpose of the Bible is not to communicate historical truths. Indeed its primary purpose is not to communicate 'truths,' i.e. propositions. When and if it does so, it does so in order to communicate the reality of God. It can do that without being historically accurate. The Bible does not have to be an authority on everything in order to mediate the reality of God and his saving grace. The treasure is in earthen vessels. The 'word of God' is expressed through the human words.

Even if all the historical statements of the Bible could be demonstrated to be true and so prove itself to be a book 100% historically accurate, it would not by virtue of that fact become a spiritual or religious authority, or even assume spiritual or religious significance. That depends upon something else.

(5) Something similar must be said about the 'argument from prophecy,' which claims that the Bible has authority because the statements its writers made in reference to the future came to pass. The accuracy of their predictions is most remarkable and establishes the authority of the Bible. Prophecy is thought of as prediction, and fulfilment as the co-ordination of event with the prediction.

This is an attempt to provide a rational proof of the inspiration of the Bible and by that means, to prove rationally that the Bible has authority. The argument is simple. Whenever the statements of the prophets are predictions they have come to pass. Therefore the Bible is reliable. Therefore the Bible has authority. It is a piece of rationalism. The problem is that the conclusion is unclear. Let us assume that every prophecy comes to fulfilment. What might we validly infer from that? If we knew of someone who made predictions and were able to say unequivocally what the predictions meant, and they always came true, we would say that he was an accurate forecaster. We would not want to say more than this. Such a person would have the authority of an accurate forecaster. No more.

The Christian church has not generally thought of the Bible as a kind of super-almanac. That is the way this argument invites us to take it. Events are believed to be fulfilments of predictions only as we stand on the far side of the fulfilment. As to the events which have not yet happened, one can only expect that they will certainly happen. For some Christians, it is very important indeed to think of the Bible in this way because certain events essential for their belief lie still unfulfilled in the future. For some the voice of prophecy is so compelling that it sets them apart from all other Christians. In this case you take the argument to show that the

Bible has authority (i.e. should be taken notice of) for the unfulfilled event, since it has shown itself trustworthy for the fulfilled predictions. The Bible is like an almanac which provides sure information about the future.

The confession of faith in Jesus Christ is not identical with belief in the prospects of a fulfilment in the future, even if Jesus Christ is the subject of that hope.

(6) Can one establish the unique authority of the Bible by appealing to the authority of the apostles as the primary historical witnesses to Jesus Christ? The question is this: Why does one accept the authority of the apostles? Note that this is not just an historical authority, but a *religious* authority. The position has not avoided the problem of the unique authority of the Bible. You are simply asking it of a different source. Unless you can give a clearer answer to this question you do not help yourself in your quest for a basis of religious authority.

(7) The supernatural authority of the Bible is proved by supernatural means. Revelation is demonstrated by miracle. The miracles are the divinely given signs that the revelation is from God. What cannot be demonstrated by reason can be proved by the miraculous. Jesus performed miracles and this established that he was a truly divine teacher. To the extent that the teaching is supernatural, to that extent there must be supernatural proofs of its truth. Hence the supernatural truths of the Bible are demonstrated by the occurrence of miracles. So one accepts the miracle stories as literal. But one must ask questions, because the miracle stories pose critical problems, concerning their historical sources and their significance.

This argument had a long currency in Christian circles. It appears in Thomas, in Hooker, in Calvin, and given its perhaps last systematic expression by Morley. So it has been popular. But it is fallacious. That miracles accompany the teacher does not demonstrate that what the teacher says is true, whatever the miracles are. The kind of acknowledgment that constitutes the Christian's acceptance of the authority of Scripture is of a quite different order than that which accepts and (perhaps) wonders at the occurrence of miracles.

(8) A further category mistake is to relate the notion of the authority of the Bible to the process whereby the books came to be written. The writer was inspired. So the writing has authority. No! These words do not have authority because, in some manner, they issued out of a process of inspiration. They may have done so. That is a problem to be settled on the basis of appeal to the available evidence. But if they did they do not have authority because they did. They have authority because they are relevant, living words, because something happens of importance when they are read and interpreted. The event of revelation happens. These words provide the means. They are the vehicle of that happening. These words are caught up in the dynamic of God's revelation. This means that inspiration is a less adequate and less important concept than revelation.

Since they are not the only writings to function in this way, they are unique in that they are the only words which have a unique historical connection with the original Christ-event, with the coming of Christian faith into the world. They are for this reason primary. They are the words which have in the history of the church proved to be the means for God's continuing revelation of himself. The church asserts the historical givenness of these and not other words. It also asserts the contemporaneity of the revelation of God these words mediate. 'The Spirit breathes upon the word and brings the truth to sight.' God revealed himself. God reveals himself.[4]

(9) One mistake we have spoken of earlier, namely to claim that the Bible is a handbook written by spiritual experts whose writing deserves respect because they were particularly competent in the religious, the spiritual life. So they are historically informative, but they also provide information and models for the aspiring spiritual seeker. 'Its (i.e. the New Testament's) authority is that of spiritual experts, and we treat it as we should treat the authority of any supreme expert.'[5] They are able to share their expertise with their

readers. But does this help us to speak about the unique authority of the Bible?

Such a comment can be very misleading. Let us pursue for a moment the analogy it suggests. If you want to learn about a subject, say Greek vases, you will find a book written by an expert on Greek vases. If you want to learn how to become a successful linguist you will read books by the experts. Eventually you may end up (if you pay attention, are intelligent enough and follow the expositions) knowing about Greek vases and knowing about the language. Does the writer really mean that the place which the New Testament holds in the Christian faith is that of informing us on a subject, the spiritual life (it seems)? If so, he has missed the point. The Bible's authority is not like that of the expert historian who informs us about the past. It does not consist in providing us with accurate information about the life of the spirit. It's not a book of instruction in the sense that the expert is instructing the novice. 'Expert' is simply not the right word. Paul was an expert in Jewish law. But he was also a devoted Christian. But there's something radically wrong in speaking of him as an 'expert' Christian. It is either a category mistake or a caricature to call him a spiritual expert, a Christian expert.

(10) Every church has a basic set of teachings. Sometimes these find expression in creedal statements, or in a series of 'articles,' in which they are formally stated, as for example the Westminster Confession, and the Thirty-nine Articles. But whether they formally state them in some such way or not, every church has such a system. The doctrinal system represents the understanding of that particular church as to what is true. The particular church requires its members to believe the doctrines. Each Christian group has a quite specific doctrinal and historical connection with the Bible, even if now separated from the Bible by a gap of twenty centuries.

The church, in demanding belief in and adherence to its teachings includes, as such a basic belief, the claim that the Bible has authority. You believe the doctrines. You believe the Bible to have authority as the source of the doctrines. One of the doctrines you believe is that the Bible has authority. In turn you believe that the Bible supports the doctrines you believe. This means that the Bible supports belief in its own authority.

Groups which emphasise the authority of the Bible often claim that there is a direct connection between their teachings and the biblical text and speak of 'Bible doctrines,' 'biblical theology.' The claim that there is an immediate connection between church doctrine and biblical text characteristically accompanies the corresponding claim that the propositions of the Bible are true. Hence the doctrines are also true and possess the authority which their source, the Bible, has.

Conviction that the doctrines are true carries with it the acknowledgement of the authority of the Bible as the source of those doctrines. Convinced of the authority of the Bible, one accepts the authority of the doctrines, and thus of the church which teaches them. But what is the initial step in accepting this authority?

Not all Christian communities claim that there is such a direct relationship between Bible and doctrine. Those that do tend to neglect important issues of interpretation, often making naive assumptions.

Let us examine the argument. We can put it quite concretely by referring to specific doctrines: for example, the Bible teaches that adults are baptized; that the soul is not immortal; that God is angry with wicked people; that God led the Israelites from Egypt; that Jesus ascended into the sky and will return therefrom; that Israelites paid tithes of their produce to support the Levites; that Jesus is Son of God; that the dead will be raised. The reason given why you should believe such propositions is that the Bible teaches them, and the Bible has authority.

On this account, you are invited to move from the system to the Bible, and accept the doctrines only if the Bible teaches them. The appeal is from the system to the Bible. The claim is that the system is *based upon* the Bible. The authority which the Bible has, and which can be established in different ways, then attaches to the 'Bible doctrines' which are derived from it. The assumption is that the system of doctrines adequately represents the doctrinal teaching of the Bible and can therefore be said to have the authority of its source.

But this assumes that the Bible has authority before you get the doctrinal system from it. The alternative is that it has authority because the teachings have the primary authority and the Bible participates in that authority — a Bible, interpreted as the system requires, shares the status of the system. Then the centre of gravity has shifted. The community is responsible for having worked out the system and for teaching it. It may even exert pressures to ensure conformity to it while asserting the authority of the Bible to back up its right to teach this doctrine and to exert this pressure.

Systems of doctrine taught in different churches differ from one another. Different and even conflicting systems are *based upon* the Bible. Once the foundations, the postulates, of the system are 'established,' the system may be more or less coherent. Two basic claims are often and easily confused. The first is that the Bible has authority, in the sense that what it says should be believed and obeyed. The second is that the Bible has been correctly interpreted and the interpretations correctly arranged, so that consistency results in the teaching derived from it.

The first of these basic claims is needed to give sanction to the second and to ensure that the teachings of the doctrinal system are invested with the same kind of authority the Bible has. So 'the truth' which has been selected and worked into a system partakes of the authority, if not the inerrancy or divinity, of the Bible from which it has been derived. A church may then claim that it has the truth, the infallible truth.

A serious problem now arises as we can see by setting out the argument:

> Authority is an ultimate source of truth.
> The Bible has authority

The teachings are derived from the Bible.
Therefore the teachings are true.

The serious error is due to 'the apparent impossibility of treating authority as an ultimate source of truth. When questioned as to why a given authority, say one of the writers of the Bible, should be accepted without question, the answer is almost inevitably a statement that the witness himself did not have to depend on authority, but possessed superior opportunities of acquiring the truth direct through some one of the other sources of belief, such as experience or intuition.'[6]

There is a central core of foundation doctrines without which the system (and the church built upon it) would not be. There are also a lot of materials remaining. These biblical materials get loosely tied into the system, but are not the hard core. When questions are raised about these, the community attempts to relate them to the system. Otherwise whole tracts of biblical material and of past doctrinal discussions in the history of the wider church lie dormant, unconnected as it were. Discussion of the question of the 'authority' of the whole Bible must include these 'dormant' sections of the canon. What inevitably happens is that the system serves as a screen or (to use Kantian language) provides a set of categories, to render the meaning of the Bible.

The doctrinal system may function to set limits to what the Bible can teach. It focuses attention on certain elements in the Bible, providing ideas and approaches which are taken as keys to the meaning of Scripture. They are like the viewfinder through which we see the landscape. Or they are like the filter which puts what we see in a certain light. Of course there's more to the landscape than the viewfinder frames. And in a different light condition we would use a different filter. The believer believes all kinds of things the Bible does not teach and may recognize that the Bible has more to teach than can be contained in the particular doctrinal system. But to the extent that the doctrinal system is of primary importance for the community, and to the extent that the community claims that the Bible is the authority for the doctrine, to that extent the doctrinal system limits the message of the Bible.

The term 'limits' in our assertion above perhaps demands some explanation. When we pay attention to one aspect of the biblical teaching we are in so doing giving more emphasis to what that leads us to see and to say. In doing so we give limited emphasis to other aspects. In certain instances a doctrinal stance will lead us to certain clear denials, and thus exclude certain alternative interpretations of Scripture. Take what is sometimes called universalism, the belief that all human beings will eventually come to acknowledge and accept the love of God. The opposing view, non-universalism, argues that human beings are created in such a way that God cannot save them if they will not acknowledge and accept his love— and it adds 'some will not.' The point is that when one accepts a non-universalist view, one then has a certain pre-disposition toward a particular interpretation of Scripture. Does one then consider that there are passages of Scripture which actually teach universalism or could be feasibly be interpreted so to teach?

But it is the angle of vision, and the set of ideas the system provides for us, that determines what is important and what is not in the biblical sources. How then, if our vision is thus pre-focused, can we be sure that the light that may fall will illuminate our way forward? Can we be sure that we do not deny truth in the name of 'having' the truth. Notice that we may deny truth and the guidance of the Spirit simply by neglect. We are looking there and the important thing is here. If the important thing is in the present and we can't see it because we're looking to the past, we cannot then speak of response to the guidance of the Spirit. We confess faith in the guidance of the Spirit in the past history. We recognize that *they* were guided by the Spirit when *they* were working out the system. So we accept the system as they have worked it out and as they have handed it down to us. We could not have done it by ourselves. What is this if it is not to adopt tradition, in the precise meaning of that term? The founders, the pioneers, worked out the system. We accept what they worked out, and now continue to affirm it. We must give attention to this fact, that *we accept their system*. Thus we view the Bible through the vision we have inherited, through the doctrinal system we have accepted from the past. That leads us fairly and squarely to the problem. If Scripture has unique authority, what are we to say of its relation to the doctrinal tradition and to the 'teaching office' of the church which promotes that tradition. That is just as much, in its way, a problem for the Protestant as for the Catholic.

The fact is that each particular religious community has worked out its own system of teachings. It came into being through an historical process. It has its own unique history, through which, in its own unique way, it confesses the guidance of God, the Holy Spirit. That unique historical process has left a deposit of practices and teachings for those who inherit them to reckon with. The very existence of that particular community depends upon the passing on of the teachings and practices and then on assent to them. As time passes the church has to come to terms with its past and the deposit of tradition which it inherits from the past.

Teachings are handed down, and where doctrine is the basis of the church's unity, the church will accept them. What the individual or the present community did not achieve and could not have achieved alone by way of interpreting the Bible, they can assent to when it is presented to them. If such a continuity of assent is not evident then the community begins to fall apart. The community continuously re-affirms what is handed on to it. In short, it depends upon tradition.

The doctrinal authority of the Bible is thus mediated to believers through their giving assent to a particular doctrinal tradition. But a shift of emphasis may become evident. The continuity of the community may be more important than the actual teachings. Assurance of assent may, ironically, become as important as the content of the propositions assented to, paradoxical as that may be. The doctrine then becomes formal. To such dogma, formal assent must be given.

Loyalty to a doctrinal system may be a form of being hidebound to tradition. In some circles it is a particularly sensitive area to talk about because what the church doctrine demands is identified with what God teaches in the Bible. This cannot be questioned. As we have seen, right at the outset, it would be in any case unduly restrictive to see the Bible only as a source of doctrine. It is further restrictive to see the Bible as teaching only what a particular system of doctrine demands. The meaning of the teachings inevitably undergoes changes as time passes. What has one meaning in one historical situation will have a different meaning at another.[7] It is an illusion to think that a system of truth can be fixed and unchanging. The words and the logic may not change. But the meaning changes. One could examine each doctrine in a system and show how as time passes the meaning undergoes a more or less radical change. It is not simply that we learn more as time passes. That is not the issue. Many Christian believers think that they possess the truth and that truth stands firm. They would enthusiastically sing, 'Forever stand the bulwarks of God's truth, unchanged, undaunted and unmoved for e'er.' But if we focus on the changing *context* of the Christian teachings rather than on the dogmatic *propositions*, we can see that the meaning a proposition has for me and *for my community*, it has *at this particular time and place*. The identical statement of doctrine in two different contexts may have two quite different meanings. In short, it is not the same doctrine. We have learnt that lesson from the Bible itself. For example it is not appropriate sometimes to say God's gift of forgiveness is entirely free. The reason is because it would be misunderstood. At other times, it has to be emphasized for example to correct an exaggeration of legal demands, or of self-righteous claims.

Dietrich Bonhoeffer in *The Cost of Discipleship* was well aware of this. On the one hand there is the threat of legalism, of thinking that by performing good works one can deserve or earn one's acceptance with God. On the other there is the threat of 'cheap grace' of a so-called discipleship without repentance, without sacrifice. Each one is a threat because they lead to distortion. One distorts the offer of the freely given grace of God. The other distorts the call for obedience and personal cost.

Bonhoeffer directed his polemic against the attitude he saw prevalent in the church that since the Christian is justified by grace he can live like the rest of the non-believing world. He wrote: 'Cheap grace is grace without discipleship, grace without the cross, grace without Jesus Christ, living and incarnate.'[8]

The church changes as the time passes, as the world changes, as the social context changes. Once, however, doctrinal attitudes have become fixed, is it then impossible to accept the fact of change of meaning without losing face, and so without compromising the authority of the church? It is, however, mistaken from the outset to be inflexible. Authority based upon inflexibility is bound to suffer when inflexibility is shown to be mistaken. There is, however, a more sinister aspect to the influence of a changing social climate upon the teaching and attitude of the church. Adjustment may be deliberate and may lead to compromise and compromise may lead to betrayal. The story of the adjustments which churches were ready to make in Nazi Germany do not make comfortable reading.[9]

When we learn or experience something significant we see what we had previously seen from a different perspective. What we newly learn makes a difference to our point of view. It makes a difference to our past. It changes the past, because we now see that past differently.

This is true not only of the individual but also of the community. A doctrinal system is an expression of the experience and of the understanding of the community. The individual is inducted when he comes to take an interest or make a decision, into that communal understanding. In fact he may be socialized into the context and only later come to make a personal judgment about it. Since his context may well be very different from earlier contexts, he will have to work out for himself the full significance of his new beliefs, attitude and context. He may find that he cannot take it in, as it has stood. He may have learned what the creators of the system did not know. He may have to relate the teachings to such things as he has learned which they did not know (and there is a whole range of such things), either because they could not have learned them or did not choose to do so.

These general principles can be illustrated by numerous examples from church history. It is empirical fact that the significance of 'the truth' that is drawn from Scripture, the significance of the doctrines which appeal to its authority, becomes different as time passes even within the 'same' community. What this implies about the meaning of authority is that it is relational. Every church has new experiences as time passes and as times and situations change. Each must come to terms with the teachings they have inherited in the light of such experiences and changes.

The group and the individual believer may find it difficult to make the adjustments called for. The group may in fact resist any adjustment and become reactionary and defensive, and lose touch with the real world by seeking to preserve its supposed integrity by otiose and irrelevant considerations. It is no wonder that when that happens theology then gets a bad name.

What will be done about the elements in the system that have become problematical? The answer which in any circumstance will be given to that question will depend upon several considerations, for example:

(1)   how radical the questions are,
(2)   how fundamental the teachings in question are to the doctrinal system and so to the unity of the community,
(3)   the degree of commitment to the system. This may range from doggedness on the one hand to a very liberal attitude on the other.

The community will consider that some teachings are more fundamental than others. If these more fundamental teachings are radically questioned then the effect will be felt throughout the system. It is when teachings questioned bear directly and explicitly upon the question of authority that response is likely to be most pronounced. The repercussions of such questioning will then be felt in the structure of the institution, since doctrine and doctrinal development always has a social aspect.

For example, if discussion on the problem of infallibility is seriously enough pursued, the very structure of authority in the Roman Catholic church will be under review. Similarly, if the authoritativeness of the prophet with her endorsement of the sanctuary doctrine and eschatological scheme were seriously enough questioned, the structure of authority in the Seventh-day Adventist Church would come severely under review.

Other questions and changes may not be so far reaching in their effects. 'Powers that be' in the community (as in the two cases instanced) will take what measures they consider needful to preserve the continuity of the community and to preserve the consensus about its past. There is in such communities a strongly (if not dominating) conservative element. The reasons why it holds on to its inherited belief system are not far to seek. Authority is at stake. To have taken a position is to put one's authority and credibility on the line. Having taken a stand on the infallibility of the teaching office, as a basis for its authority, or on the inspiration of the prophet as a basis for the prophet's authority, that sort of claim is most difficult to modify, perhaps impossible to abandon.

But the meaning of the Bible is not exhausted by being made the basis of a system of doctrine. There is much that escapes when Bible and system of doctrine are practically conflated. In fact, while by no means denying the importance of doctrine (why should a theologian do that?), one must say that if the importance of the Bible is made to consist in its being construed as a source of doctrine, it is being severely reduced, misunderstood, and indeed distorted. Revelation is not reducible to the communication of propositions, and faith is not identical with assent to propositions, in this case propositions repeating biblical statements, or being inferred or worked out from them.

It is also a category mistake to assert that the Bible has authority in and of itself apart from the church that is interpreting it. Of course we shall not be able simply to equate the revelation of God with the activity of the Church, any more than we shall identify the revelation of God with the words of Scripture. The meaning of Scripture is mediated through the interpretation of the church.

This is an active process which selects and decides what is important, what is to be said and what to be left unsaid. The church does not appeal to the Bible in and of itself. It always has its own interest in what the Bible teaches and shall teach. There is, of course, a certain objectivity. The church inherits these books, these words, not others.

But the church cannot pretend that it does not intervene between what the Bible contains and what it pronounces that the Bible teaches. To pretend so is to commit a fallacy of the utmost importance as the following line of argument shows.

Consider two lines of argument:

ARGUMENT (1):

> The Bible contains such and such teachings.
> The Bible has doctrinal authority.
> Therefore, these teachings have authority.
> Therefore, the believer must accept these teachings if he accepts the doctrinal authority of the Bible.

The statements of this argument must be prefaced with the words, 'I say,' 'we say,' or 'the such-and-such church says . . . .' Only then can we appreciate the importance of the intervention of the interpreter. The argument then looks, and is, a rather different one:

ARGUMENT (2):

> The Bible contains such and such teachings, which we have selected and listed.
> The Bible, in the context of a particular church, has doctrinal authority.
> Therefore: Such and such teachings based on the Bible and drawn from it by this particular church have authority.

Therefore: the believer, *in the context of the particular church,* must accept the teachings.

The serious error of argument (1) is that it omits all reference to the process of interpretation, to the interests and presuppositions of the interpreter, and to the social context.

By omitting the reference to the church as the interpreter one seeks to gain an easier admission of the authority one asserts of the Bible. But one is but doing so in such a way as not to make it obvious what the real issue is, namely, the issue of interpretation within the context of the interpreting community, the church. The cogency of the argument and hence the force of the conclusion depends on the acceptance of the assertion that the Bible has authority *and* that the church has the authority to interpret the Bible *and* that when it does so the particular interpretation it makes has authority. Argument (1) is a truncated version of Argument (2).

The argument has force only when used *within* a community of belief that respects the Bible as a doctrinal source. It has no force to someone who does not accept the authority of the community. For such people different arguments, pointers and approaches must be used. They may not be available to the particular community.

But internal crises *do* take place within such communities. This happens when there is dissatisfaction with current interpretations and the claims to authority which accompany such interpretations, and when there are alternative interpretations. It happens when people start asking such questions as the following.

First, is one not being asked to accept the *teaching authority* of the church gratuitously, on the strength of accepting the authority of the Bible? Is it not as if the authority of the church slips in between the claim and its acceptance? This must be brought clearly out into the open. We can't avoid the question: Who says so? That means we cannot avoid the question, *How* does the church derive its teachings from the Bible? That is the question of interpretation. An essential element of the Protestant stance is not to accept the teachings because *church*, even if it is my church, says that these are the teachings to accept. It is to ask: 'Are you, is the church, interpreting aright?' We do not simply ask 'What do *we* believe?' but also ask, 'On what principles of interpretation are such beliefs derived and in what manner are they put forward for acceptance?' That is what it means to be a Protestant, to say nothing about what it means to be intelligent. It is to have the right of private judgment.

It is to believe that the Holy Spirit guides the individual believer in making judgments and that means not simply and only when his judgments agree with what the tradition teaches or what the elders teach. In seeking to dominate and pressure private judgment, there is present a denial of the important Protestant principle. For the Protestant the teaching authority of the church represents a consensus of interpretation, and that can only emerge where the recognition of the principle of the guidance of the individual by the Spirit is present and the right of private judgment is acknowledged.

If someone were to say to me: 'You must accept what this book says,' I should ask, 'Why? Is it because the book says so? Or, is it because you say so? I mean: does the authority reside in the book? Or, does the authority reside with you?'

So when the church says, 'You must accept these as the teachings of the Bible,' one must sometimes ask, 'Why? Is it because the book says so? Does the authority reside in the book? Or, is it because you say so; 'you' being 'the church'? If so, where in the church do I locate who has the authority to tell me what I should believe? Does the authority reside in the church? Should I be told what I am to believe ?

The problem that I would then have would be to ask first whether the authority of the church lies in some official, or group of officials, or in some official pronouncements, and, if so, I would like it to be made quite specific. I want to be quite clear that there is adequate and widely accepted machinery for discussion and presentation of the issues.

A second important question concerns the question of change. Must the church sometimes change so as to preserve the authority of the Bible and to experience the guidance of God? Or, put in another form: When the church experiences the guidance of the Holy Spirit, will it not sometimes have to change? That this is the case is readily acknowledged in the formative period of the church. But when practices, doctrines and interpretations become fixed, there is a growing tendency to become inflexible and formal. Often intolerance follows in its wake.

To change would have interesting implications. First, to change might mean that the past interpretation was wrong and therefore the church had erred in the past. What assessment is to be given when such error is admitted?

The second problem when such error becomes evident concerns the Bible as the source of the church's teaching. Does change mean that the Bible on which the teaching or demand was based does not have the authority it was claimed to have?

But third: the basic question at issue is not the authority of the Bible but of the church and of the *present* basis for teaching. The question becomes more complex when there is either an explicit or implicit claim to infallibility. This is explicit in traditional Roman Catholic teaching. It is implicit in conservative Protestantism. But one does not have to go so far as to speak of infallibility. One simply recognises that the teaching was considered to be right in the past by the authority. It means that in the present the church will have to make changes in how it understands and is to reckon with the sources of present teaching in the community, how it is to achieve agreement on the question of authority, and on the teachings in the present. The issue is that of authority in the church. It is as much a sociological as a theological problem.

In concluding this section we might indicate different possible kinds of doctrinal change which are appropriate for discussion at the present time.

(1) There are those teachings which were once relevant but now are no longer relevant, relevant in a particular context but not outside that context. I am thinking of arguments for the existence of God, of salvation conceived in terms of the symbol of substitution, of the conception of God as Judge. What relevance can such teachings have in a humanistic, atheistic context where the idea of God or of salvation or judgment has no meaning? Are the traditional frameworks to be retained?

(2) When there is a change of circumstances there is the erosion of meaning for the particular community. If one

says, 'Jesus is coming soon,' 'The Kingdom of God is imminent,' but does not define what 'soon' and 'imminent' mean and a century or two or a couple of millennia pass, then the meaning of the expression becomes problematical, and there is a dilemma to face.

(3) Evident shift in doctrinal teaching occurs when the emphasis changes. It may be by changing what, or part of what, was formerly affirmed. In any case the significance of the doctrinal system is thereby altered.

(4) Sometimes a change of basic symbolism takes place. Some symbols are central to a doctrinal system. Should those symbols lose their centrality or become otiose, the system undergoes a change of meaning, or loses its meaning.

Take for example the symbol of the 'lamb of God' which pictures graphically the concept of substitution following death. He 'takes away the sin of the world.' The symbol is taken from the sacrificial system of the Jewish Temple where death occurred daily. The lamb was slaughtered before its blood was sprinkled on the altar. It combines with a further symbol, that of a God of strict justice who cannot overlook the gravity of human sin, who must be appeased before sin, the very serious offence against him, can be forgiven and wiped away. That is achieved by the death of the Son of God the divine human intermediary between sinful man and a just God.

The theory of substitutionary atonement worked out in detail by Anselm and widely taught in the Christian churches for centuries requires such symbols. When rejected, on whatever grounds, ethical or theological, it can no longer take central place in accounting for human redemption. Further symbols which depend on it and illustrate are to be abandoned with it.

Following these observations about doctrine and doctrinal systems, it is time now to return to our main issue, the argument from the authority of the doctrine, taught and accepted, to the authority of the Bible. The argument appears to have appeal, provided one accepts the premises and assumptions on which it is based. But there is a rather different case. Again we shall put it in the form of an argument:

> The doctrines (= system) are true (for whatever reason they are accepted as such.)
>
> The doctrines are based on (derived by a process of interpretation from) Scripture.
>
> Therefore Scripture has authority (i.e. Scripture as required by, and interpreted as required by the doctrinal system).

We spoke earlier of categories of interpretation. Let us specify some examples: atonement as sacrifice and mediation; the work of Jesus as substitute; prophecy as prediction; Jesus as fulfilment of Old Testament typology. If the doctrinal system requires a literal interpretation of ascension, descent into hell, pre-existence of the Son then literal interpretation there will be, not only of these but of as many passages as it seems reasonable to interpret literally. The interpretation of the Bible will be made in the light of these dominating concepts. The Bible gets read in the light of these concepts, and becomes a source for the elaboration or interpretations fitting in with and supporting such teaching. The Bible materials are then supportive of the doctrinal scheme. The Bible supports the church's doctrines. One searches for 'texts', and arranges them into a supportive scheme. The Bible thus becomes a doctrinal textbook, or a doctrinal sourcebook. It is a book full of 'truths' that have to be discovered, culled and arranged. The community which supports both the procedure and the doctrines so derived will support both the method and the system and shield it from threat and question.

Each of the ten reasons we gave above is in error. Are there then ten different category mistakes? Perhaps the reason there are so many is that they are all making a common mistake. What is common to all of them is (1) that they seek to establish the authority of the Bible on the basis of something other than the actual effectiveness of the Bible in the church and in the world, and (2) they assume that this authority can be established by an appeal to facts other than the intrinsic one. The pattern of argument common to each argument is:

> *E*, i.e. something extrinsic, establishes the authority of the Bible
> Therefore, the Bible has authority.

What is missing is an understanding of the *intrinsic* nature of the authority of the Bible. *E* in each case is something *extrinsic*: e.g. a claim the Bible makes, or a claim Jesus makes, or a claim the church makes. Authority which has to be demonstrated and then attributed to the Bible is secondary and not primary. Christians do not believe the Bible because of something else, this *E*, this extrinsic thing. They believe it on account of its effectiveness. That is the kind of authority it has. They have already experienced its effectiveness. They do not need persuasion by argument. The point of argument in this context is to *explain* what they already know. Faith has come into being. Now we seek understanding. That is a good definition of theology: 'faith seeking understanding', *fidens quaerens intellectum.*'

3 RECOGNIZING BUT NOT CONSTITUTING AUTHORITY

These are then ten versions of a basic mistake in conceiving authority.

It is not a question of saying what attitude we ought to take to the Bible. The Bible does not do what it *ought* to do. It is not that sort of thing. We do not determine the limits of the literature. We reckon, after the event, that it is these books that have been the instruments of the event. We then can anticipate that they will be so again. Having happened in the past, and happening from time to time and from place to place in the present we can then acknowledge the unique agency of the Bible. We *recognize* that it has this status, this function. We do *not constitute* it as such. It is not that the church sets up the canon and then the Bible does such and such. The order is quite the reverse. God reveals himself. The literature of the canon is the instrument. The church is constituted by the revelation of God. It confesses that it is, and so is an article in its own creed. It confesses that it is because of the revelation of God within it. It confesses the essential role which the Bible plays in providing the means for God's revelation of himself. Its very being has depended and depends upon that.

It then follows that all attempts to *prove* the status, the authority of the Bible, which omit reference to the revealing, saving, and community-creating, activity of Jesus Christ within the church are misguided. We cannot hope to *demonstrate* the unique authority of the Bible on the basis of showing the trustworthiness of the Bible on historical grounds; nor on the basis of an argument from prophecy to fulfilment, nor on the basis of its own testimony to itself, and then on the basis of that demonstration demand that the authority of the Bible be acknowledged and its concepts be obeyed. To do that is to enter a quite different realm. Where God is known he makes himself known. The Bible is the instrument, the means of that revelation. As such there can be no talk of demonstration. The Bible whose authority can be demonstrated is not the church's 'Word of God.' Archaeological evidence is interesting. Here it is irrelevant. Between historical demonstration and religious authority lies an unbridgeable gulf.

4 AUTHORITARIANISM

We are looking for a concept of authority that avoids authoritarianism. We want to define an attitude which accepts authority without succumbing to such authoritarianism. We may define 'authoritarianism' as (1) the attitude of demanding unquestioning dependence for the knowledge of matters we cannot find out for ourselves, of assuming unquestioning reliance on the testimony of others for discovering truth. Of course we rely on witnesses for our knowledge of the past. Historical knowledge is like that. But we can test the witnesses, not uncritically accept their testimony. We can question the assumption of authoritarianism. We are nevertheless dependent on others for whatever knowledge we have of the past. I must accept the authority of others to get information about Julius Caesar, John Locke, Napoleon. They (those others who have provided such information) were in a position I could never be in. So I depend upon them. But I do not just accept anything any purported witness or historical source says.

By authoritarianism we also mean (2) the acceptance of beliefs and demands on someone's authority, the shifting of the responsibility for the belief from the person believing it to the authority teaching it. We can consider authoritarianism from a logical, a psychological and a sociological point of view. In doing so we might answer such questions as: Is it reasonable? What state of mind does it demand? Where in any group of people does the centre of authority lie? Why and how does the group or the power centre in it try to retain its authority?

Most of us accept most of what we believe most of the time on someone else's authority. We have to. We can't learn everything we need to know from experience. We just rely, and rightly, on the word of others who are in a better position to know than we are. We readily support institutions which pass on, often in a very authoritarian way, the traditions which we believe in, for example, to young people in school, who are in no position to raise questions about what they are being taught. But we believe in the trustworthiness of those whose word we take to be true. Such trust is not always evident and explicit to us. But it is always implied whenever we believe what we are told without questioning.

Is such acceptance of authority reasonable? If we wish to test the authority we can raise questions at certain points, test its statements where we are able to test them ourselves. If that satisfies us we could then reasonably trust claims we are not able to check.

When authorities conflict you have to find a reasonable way of deciding between them. Otherwise your adherence to one particular authority would be irrational. Disagreements between authorities over the question of authority are not to be settled by appealing to their authority. That is the very thing that is in question. The Christian appeals to the Bible as authority. The Moslem appeals to the Koran as authority. Both may appeal to their book to establish the authority of their book. But obviously that will not do. If there is a rival authority we cannot accept the claim of an authority on the basis of the claim that it is an authority making the same claim. We shall have to seek for other grounds to establish it. This leads us to an important conclusion: We cannot accept authority as an *ultimate* source of truth.

The psychological appeal of authoritarianism for a certain type of mind is irresistible. To rely on someone else to tell you what to believe, how to act and what to think, relieves you of the task of thinking and deciding for yourself. If the authority assures you that there is no need to think for yourself, that all that needs to be decided has been decided, that may well confirm you in your credulity, sloth, timidity and intellectual laziness. Many people like such assurance and are prepared to pay a big price for it.

> The chief reason for the continuance of author-itarianism as a method lies not in its logical but in its psychological appeal. Men who are intellectually lazy or timid will always welcome the appeal to cease thinking for themselves and to believe what they are told to believe. Such men enjoy the freedom from responsibility which their conformity brings. So far from being ashamed of accepting a doctrine on the mere say-so of someone else, they actually make a virtue out of their weakness, and singing the praises of blind faith, they proceed to persecute those who seek truth for themselves. . . . He who repudiates this gift and the responsibilities which it brings, and binds himself over to the blind acceptance of authority, has exchanged his birthright for a mess of slave's pottage. He may be more comfortable, for the search after

wisdom often brings sorrow and disillusionment, but his soul's comfort will have been purchased at the cost of his soul's honour. Better to raise one's eyes to the sky and seek humbly for the truth, even though the search result in failure and unhappiness, than to give our beliefs into the keeping of another.'[10]

All institutions in human society have their structures of authority. The church is an example of this familiar social phenomenon. In any hierarchy there are leaders and there are the ones led, those who exercise power and those who accept as rightful the exercise of that power. There are those who lead. Some have more prominence than others. These wield authority in matters of organisation. But they also exercise authority regarding matters of doctrine. The centre of power in any church would have the authority both to designate what is true teaching and to see to it that such teaching is taught by its clergy. Since clerics must be supported both financially and ideologically in order to carry out their duties of teaching, the authorities in a church have several sanctions which can be used to get their will done. The authorities have power, in this context the capacity to get someone to do what you want them to do and to believe what you want them to believe.

Now, it is a principle (well known to sociologists) that those who have power and prestige will take whatever means they believe they are able to take in order to preserve these structures that give them their advantage, and to preserve themselves in the positions of power. Since the word 'authority' implies the acceptance and hence the legitimisation of the position and activity of those who have power, they will see to it that those who accept them are given grounds (convincing reason?) for maintaining the attitude of acceptance. They will try to demonstrate that the structure is divinely ordained, that the particular teachings they are promoting currently are divinely initiated and underwritten, and that structures and teachings coming from the past — the tradition — are believed to have the divine approval.

Not every Christian community explicitly works out a doctrine of infallibility. But there is something equivalent to it in many, many groups. Whatever the particular teaching or practice which the authority wishes to endorse, promote, retain, or introduce, if there is a *general* acknowledgment of the authority's right to promote it, the authority is free to proceed. It can then promulgate the teaching. It can require its acceptance as it can of whatever it deems to be important or essential. Then a two-fold acceptance is necessary: of the right of the authority to make decisions, and of the right of the authority to demand acceptance of its decisions. Given such acceptance the authority does not need to work out and state explicitly that it does not err.

To *accept* this right involves commitment, i.e. an *act* of acceptance. The question is whether the act will be made consciously and rationally, or only implicitly.

If I can be sure that some group is always going to accept without question what I teach them and give them to accept, there would seem to be little point in my trying to convince them that they should do so by producing a doctrine or a theory which justifies my authority. If I have unquestioned authority, so be it. There is no need to justify it to those who accept it without question.[11]

If the church rejects the principle of infallibility or incorrigibility but maintains its right to define orthodoxy i.e. state what ought to be believed, pronounce as to correct and so acceptable teaching, let that be carefully explained. A start might be made by putting practice into theory and examining the theory. That would be all to the good. The theory might sound like this.

(1) God has called and appointed the elders as custodians of the truth. God has ordained the leaders of the community and given to the group (committee, council) special guidance. This calling, these gifts, this group have warrant so that their decision, their pronouncement has authority i.e. is to be accepted as the true expression of doctrine. That means that it should become the orthodox

teaching of the particular community. When that
acceptance takes place the teaching assumes a kind of
fixity. The group may not originate the teaching, but
endorse it, sometimes in face of alternatives, indeed
sometimes because of the threat of heresy, defined as
such by the 'authority'!

(2) God has granted certain gifts to one particular person to
enable that person to function as teacher, leader or
prophet.

Illustrations can readily be found of binding authority but not
infallibility claimed for teachings. For (1) Church councils, e.g.
Nicaea, Chalcedon, framers of the Westminster Confession and
of the Thirty-nine Articles, contemporary doctrinal committees
within the particular community.. For (2): outstanding individuals,
e.g. Luther, Calvin, modern 'prophets'.

In every case the authority of the proposed teaching depends
upon acceptance within the particular community of the status of
the proposing group or person. That is often assumed. This
provides another case where practice demands justifying theory to
explain why such status is granted.

5 WITNESS TO JESUS CHRIST

In many respects the Bible is no different from other books. It
has a history and so may be studied historically. It was written, i.e.
compiled, edited, transcribed and translated as other books from
the ancient world have been. It is not the only book which speaks
of God, even speaks of God in personal terms. Other books too
have become the focal point of other religions and the source of
religious teachings.

The authority of the Bible does not derive from some other
source considered to be more basically authoritative,[12] for example,
the church, the inspired writer, the religious experience of the
believer; the loftiness of the ethical teaching; its literary qualities;
its reflection of religious genius.

The Bible is unique in that it bears witness to Jesus Christ. It is both the primary witness to Jesus Christ, and the means by which God is mediated through Jesus Christ to the believer in the present. Thus we may speak of the Bible as the Word of God, recognizing that this is a figure of speech. Through the human words of Scripture, God makes himself known, and the believer experiences the knowledge of God in reconciliation, peace, fellowship and demand. Thus, for the Christian, the Bible is *effective*. Its special place, its uniqueness, is in its effectiveness. These words are the instrument of God's continuing activity in the world.

So the Christian who confesses Jesus as Christ can acknowledge the unique status of the Bible. It is within the context of faith and of the community of faith that such a confession is made. It is not a matter of demonstration. It is a matter of witness. This is something quite different from acknowledging the factual trustworthiness of the Bible and fortunately does not require it.

6 THE AUTHORITY OF THE OLD TESTAMENT

We must raise the question of the authority, or the status, of the Old Testament for separate treatment, since the Old Testament was not a Christian book. It both is and is not a Christian book. It is the sacred book of the Jews, and the Jews would quickly and rightly claim the *Tanach* as their book. This book, 'The Law, the Prophets and the Writings,' had been their book and nurtured their piety for a thousand years, long before there were any Christians. (The name *tanach* is derived from the Hebrew words for *Torah, Nebiim, Kethubim*: Law, Prophets and Writings.)

The second important fact is that this book became a Christian book only when the Christian community came into being and began to read it and to interpret it. When Christianity came into being this book became part of the Scripture of the Christian community.

The third important fact is that when it became part of the Christian Scripture it remained the Scripture of the Jews. Since then it is thus Scripture for two religions. Moreover, Christians renamed this collection of books. They called it the *Old* Testament. Meanwhile, that is to say by the end of the first century A.D., a number of Christian writings had appeared and Christians called these the *New* Testament. The Hebrew and Greek words behind the English term 'testament,' mean 'covenant,' and this more readily than the more familiar, if no better understood, designation 'testament' suggests why it was that the sacred writings of another religion became part of the sacred writing of Christianity. They both agree in crucial respects concerning God's relation to mankind.

For we may ask whether there is anything distinctively Christian about the Old Testament. Certainly there is one important difference between the Old and New Testaments. The Old Testament is the book of a religious group which is also a nation. It is the book of a people which has and always had an existence separate from that of the Christian Church. Its teachings can be worked out and presented without reference to the New Testament and the figure of Jesus and the fact of Christian faith. There is nothing distinctively Christian about the teachings of the Old Testament. When Christians endorse and teach what the Old Testament teaches they thereby share teachings which are not distinctively their own, in the sense that they originated before the existence of the Christian community. The Old Testament teaching of sin, of God as Creator, of the law as the basis of covenant, of man as fallen creature, for example, are not uniquely Christian. They had been taught for many centuries before the coming of Christianity. They became Christian as Christians inherited them and put them in a new setting.

Christians agree with and proclaim teachings they did not originate. Christians adopt and interpret a book they did not write. They endorse and promote doctrines and attitudes contained in the book which they adopted. To understand this we must try to reconstruct the situation of the early Christian community and consider its attitude to these Hebrew writings. The first Christians were Jews. They had faith in Jesus, who was a Jew, who lived, taught, died and was widely known in Palestine. Jews believed that God is one. That firm monotheistic belief was the foundation for everything else. They believed that God is one because they interpreted the multifarious events of their long history as a continuity, indeed as a unity. How could they have possibly done that? Since it was an extremely diversified history, how could they come to see it as a unity? The history of the Jews in biblical times took many twists and turns. There was very great variety indeed. From the evidence of the Old Testament it is quite clear that at different times and even at different points in that history, Jews took very different attitudes to life. They had very different, even contradictory, ideas of God and of man's relationship to him. They endorsed opposed ethical ideas and ideals. The possibility of the Jewish people being split into many segments was always present. But these people with this varied history came to believe in one God and came to look back upon a unified history. It was a lesson that took them a very long time to learn. It was certainly not an inevitable development. Why did they not continue to think of Yahweh as a tribal god, or a fertility god, or as a national god? Why did not elements of all of these continue to exist side by side? Why did it not happen that Israel splintered into many fragments?

The fact is that they came to look on that very diversified history as a whole, as a unity. They found their unity as a people in the unity of their history, and that history pointed them to Yahweh. They came to believe that in the whole of their diversified past, God, Yahweh, had revealed himself to them. They had learned to think of Yahweh, and to experience Yahweh, not as a tribal God who preserved them from their enemies, not as a fertility god who gave them prosperity by ensuring that their crops grew, not a national god for whom there was only one people, but under the guidance of the greatest of their prophets, who while they lived wielded the real authority in the nation, as the God of the whole earth. The process that had taught them this lesson was a long historical one. Yahweh had guided them through their many experiences to a more adequate understanding of himself. They had believed many things. They now believed in one God. They also believed that their very coming to believe in one God, a God of *hesed*, loving kindness, was itself the product of God's activity. We see this process of development taking place as we read the Old Testament.

When Christians spoke of these writings as the *Old* Testament they were relating themselves in an explicit way to the history which those writings represent and to the God who revealed himself in that history. The Christian movement was not another Jewish sect. Jesus was not simply one more in the line of the prophets. A new and decisive revelation of God had taken place. This was continuous with the revelation of Yahweh in the long history of the Hebrews, but it also surpassed what had gone before. There was continuity and there was discontinuity.

In view of their new experience of faith, Christians began to read the writings of the Hebrews in the light of Jesus Christ. They saw those writings in relation to their community which had newly emerged and which was different. That is to say, their community was not simply an extension of the Hebrew community. Jesus Christ made the difference. 'Jesus' is a Jewish *name* (Joshua) and 'Christ' is a Jewish *title* (Messiah, Anointed One). Jesus is an historical figure, and 'Christ' is the clue to understand him. So Christians used Jewish terms from the beginning to show the uniqueness of Jesus, the Jew, for that community which separated itself from the Jewish community and became the Christian movement. In a word, Christians found that these writings made sense and helped them to make sense of their new experience. There was continuity in history, while something quite new had now emerged. The word 'old' in the term 'Old Testament' suggests that while Christians took these writings as their own, they at the same time recognized their limits.

Christians read the Old Testament from the perspective of faith in Jesus as the revelation of the love and grace of God. They therefore developed methods of interpretation so that they could make connection between their experience and that of the

Hebrews, their faith and Hebrew faith, their convictions about Jesus and the writings which had currency among the Jews. This meant that the history of The Old Testament had to be related to the history of Jesus Christ. It meant that the ideas drawn from the Old Testament were duly modified as they were applied within the 'new' context. For example, the idea of 'priest,' of 'high priest,' of 'prophet,' and of 'king' were drawn from the Old Testament. But they were reset in such a way that, as they served the Christian purpose, the limits of the Old Testament concepts became clear. Negations and qualifications were necessary. Jesus is in crucial respects not like the Hebrew High Priest — that is the message of the book of Hebrews. So while the imagery may be duly applied in the Christian context, it must be modified in relation to the new experience and the new history. Then, i.e. later, it means what it did not mean before. In such a way the Hebrew ideas become Christianized. In such a way the Christian consciousness and identity is reinforced.

Christians used various methods to interpret the significance of Jesus Christ and of Christian faith when reading the Old Testament. The New Testament is replete with Old Testament imagery and with references to people, events and ideas from the Old Testament. Once Christians as a group had accepted these writings as their own, and had in practice, if not by official pronouncement, adopted them as Christian Scripture, Christian interpreters assumed that they could read them as a Christian book and produced methods to accomplish this. They saw the writings as types, as allegories, as predictive and accordingly made connection with their Christian convictions.

As the Hebrew writings were instrumental in illuminating the meaning of the Christian experience, and in explicating a monotheistic understanding of the God whom Jesus reveals, they have, in the practice of the church, ensured their permanent place in Christian Scripture.

A warning is necessary. We have pointed out that these writings were not Christian. They were a deposit of that long Hebrew experience which led to and provided the grounds for the understanding of the decisive manifestation of God in Jesus Christ. They prepared the way for that revelation in Jesus Christ. But it is always possible to take these writings (or parts of them), to take concepts from them, in isolation from that new revelation. Then two possible results may follow. (1) One may find oneself with ideas and teachings Christians would have to deny, or (2) with ideas and teachings with which Christians would agree but which are not distinctively Christian. Examples come readily to mind. Christian theologians have found a deep meaning in the Hebrew stories of Creation and of the Fall. These make profound sense but are not specifically Christian. They become part of a Christian theology when the meanings they suggest get related to the event of Christian faith and its source. In short, the Hebrew doctrine of God (at its highest point) is not (of course not) Christian. But it becomes Christian as it gets related to that history and to those concerns which come to expression in the New Testament. The teaching drawn from the Old Testament is affirmed but is not yet distinctively Christian until it gets interpreted by being related to Jesus Christ. The task begins in the New Testament. It is the continuing task of Christian theology to produce distinctively Christian interpretations of concepts which are available to the Christian and which are seen as congenial to the expression of the meaning of Christian faith.

Now for a few concluding and summary observations.

The collection of writings we now call the Old Testament *was* not a Christian book. It can be read as such a non-Christian book. Any Jew knows that. It *was* not a Christian book, and (except that the Christian claim can be made good) it *is* not a Christian book. That seems to be a contradiction. Viewed in one way the same book is not Christian. Viewed in another way, it is.

There is no problem with the collection of Christian books called the New Testament. That is a Christian book because it was written exclusively within the Christian community, and is in its various forms an expression of Christian faith.

The Old Testament is a Christian book when and because, written exclusively outside the Christian community and indeed before that community came into being, it is adopted by the church, read, interpreted in relation to Jesus Christ, and in relation to Christian faith in God. It is Christian in that Christians deliberately read themselves into the history of the Jewish people at the point where they (Christians) have faith in God through faith in Jesus Christ. They then read the Hebrew history in the light of that faith. They relate that Christian faith to the long history of the Hebrew experience before that faith came into being. The basic confession is that the same God whom the Hebrews worshipped and came to understand is the God whom in faith in Jesus Christ they too worship and understand.

The writings of the Old Testament, in short, are used in the Christian church. What constitutes the authority of the Old Testament for the Christian is that Christians accept it as illuminating and as important for their understanding piety and action, use it in the worship of the church, read it in private and interpret it in public. In short, it has influence in the Christian church because the Christian church chooses to use it in various ways.

CHAPTER IV NOTES

[1]*Conceptual relativism* is the teaching that since the meaning of a word is relative to the society in which it is used, there can be no communication between different societies or between different realms of discourse, for example between science and religion. Cf. Roger Trigg, *Reason and Commitment*, pp. 14-22.

[2]Gilbert Ryle, *The Concept of Mind*, p.17. A category mistake occurs when facts belonging to one category get presented 'in the idioms appropriate to another.' *Ibid.*, p. 16.

Ryle defined the task of philosophy as 'the replacement of category habits by category disciplines.' *Ibid.* He was seeking to correct the grammar that led to unwarranted beliefs. He wanted to rectify the logic which was being misused. In his case it was the misuse of mental-conduct concepts. It is a category mistake to assert that there is an additional entity called 'mind' within the body, in addition to describing the activities of the body. Ryle's particular target was the teaching of Descartes, the para-mechanical hypothesis which speaks of mind ('soul') as an entity in addition to the body and separable from it. Ryle calls it 'the ghost in the machine.' It is the category mistake of thinking of the operation of the whole as requiring a separate entity. The mind is not another thing in addition to the body, any more than the university is another thing beside the colleges and museums, etc.

In our case what needs rectifying is the use of authority concepts. Our argument serves to correct the misuse of the concept of authority when it is derived from or identified with concepts of a different category, e.g. inspiration, factual accuracy etc.

[3]For further discussion of the point see Barr, *Fundamentalism*, pp. 72-78.

[4]The issues raised by this section are taken up in greater detail below. See Chapter VI: sections 3-5.

[5]A. H. McNeile in F. Bertram Clogg, *Introduction to the New Testament*, p. 14.

[6]W. P. Montague, *op. cit.*, p. 40.

[7]What Barth said of Bultmann's approach to the New Testament may *mutatis mutandis* be appropriately quoted here:

'With regard to the New Testament can there be any genuine understanding of the text if we presuppose as our norm a fixed canon of possibility, truth and importance — the prior understanding, as Bultmann calls it? . . . Of course, everyone approaches the New Testament with some kind of preconceptions, as he does any other document. We all have our prior notions of possibility, truth and importance . . . . Let the New Testament serve as the catalyst of our capacity to understand. Do not make our capacity to understand the catalyst of the New Testament . . . . It is impossible to understand another . . . text . . . if we do not allow it to question us with the utmost frankness . . . . If our aim is to understand it, we must surely try to approach it as open-mindedly as possible.' Karl Barth, 'Rudolf Bultmann — An Attempt to Understand Him' in Hans-Werner Bartsch, *Kerygma and Myth*, Vol. II, pp. 123, 124, 125, 126.

[8] Dietrich Bonhoeffer, *The Cost of Discipleship*, p.36.

[9]Accounts of adjustments churches were prepared to make under the Nazis are readily available.

[10]W.P. Montague, *op. cit.*, pp. 48-49.

[11]But if everyone accepts the right of the authority to teach them, a definition of that authority would (it would seem) be universally accepted if worked out. So, of Vatican I, Hans Küng remarked: 'What then was the decisive factor that led to the definition of papal infallibility? It *was* simply that most of the bishops took it for granted before it was defined.' Hence there was no risk in producing the definition. By the time of Vatican II there was a rather different atmosphere. Something analogous could be said of many a Protestant community's leadership. Cf. Hans Küng, *Infallible*, p. 100.

[12]For a brief but sustained argument to this effect see Alan Richardson in George Arthur Buttrick, *The Interpreter's Dictionary of the Bible*, Article: 'Scripture, Authority of', Vol. IV, pp. 248-251.

SUMMARY OF CHAPTER V

INSPIRATION: THE DOCTRINE.

A doctrine of inspiration, if it is to be at all satisfactory, must take into account the facts about how the books of Scripture came into being and how they were recognized as special books. Different writers have understood the idea of inspiration in different ways. We examine some views and consider carefully, possible meanings for the term, *inspiration*. Does inspiration have to do with the process i.e. the composition of the book or the product of the writing, or with both? The great diversity in the writings, and the practice within the churches in using and valuing some portions of Scripture over others, means that a 'flat' doctrine of inspiration is unsatisfactory, i.e. one which claims that all parts of Scripture are equally inspired.

V

INSPIRATION: THE DOCTRINE

1 THEORY AND FACT

The incentive for constructing theories of inspiration is to provide a basis for asserting the authority of the Bible. The Bible, so the argument goes, has authority because it is inspired, and it is inspired in the way the theory of inspiration accounts for it. Since we know *how* the scriptural books came into being and how they became part of the canon, we simply have to reject any theories which do not take this process into account, or which do not take it sufficiently into account.[1] The question how in fact a scriptural writing was produced is decisive: 'the real question is whether in fact such a writing was ever produced to form part of the Bible as we know it today. It is by this criterion, and not by its inner logic or consistency, that the relevance of the scholastic theology of inspiration must be judged.'[2]

The question how in fact a scriptural writing was produced is decisive. It is the criterion by which we must judge not only a scholastic theology of inspiration but any theology of inspiration. What is at issue is the *relevance* of any theology of inspiration. In view of what we now know concerning how the book came to its final form, we ask how a theory of inspiration can be helpful and what it is that it explains. We must keep the demands of what we know about the actual production of the literature always before our minds. We go seriously wrong if we do not constantly keep in mind what happened in the long story of the composition, compilation and acceptance of the Bible.

A theory of inspiration may make claims that are easily shown to be false by carefully examining the facts. It will either ignore or explain away the facts. Any satisfactory doctrine of inspiration will take account of these data, and be compatible with them. It will take notice of the history of the Bible, and its great complexity. It will not take as an a priori principle that the Bible is inspired, and then proceed to build on it, saying something like, 'The Bible is inspired, therefore . . . .' and then proceed to fill in the claim, e.g. to conclude that there were certain ways in which it could not have been written. The last time I confronted the argument it went: 'The Bible was inspired, therefore its writers could not have borrowed or copied from other sources in any shape or form.'

Rather one asks first: What, according to the evidence which is available, are the stages and the processes which took place before the end-product resulted? If you ask this historical question, you will have to keep an open mind. It is not fitting, nor is it honest (even if one is sincere) to say, 'Scripture is inspired: therefore such-and-such did not happen.' We must seriously take account of the historical data. We may not overlook any significant facts in building a doctrine of Scripture.

2   SOME WELL-ESTABLISHED FACTS ABOUT SCRIPTURE

Here, then, is a short list of some well-established facts about the Scriptures. They represent the dedicated efforts of competent and devoted scholars over several centuries:

(1) There is an enormous range of styles in the Scriptures. Some is literature of the very highest rank. Some is ungrammatical.

(2) There are *literary* relationships between some of the Scriptural writings. That means that the similarities are so close that they come from common *literary*, i.e. written, sources. Simply, the writer copied from other people.

(3) Oral traditions lie behind our written documents.

(4) The traditions were reworked, often several times, before the product resulted as we now have it. The process of redaction was complex.

(5) It was a common practice for ancient authors to use pseudonyms. They hoped to give distinction to their work by connecting it with well-known figures.

(6) It is at times impossible to harmonize some biblical narratives with others.

(7) Each piece of writing has come from a quite particular historical setting. In the majority of cases we can reconstruct that particular setting and relate the writing to the setting.

(8) Often, e.g. in Genesis, Kings, Deuteronomy, several oral traditions were set side by side.

3   HOW THE BOOKS WERE PUT TOGETHER

The following is a very brief and simplified summary of the series of events that went into the making of a book.

'Literary studies lead to the conclusion that the process of composition of a typical Old Testament book was as follows:

   a. groups of unknown people composed oral forms to help them with their work, their worship, their teaching;

   b. the oral forms were passed on through the generations, undergoing small changes from time to time;

   c. local men of letters wrote down the oral forms with which they were familiar;

   d. In some period of great literary activity, an editor collected these various literary products and combined them into one large work;

e. The large work might be combined with others to make up a complete roll.'[3]

Any doctrine of inspiration must reckon with these facts, take into account this complex process by which the books came into being *and* the manner in which they came to have a special recognition in the church.

4 POSSIBLE MEANINGS OF INSPIRATION

We may now explore the possible meanings of inspiration which have been put forward in the interests of preserving the uniqueness of the Bible and its authority. To understand, we shall need to consider the vocabulary and the range of analogies people have used in the history of the doctrine. We might then test such theories of inspiration against the historical facts concerning the composition of the literature and in view of its very evident diversity.

For the Bible is a book of great diversity. We cannot speak fairly and adequately if we do not do justice to this important fact. When the concept of inspiration has been used as a theory of the authority of the Bible, it has too often been presented in an over-simplified way. In view of the complexity and the variety of the Bible's literary history, we shall only mislead and confuse if we try to present a monolithic model of inspiration. Inspiration must be as complex as the 'writing' of the books and their contents are different.

It is therefore a mistake to take the prophet as the model of inspiration and make every writer and writing 'fit' the model. When that is done the model gets stereotyped. God 'speaks' to the prophet. The prophet 'hears', and writes down what he 'hears.' Sometimes the 'speaking' and 'hearing' are taken more or less literally. But there is great variety in the phenomena of prophets. 'In many and various ways God spoke of old to our fathers by the prophets.'[4] Not all the prophets fit the stereotype of 'prophet.' It is a serious mistake to try to force the process of revelation into this limited and limiting mould.

There are *many* other writers and writings besides prophets. There are no visions or auditions or unusual experiences behind the writing of a Gospel, say Luke's for example. For he tells us how painstaking was his examination of existing sources, both written and oral. And as for Paul, you can, if you have any sympathy for the text at all, sense him thinking through the problems as best he can, even when (as he says) he has no explicit word of the Lord. What he writes, or better dictates to his amanuensis, is later to become Scripture, even if we cannot fit his (and other) New Testament writings into the model of the Hebrew prophet.

So if we cannot tie the idea of inspiration to the prophet model, we must use many models. Some writers have claimed that inspiration was the process by which God, in a vision or audition or by creating thoughts in the prophet's mind in a unique way, gets into the prophet's mind what he wants him to write. The fact is that each writer and each book has its own way of mediating the revelation of God. So we should not think of one book as more inspired and another one as less inspired. 'We must learn to think of one book as inspired differently from another, as therefore being, or mediating, the word of God in its own proper fashion.' [5]

We shall be able to give proper weight to what are the obvious facts. The writers were very different. Their experiences were very different. Their writings are very different from one another. What they all have in common is that in their different ways they mediate the purpose and will of God. This some of them call 'speaking the Word.' So we cannot speak of degrees of inspiration.

Proverbs and Genesis are very different pieces of literature. Indeed Genesis 1-11 is different from the closing chapters. Job and I Kings are very different. Mark and John, while both called Gospels, have very different interests. An epistle of Paul (getting down to the brass tacks of serious church problems in First Corinthians) is very different from the Apocalypse (giving encouragement through strange symbols to a small persecuted church). Different kinds of *human* inspiration underlie the production of these very different writings. We had better not speak of degrees of inspiration.

The weakness of William Sanday's important book on inspiration is that he seems to want to have it both ways. He can on the one hand say, '. . . the prophetic inspiration seems to be the type of all inspiration.' and 'We are constantly being brought back to prophecy and the prophetic inspiration which I have already described as "typical of all inspiration."' But he can then, at once, so qualify the claim as to lead us to wonder whether he had seriously considered the implications of his qualification. So he wrote: 'It is not strictly safe to transfer what is said of this (i.e. prophetic inspiration) to all other kinds of inspiration . . . . The inspiration of the prophet was a special gift bestowed upon him at particular times and for particular purposes.' He then makes the interesting and significant contrast: 'But the inspiration of the prophet was remote from the writing of history.'

He believes that the inspired knowledge of the ways of God 'might' give an insight into the meaning of history. He then adds, 'But there is no evidence to show that it, i.e. insight, acquired in inspired moments, in any way superseded the ordinary use of historical materials, or that it interfered with that use in such a way as to prevent possibilities of error.'[6]

Sanday is aware that the concept of inspiration needed careful refinement, needed 'more precise definitions.' For example, he suggests that we use the term 'inspiration' of the New Testament in a way different from the way we use it of the Old. We apply it, he suggests, to 'a body of connected truths', to 'a system of theology' rather than to the single truth.[7]

We seem to have a shift of ground here. But rather than take Sanday to task for his inconsistencies and inadequacies, we will point out some serious questions arising from the discussion.

Is inspiration to do with truths? Is inspiration the communication of truth or a system of truth? If it is necessary to distinguish the phenomenon of inspiration as it occurs in different instances does not the type then become less typical? If we must distinguish the prophets as inspired and the historians as not inspired, according to the type, we cannot then apply the concept of inspiration unequivocally to the whole Bible. If the concept of inspiration as defined on the model of the prophet is therefore misleading, some more adequate concept must be found, either of inspiration or of another model.

An account of inspiration will be satisfactory only on condition that it can be applied to *all* of the literature and not simply some selected portions. It is a common mistake to veil the variety of viewpoints, teachings, aims, styles, approaches, theologies, by simply speaking of 'the Bible.' When people use such clauses as 'the Bible says,' 'the biblical teaching,' they are making the assumption that it is easy to put all this diverse literature, spanning many centuries, millennia even, and cultures, under one rubric. We must not create an over-simplified version of the unity of the Bible and then think we have provided for an adequate theology of inspiration. The disparity of the biblical materials is a primary datum not an inconvenience to be glossed over and tacitly ignored. You cannot simply *assume* such unity, It is a fatal weakness of traditional inspiration theories that they either chose to overlook, or just did not see, the diversified character of the Bible itself. They used the term 'Bible' to refer to a book which did not exist as their theory required. That book existed only in their imagination. Theories of inspiration have constructed both the Bible they are explaining and the explanation of how that Bible came to be. They were little concerned with its actual history with the process by which the books actually came to be. They also failed to understand what the biblical writings themselves say on the issue.

In short, we are not permitted to take an unhistorical view of the matter.

Such phrases as, 'The Bible *speaks*,' 'The Bible *says*,' 'God speaks,' 'the *word* of God' are figures of speech. We should not allow our imagination or our thinking to be misled by what figures of speech seem to imply. This particular figure of speech is that of 'personification.' It is only persons who speak. We have plenty of experience of people speaking words, ourselves hearing the words and as a result mutual understanding, communication taking place. When we then extend the range of the word 'speak,' we usually know that we are doing so, and what we are doing. A picture or a book may 'speak' to us, but we have personified the picture or the book when we talk this way. When we say 'The Bible says,' we are using a figure of speech. If we are aware that this is what we are doing, we shall be careful to avoid taking the metaphor literally. 'God speaks' is suggestive precisely because it is *not* literal. It is an anthropomorphism. A human word about a human experience is being used of God. Due care and serious qualification is needed.

5   VERBAL INSPIRATION

The theory of the inerrancy of Scripture is a case in point. This doctrine holds that the Bible contains no error of any kind, and that it is for that reason that it has authority. The reason it does not contain error is that God is its source and God is truth itself.

An inerrant Bible is purely a theoretical construction. The Bible is not inerrant. This theoretical construction led to and was supported by other theoretical constructions, e.g. an explanation of how the words got on to the page. The doctrine of verbal inspiration as dictation was the most extreme of these.

Verbal inspiration is the theory that the actual words of the books, as those words were written, came to the writer from beyond himself. God provided the words the biblical writer set down. The writer was merely the instrument through which the words were transcribed.

We have been given analogies to explain how God put the words phrase by phrase or idea by idea into the minds of the 'writers'. Illustrations are of the flute player and the flute (God using the 'writer' as a flute player uses a flute), of the writer and the pen (God using the 'writer' as a writer uses a pen), of the author and the 'pen men' (God using the 'writer' as a person with a message might use a scribe). A biblical metaphor was that of the spirit influencing a person and producing the desired result. The spirit (or breath) came upon him and he prophesied. But this does not have to be taken as requiring these kinds of verbal inspiration.

We have also been provided with such terms as 'accommodation,' 'assistance,' 'dictation,' 'instrumental causality.'

Our knowledge of how the books came to be produced is now well established. It is only ignorance of the historical facts, the looking at things in an unhistorical way that makes it possible to pin inspiration to the activity of the 'author' in the process of actually 'writing' the book. We know quite well that often books were not 'written' in the sense that they came out of the author's mind as an original product. In many cases there is a long pre-history. The 'author's' activity is one activity in a long process, and may not be the last in the line. In most cases, it is certainly not the first. Only if this one activity is isolated from all the others can the divine movement be connected with it alone. But that is to do violence to what are very often the facts of the matter. The production of a book is the result, in many cases, of a long process. The traditions are shaped, handed on, recorded, revised, edited. The sources are collected, reworked, translated. Finally a text is formulated and is transmitted through the centuries to the contemporary reader. Moreover since one text was copied and recopied over and over again, variant readings came into being and get incorporated into some texts but not others. Then there is a multitude of translations. One only has to consider how many there are now in English to realize what a great variety of versions of the Bible there are. But even in cases where there may have been one 'writer,' the above account would not be satisfactory.

To locate the activity of inspiration in the writing of the first draft of the text, or of any draft of the text, is to fail to do justice to the complex history of the Bible, let alone to the actual function which it performs in the ongoing life of the Christian community. A doctrine of inspiration would have to apply not to an original autograph but to a process, a whole textual tradition. It would have to include the preservation as well as the production of the text. For there would be no point in speaking about the inspiration of an original text if that text were not now available to us, or if it were inaccessible to us.

Moreover it would be purely theoretical to speak of the inspiration of a book which was never read, even if it were available. What is the point of saying a book is 'inspired' (in the sense we have examined) if it is virtually ignored (as some books in the Bible are)?

The 'original text' is not available to us. So it is only a theoretical possibility to speak about the inspiration of the original text, unless we can say with some assurance what the actual readings of that original text were. But what does 'original' mean in view of the complex process of composition? Is it the product of the first scribe or the last one? Is that also just one more theoretical possibility and not a real one — one which moves us away from rather than into the realm of historical inquiry?

Only those who were competent to read the original text would have the inspired text (if it had survived) available to them. It hardly needs to be said that it is quite illogical and even irrational to select a particular translation (say the King James version) and make that the normative version. Since we do not have original texts, we rely upon the work of textual (i.e. lower) criticism to work over the texts available to us, with the goal in view of reconstructing as nearly as possible, according to the best of the scholar's knowledge and judgment, what the original text said. But we can make no absolute and indubitable judgment in every case as to the wording of the original text.

Any account of the Bible that is at all reasonable and adequate will recognize this fact and as a result will not be able to speak of the Bible in terms of verbal inspiration leading to an inerrant text. It will take into account the whole process of composition and also give due weight to the way in which the Bible functions within the Christian community. But traditional theories of inspiration either did not take adequate account of how the Bible actually functioned in the church's life, or gave a truncated version of that function. For example, they see the Bible as a textbook of doctrine from which a doctrinal system could be derived, and which would be duly guaranteed by the inerrancy of their source. So we have returned again to the idea of inerrancy.

6 The Diversity of the Bible

An obvious fact is the diversity of the Bible. To take samples: The teachings differ: e.g. Romans and James. Luther's strictures on the book of James and his preference for the Pauline books are well known. He was prepared to see James out of the canon. But it is in the New Testament. If we do not choose to do as Luther did and abandon James, there are two courses open, it would seem. (1) Say that Luther was exaggerating and then try to show a harmony between the teachings of the two books; (2) Acknowledge the diversity, even opposition, and let it stand as a datum.

Concepts differ. Concepts of God we find in the Old Testament are very different from one another. God is the tribal, war god; he is the god of the nation; he is the God of the whole earth, the creator. We cannot pretend that such concepts are compatible with one another. They are not. The different 'writings' of the Old Testament are not in agreement. 'It is impossible to conceive of Jeremiah and Ezra for example, had they been contemporaries, as not having been completely at loggerheads over the first principles of man's relation to God.'[8] That is precisely the point. They were the products of a different age, a different historical context. They were different kinds of men, different kinds of Jew. We cannot try to harmonize their teaching. Once again we must take the divergence as given.

Even in the same book we find contrary statements side by side, as for example in the Book of Ecclesiastes. Is the author arguing with himself? Is a later edition arguing with an earlier author?

7 Infallibility

Sometimes, to support a high theory of inspiration the claim is made that the Bible is infallible.

Infallibility involves that what is written is true and is incorrigible. The two concepts of truth and of incorrigibility are not identical. If the pronouncement is a demand, infallibility presumably means that it is binding without question and continues to be binding. To say the Bible is infallible means that its propositions are true and that its directives are absolute. A similar claim may be made for pope or for church.

This leads to the further claim that there can be no inconsistency between the statements of the Bible. It also means that the ethical demands must be consistent with one another. The Protestant Christian who commits himself to the theory of the infallibility of the Bible must take responsibility for defending the consistency of all its statements with one another and for defending the consistency of its ethical demands.

Similarly, the Catholic Christian who commits himself to the theory of the infallibility of the pope, or of the church, must defend the consistency and the incorrigibility of the doctrinal and ethical pronouncements. You cannot claim that a pronouncement was infallible and later question it. That would be inconsistent. When a high-sounding doctrine of infallibility gets qualified to allow for inconsistency, for corrigibility, it is no longer what it appears to be. The appeal of a theory of infallibility is that it can be applied without qualification. As soon as one says: 'infallible under such circumstances,' 'infallible with such and such limits,' or 'infallible then but not now,' one begins to relativise the idea and then one erodes the claim.

Hans Küng, the Catholic theologian, demands that when the history of the Catholic Church is considered, the idea of infallibility must be adjusted accordingly. If the word 'infallibility' is to stay it must be made clear that it does not mean inerrancy or incorrigibility. Küng suggests that the Catholic uses the term 'infallibility' in the sense of *indefectibility*. However defective the church is, however many errors she has made, however many false propositions she has endorsed, the church continues in being. So we should not speak of the church's infallibility or even of 'the indefectibility or perpetuity of the church, but of its indefectibility or perpetuity in the truth.' What he means by this is that the church remains in the truth, and that it is not affected by any errors in 'detail.'[9] The truth is God's truth. The church continues in being as the guardian of that truth. The church is the guardian and locus of that truth as she continues in being. The church's continuing existence as the instrument and guardian of God's truth is the sign of the presence of God's truth in the world. In other terms, the church is the continuing instrument of God's revelation in the world.

The church may err. But the church remains in the truth in spite of error, mistakes, corruption, crime. Its story is one of revival and retrogression. But the church has survived and continues to survive. The faith of the church, and this means the faith of the countless numbers of unnoticed believers, not that of leaders alone, has been maintained. The continuance of faith and witness in the church is, in spite of its defects, the important fact. Faith in Jesus Christ is primary. There is no need to claim, and to make it of first importance, that the propositions which express faith are infallible.

Clearly, Küng's demand for a re-expression of the traditional position of Vatican II and following involves not simply adjustment in detail, but a fundamental reassessment of the dogma of papal infallibility. There are elements in Catholic tradition which support the change and to which appeal can be made. But that does not alter the fact that such change, if made, would be a fundamental change. It would reflect a radical change in attitude within the church as a whole. Whether that change in attitude within sections of the church is far-reaching and evident enough to influence such a change in doctrine remains to be seen. At least the way forward has been mapped out by the theologians of the church.

But why did such a dogma of verbal inspiration[10] leading to an infallible Scripture ever develop within Protestantism? In the main there were two incentives which produced it. One was polemical: to produce an unquestionable authority which could be opposed to the Catholic doctrine of papal infallibility, and of which it was the counterpart. The other was dogmatic: to provide an unquestionable foundation for the doctrines which its proponents taught. The prophets and apostles are 'authoritative didactic functionaries.' What they teach is unquestionably true doctrine. The heart of the classical fundamentalist doctrine of verbal inspiration seems to be that the Bible is part of a movement of true doctrine from God to man. The function of the prophet and the apostle is to teach true doctrine to the religious community.

The complementary function of the interpreter is to put together the true doctrine in a systematic form and present it to the church. To perform this task he must take a particular attitude to the Bible. It is a storehouse of true doctrine. His job is to cull out of this variety, here a little and there a little, an arrangement of teachings which will indoctrinate and duly edify the church.

Now, the securing of the text (even if it were possible) would not secure a particular interpretation of the text. And even a co-ordination of selected passages from different parts of the text presented without comment is of course interpretation. Why choose them and put them together in that way? Selection is interpretation.

So there is no gain in having an infallible text when it gets interpreted (even in such a way that the interpreter would like to think lets the Bible 'speak for itself') so that different doctrines which are incompatible with one another result. If incompatible doctrines result from reading an infallible Bible what advantage is there in its being infallible? Is it a question of authority? The interesting fact is that people in the same tradition can draw different meaning from the same passage(s). If both claim that their teaching has authority because it is based upon the biblical text, a doctrine of inerrant Scripture does not help, nor does a doctrine of inspiration. An adequate teaching concerning the Bible must account for what actually happens in the church with the Bible. To give such an account, the concepts of the inspiration of Scripture, even of its inerrancy, are inadequate and so unsatisfactory. They do not secure unanimity of interpretation, and in consequence do not provide a basis for the authority of the particular interpretation. *Inspiration and infallibility are quite neutral with respect to the doctrines derived from Scripture,* in the sense that they do not influence their derivation from Scripture. The same doctrines would be derived from Scripture whether inspired or infallible or not.

If you want to claim that you have the truth, i.e. the doctrinal truth, and that that doctrine has authority, you will have to do more than provide an account of the Scriptures. You will have to defend the method of interpretation you use and also the particular interpretation you give. That means coming to terms with your past. To *assume* the one is correct and the other is true is to take too much for granted.

8 INERRANCY: THE ISSUE WITH FUNDAMENTALISM

It is the doctrine of the inerrancy of Scripture that divides modern fundamentalists from other Christians. We hesitate to speak of this difference as an issue, since that suggests that it is a live option, and that we are discussing it as such. Many Christians today do believe in the inerrancy of the Scriptures, and the doctrine of verbal inspiration which is its correlate. The inerrancy of Scripture is of little value however, unless the interpretations which are based on Scripture yield also true propositions, true doctrine. Hence a method of interpretation which produces this result must be guaranteed. We shall discuss this point further in speaking of interpretation. It is not then a question for the fundamentalist that the Scripture be taken literally. It must be taken so as not to compromise its inerrancy. That may well require an analogical, a typological or a metaphorical interpretation.

> The point of conflict between fundamentalists and others is not over *literality* but over *inerrancy*. Even if fundamentalists sometimes say that they take the Bible literally, the facts of fundamentalist interpretation show that this is not so. What fundamentalists insist is not that the Bible must be taken literally but that it must be so interpreted as to avoid any admission that it contains any kind of *error*. . . . In order to expound the

Bible as thus inerrant, the fundamentalist interpreter varies back and forward between literal and non-literal under-standings, indeed he has to do so in order to obtain a Bible that is error-free.[11]

9   WHY VERBAL INSPIRATION IS WRONG

We shall now quite simply list reasons why a verbal or dictation theory of inspiration is in error. Such a theory is very often, but not in every case, provided as the support for a doctrine of scriptural inerrancy.

(1)   The 'writers' do not claim to be inspired in this way.

(2)   Only the originals would be so inspired. We don't have them. Translations are of secondary value.

(3)   It has nothing to do with the function of the books. Suppose they were inspired in this way and then had been left in a box and had not yet been discovered?

(4)   'Verbal inspiration implies a dictation theory' is a caricature of the actual process of composition and transmission which is very varied indeed: 'in many and varied ways God spoke.' Luke listened, gathered and copied from various sources, 'having followed all things closely for some time past.'[12] Mark was copied from. The theory of accommodation is an   obvious enough rationalisation.

(5)   It makes the writers into puppets.

(6)   Evidence from the writings themselves contradicts a verbal inspiration/inerrancy theory. Paul flounders around when telling how many people he baptized in Corinth. He says sometimes, 'I have no word from the Lord but I'm giving you my advice', etc., etc.

(7)   It misconceives the concept of authority.

(8)   It does not, even if true, establish the authority of Scripture. It only tells us how the words got onto the page.

(9) Verbal inspiration in implying a dictation theory also implies inerrancy. The writings are not inerrant.

(10) It fails to consider the historical evidence, and in doing so distorts basic definitions, e.g. 'writer,' 'author.'

(11) It fails to do justice to the diversity of the biblical materials.

10 BIBLICAL TEACHING

We begin this section with a caveat. We are speaking in what follows of individual writings speaking about other writings. The term 'writings' (or 'scriptures') in the New Testament is the Greek word *graphai*, a plural form, from which we get such words as graph, graphic and all the other words of which these form a part (e.g. photographic, lithograph). This word, *graphe*, has a general and so a rather vague reference. We cannot therefore, as some people would like to think, speak about 'the Bible's view of itself'. When some of the statements were made the Bible did not yet exist as a whole. Moreover the *recognition* of a particular body of books was in the future. Only when that recognition was established was it possible to speak of 'the Bible.' That was, of course, after the production of any particular writing. What we should rather say is that some writings talk of other writings. One may, of course, take what these writings say of those others as true of the whole. But that is *an* interpretation. It was not the intention — how could it have been? — of the writers themselves. This will become clear as we consider the particular passages themselves in some detail. We shall have to ask whether we can say for sure which writings are being spoken of, when the term 'writings' is used.

It is therefore misleading to say, 'the Bible claims' to be inspired.

> There is no "the Bible" that claims to be divinely inspired. There is no "it" that has a "view of itself". There is only this or that source, like II Timothy or II Peter, which make statements about certain other writings, these rather undefined. There is no such thing

as "the Bible's view of itself" from which a fully authoritative answer to these questions can be obtained.[13]

It is wrong to claim that the New Testament states clearly and unambiguously that 'it' is inspired. As we have seen, the canon has a history. Some books were considered secondary, even disputed. II Peter was one of these secondary books and II Timothy was considered marginal. This means that two of the less important books make claims about source writings which they know. The term 'scripture'means 'writing,' simply 'writing'. We have no means of knowing which books they are speaking about. We cannot, must not, assume that II Timothy 3:16 is referring to the twenty-seven books of the canon which we adopt. We do not know how many such writings II Timothy knew. We cannot say that this passage represents the New Testament teaching about itself. The passage reads: 'All Scripture is inspired by God and profitable for teaching, for reproof, for correction and for training in righteousness.' The marginal note correctly indicates that the language is ambiguous. It reads as an alternative: 'Every Scripture inspired by God is also profitable. . . . The ambiguity is inherent in the Greek construction. The text reads: *pasa graphe theopneustos kai ophelimos pros didaskalian*. There is no verb, no 'is' in the sentence. Rendered word for word, which in this case is not misleading, the passage reads: 'every writing inspired and (or also) profitable for instruction.' We have to supply 'is'. But the writer does not indicate where we shall put it, and so we do not know which of the following alternatives he intended. We can read either: (1) 'every writing is inspired and profitable' or (2) 'every inspired writing is also profitable'.

In the first case we have supplied 'is' after *graphe* 'writing.' In the second case we have supplied it before *kai* (and), which, since it then introduces a second adjective *ophelimos*, is translated 'also,' as it often is. There is no stretching or distortion. To translate the passage as in (2). is to render into English a perfectly normal usage from Greek. The sentence is ambiguous in Greek and requires consideration of both (1) and (2) to render that ambiguity. So much for the language.

Therefore, first, we cannot say which books the writer refers to either from the meaning of the words of the passage, or from its context. We cannot, therefore, construct from this *one* use of the term 'inspired' a theory of the authority of the whole Bible. Second: the term is used only once, and the associations with the Greek culture render it unsuitable for use as the basis of a doctrinal theory. It is only as the concept of inspiration is duly qualified that it may be used as a theological principle. Even then it has serious limitations. This is because the biblical materials are so diverse that we cannot impose one and only one model of inspiration on them.

Even if it were the case that the Bible claimed that the Bible had authority, that the Bible was 'inspired,' holy, set apart, that would not prove that it was. We just cannot take as a general principle: What a book, claims to be it is. Nor can we say that if someone makes a claim, that person is the something he claims to be. We must establish that on other grounds. Not all those who claimed to be prophets inspired by God were prophets inspired by God (Jeremiah 23:30-32). Several stories in the Old Testament make the point that other considerations than that a person makes a claim have to be carefully weighed before a decision is reasonably made about the claim.

We mentioned the Greek concept of inspiration. The word *theopneustia* itself is not biblical. It is not found in the Septuagint but it is part of the religious vocabulary of Greece. Inspiration is a kind of possession. The state of mind is readily identified. It is a kind of madness, dementia, loss of wits and remembrance. The accompanying behaviour is unusual. The person has visions and utters words, is beyond consciousness and needs an interpreter to judge of their sanity and of the truth or falsity of the matter. When they speak they do not know what they say. 'No man, when in his wits, attains prophetic truth and inspiration, but when he receives the inspired word, either his intelligence is enthralled in sleep, or he is demented by some distemper or possession.' So it is necessary to 'set up spokesmen to pronounce judgment on inspired divination.'[14]

Christian theology of revelation could be developed along such lines. Were that done, the unusual behaviour of the individual would then have to be explained. If one took the problem boldly in hand, the unusual phenomena accompanying the visitation might be taken as evidence that it was authentic. The physical or psychological state would then be interpreted as positive evidence of the divine activity. But that is the very thing in question. It is illogical, and so irrational to argue from an unusual psychological or physical state for support of the trustworthiness of the sayings delivered. Plato knew that. An interpreter or 'spokesman' (*prophetes*) was needed to assess the whole business.

There were ecstatic 'prophets' in the Old Testament story, and they were considered to be mad. Their ecstasy was wild and contagious. It is as if something enters into a person from without and he becomes another person. Such is the literal meaning of 'possession' and 'ecstasy.' 'The spirit of the Lord will come mightily upon you and you shall prophesy with them and be turned into another man.'[15] That was said of Saul. And when the 'prophet' comes with a notorious message to Jehu, his servants ask him, 'Is all well? Why did this mad fellow come to you?'[16]

But the Hebrew understanding of prophecy did not in the main develop along these lines, the lines of mantic possession. Nor did the Christian understanding. It could have done, and later to some extent it did. Philo the Jew spoke of the divine possessing the human and shaping words within the man. Many Jews treated their books as though they had been produced in this way. Some Christian writers use metaphors which suggest possession of the human by the divine. Athenagoras speaks of man as the flute and God as the flute player. The Holy Spirit is like a player blowing into the flute.[17]

There is no suggestion on the part of the New Testament writers that this was the way they thought about the matter. They do not think of possession, nor of a verbally inspired text, nor of inerrancy as Philo had done.[18] That was left to much later Christian writers for whom inerrancy and verbal inspiration was crucial. But from the beginning that was not the case. The reason for this is that they do not think of the activity of the Holy Spirit in this way. The Holy Spirit is active in the many and varied activities which make up the whole of the church's life and witness. The whole Christian movement is inspired. Without the Spirit there could be no witness, no love, no unity.

The term used of 'the writing' in II Timothy 3:16, *theopneustos,* means literally 'God-breathed.' It is a combination of the words for 'God' and for 'breath', 'breathing.' The term 'inspiration' is a very free translation, and is thus inexact. As we have seen, the term, once used of the writings, calls on a whole range of meanings which are not suitable here.

Nor does the text claim a great deal for the 'inspired' writings. They are 'profitable for instruction and for edification.' That does not particularly set them apart from many other writings. The later high sounding claims made in the name of inspiration have no basis whatever in the modest association of *theopneustos* with edifying.

Writers up to and around A.D. 200 have various ways of describing what it is that makes New Testament Scripture different. The writings are sacred because they are inspired by the Holy Spirit. The terms used vary. The writers are *pneumataphorioi* 'bearers,' i.e. instruments, of the Spirit. Their minds are 'flooded' with the Holy Spirit. Sometimes the source of inspiration is the Holy Spirit. Sometimes the writings reflect the authority of Christ. The writings are *kuriakai graphai* (the Lord's writings). Christ speaks through the writings. Some speak of the inspiration as having to do with the very words, and of the Spirit as foreseeing what would happen, e.g. that heresies would arise, and speaking appropriately to the situation they foresee. Sometimes Scripture is said to be perfect and infallible.[19] Scripture is holy.

The term for 'spirit' in the Old Testament is *ruach*, in the New Testament *pneuma*. In both cases the term means 'breath,' 'wind.' Breath is air in motion, and without inbreathing air there can be no life. Breath is life-giving. Without breath there can be no speech. When the breath moves over the vocal cords and articulate sounds are produced, communication becomes possible. It is itself invisible but its results are quite visible and tangible. The term *ruach* is in the Old Testament books used of the life-giving power of Yahweh, and of the revelation he makes through the prophets to man. He breathes the 'Spirit' into the lifeless form and man becomes a living being. He sends his 'Spirit' and the prophet speaks the 'word of the Lord.'

Since the term *ruach*, spirit, is a way of speaking of God, the writers of the Old Testament recognize that God is in some sense present in the very process by which he comes to be revealed. God is in some way present in the events which make possible the speaking of the prophet.

So the metaphor of inspiration, in-breathing, has connections with this process of revelation. The word of the Lord and the Spirit of the Lord are dynamically one. When *ruach* is used metaphorically, at its root is the idea of movement, creative and revealing movement. Breath is air in motion. So there are remarkable and sometimes devastating results. The wind moves mightily. Storms follow, and leave their trace. So it is with the Spirit of God.

It is clear that the *ruach* has many different meanings, and can express in concrete terms, physical terms, a quite basic conviction of the Old Testament, namely that God is active in the midst of his people in many different ways. The idea of God's spirit influencing persons and events through persons underwent change and refinement as time passed.

The earlier prophets behaved in very strange ways. On those occasions when the *ruach* came upon them, entered into them, they were filled as the lungs are full of breath. So possessed, they did strange things. Then the spirit left them and they resumed their normal personalities and more normal activities.

CHAPTER V NOTES

[1]Cf. Leo XIII (Nov. 18th. 1893).

[2]Bruce Vawter, Inspiration. 3.1. p. 75

[3]David Stacey, *Interpreting the Bible*, pp. 44-45.

[4]Hebrews 1: 1.

[5]Vawter, *op cit.*, p. 164.

[6]W. Sanday, *Inspiration*, pp. 128, 268-269.

[7]*Ibid.*, p. 353.

[8]Vawter, *op. cit.*, p. 3.

[9]Hans Küng, *Infallible*, p. 150.

[10]James Barr, *Fundamentalism*, pp. 289ff. Barr finds fundamentalists' denial of dictation as the mode of God's communication, in J.I. Packer for example, to be inconsistent. They do not, he suggests, want to be saddled with too big a miracle. *Ibid.*, pp. 290-291. They want to be modern, but (at the same time) cannot bear the implications of the analytical questions which may be raised about the composition of the writings.

[11]*Ibid.*, p. 40. Italics in text.

[12]Luke 1:2.

[13]James Barr, *op. cit.*, p.78.

[14]Plato, *Timaeus*, 71e. Plato places the seat of inspiration in the liver. That portion of the soul which resides in the liver has no share in mind and reason. Inspiration is irrational.

[15]I Samuel 10:6. Cf. the even more bizarre incident of I Samuel 19:24,25.

[16]I Kings 9:11.

[17]ca. AD 177. *Legato pro Christianis*, 9, Migne, *Patrologia*, 6: 905-907.

[18]Philo, 'in the most uncompromising manner, expresses his conviction that the Old Testament came solely from God. He uses the strongest language in regard to the process, a conception of inspiration which is nothing short of verbal. The recipient is passive in the process. Josephus says something similar: 'He causes us to utter words such as he wills and speeches without our knowledge . . . when He has entered into *us* nothing that is in us is

any longer our own.' Cf. Sanday, *Inspiration*, pp. 72-78. On this whole question see the excellent account in Vawter, *op. cit.*, pp. 8-19.

[19]For the evidence for these statements see Sanday, *Inspiration*, pp. 28-58.

SUMMARY OF CHAPTER VI

INSPIRATION AND THE CONTENTS OF THE BIBLE

Writers who hold firmly to a theory of inspiration readily admit that it does not have to do with the content of the book, i.e. the content is the same, whether you say it is inspired or not. To say that a book is inspired rather serves to give the content a special status. But to claim that the Bible has authority *because* it is inspired is an error.

VI
INSPIRATION AND THE
CONTENTS OF THE BIBLE

1 A SELECTIVE HISTORICAL COMMENT ON THE TEACHING OF INSPIRATION

The teaching of the inspiration of the Bible has a history. Today, conservative Christians teach it in a particular form. But they did not originate it. They inherited it. It is a heritage of both Protestants and Catholics, who over a long period of history would agree regarding a doctrine of inspiration. The nineteenth century was the turning point.

Christians inherited the Jewish theory of inspiration. That theory supported the esteem in which the recognized books were held. The writings were inbreathed by the Spirit of God. So the analogy is made to the act of creation where God breathes into man the breath of life and he lives. The Old Testament is a unity through which the Spirit of God speaks to man. The writings were produced as a consequence of the divine influence upon the writers. This is reflected in the New Testament passage: 'no prophecy ever came by the impulse of man, but men moved by the Holy Spirit spoke from God' (RSV).[1]

Many Jews thought of the process of inspiration as one of dictation. In fact, it was a Jewish teaching that the process of inspiration extended to the very syllables, and even to the very vowel points. The doctrine of dictation did not originate on Christian ground. Nor did the accompanying belief that a supernatural origin and series of events accounts for the composition of Scripture. The myth of the translation of the Greek version of the Old Testament illustrates this. Greek-speaking Jews accepted books the Palestinian Jews did not. These Greek-speaking Jews produced a translation of the Scriptures into Greek, and included in it more books than did their Palestinian counterparts. According to the story, seventy translators worked on the translation independently of each other and when, at the end, their translations were compared they were found to be identical. That being so, there was no alternative but to accept its divine endorsement.

The Reformers spoke of the Bible in dynamic terms. It was the Word of God. They recognized the particular writings which had been handed down to them from the ancient church and acknowledged the canon of Scripture to contain Old Testament and New Testament. But there was no automatic and artificial endorsement of these contents. The book of Scripture was not a series of propositions making up a system of teachings. It was the vehicle of God's word. It was the means through which Jesus Christ became a living reality in the church. Not all books were thus of equal merit. Nor were any of the books effective without the witness of the Holy Spirit, which was another way of saying that God comes to human beings through the books.

The Protestant Scholastics, as they came to be called, took the Bible to be God's word in a much more rigid sense than the Reformers themselves. There were two strands in their fabric. One was that the process by which the words got on to the pages could be specified, and the manner in which this took place led them to the belief that there could be no error in the writings which resulted. God used the writers as passive instruments. He wrote with them as with a pen. He played upon them as upon an instrument. They were his pen, his lyre. So the words of the Bible are the words of God. God inspired the writers so that his words were set down on the pages of Scripture. This process of inspiration guaranteed the total truthfulness of the resulting writings. The dogma of infallibility accompanied that of the inspiration of the writers. Inspiration, the term, refers to the process by which the words got on to the page.

In the eighteenth century another argument became popular. Since a whole series of prophecies from the Old Testament came to be fulfilled in the New Testament, and since the miracles of the Gospels could not have had any source other than the divine, you could argue from the fulfilment of prophecy and the occurrence of miracles (both supernatural occurrences) to the authority of Scripture. Once that had been established, you could move to conclude that the book had moral and religious authority.

The nineteenth century saw the emergence of the historical method, the revolution in historical studies. It brought about changes in the understanding of the Bible as great as any in the history of the Christian church. The hope was that now a firm basis for the Christian faith would be found by applying the historical method to the Scriptures. People turned to the synoptic Gospels to derive from them a 'Life' of Jesus. It was a magnificent achievement. Schweitzer sees it as the grandest failure in German theology. A multitude of Lives of Jesus emerged.

It became necessary to decide what relation the truths of history bore to Christian faith. The particular question of the nature of the authority of the Bible thus became urgent, in view of the results of such historical exercises. Add to this that there was wide agreement about the composition of the Bible, Old and New Testaments, about he way in which the materials came to be produced, collected, put together, recognized as canonical. Dedicated scholars painstakingly studied the great variety of forms of writing, and how the text of Scripture was transmitted. They made it their lifework to examine and assess answers to difficult historical questions. Much knowledge was gained about the surrounding cultures and it became possible to set the story of Israel into a historical setting with a considerable degree of confidence.

What this meant was that a doctrine of verbal inspiration and of the inerrancy of the Bible was done for. Another question became much more important, and continues to be much more important, the question of the relationship between history and faith. One rearguard action was fought. Could one not demonstrate the historical trustworthiness of the historical accounts of the Bible, and having done so go on to claim that the historical trustworthiness of the Bible provides a compulsive ground for its spiritual authority? Do not the positive results of for example archaeological research demonstrate something important about the Bible? Why not now move easily from historical trustworthiness (assuming that a good case for this was made out) to religious or spiritual authority? To come to that conclusion was to move from a false assumption. The idea was that if you could establish the essential facts concerning the life of Jesus, there would be a basis for faith. That would be an alternative to accepting the dogmas of the tradition. It was with some enthusiasm that such enterprises were undertaken. One question had to be settled, Lessing stated the problem. Facts of history were relative, contingent. The demand for faith was absolute. What then is the relation between historical assent and Christian faith? He insisted that contingent facts of history cannot serve as a basis for the absolute that faith requires. Between history and faith there yawns an ugly, wide ditch.

Meanwhile there were attempts to rehabilitate a doctrine of inspiration. In England, Jowett wrote in the 1860s that the Bible was to be treated, from the point of view of historical research, like any other book. He believed that if it were it would show itself to be unlike any other book. Sanday, at the end of the century, reinterpreted the doctrine of inspiration, taking account of all that had taken place in the nineteenth century. Could there be a kind of inspiration that was not verbal and which did not lead to an inerrant Scripture? Could there be a doctrine of inspiration which could make full allowance for the humanity of the biblical writers, and which might provide for the uniqueness of the product which came from their hands? It was now a question of deciding where the uniqueness of the Bible lay. Wherein lay the special character of these writings? Wherein lay their authority? Could such authority be established by an appeal to a modified doctrine of inspiration? Sanday had his own answer to the question about the status of the product of inspiration, to the question as to what was unique about the Bible. He claimed:

> What has come down to us is Revelation, i.e. a number of concrete truths contained in written books on the subject of God and religion. And they are truths because these books are the work of inspired men, so that even through the printed page there speaks the Spirit of God.[2]

We study in greater detail Sanday's particular doctrine of inspiration shortly. Suffice it to say here that his restatement did not answer the problems of the nineteenth century.[3] Was there an alternative approach? Sanday (and others in agreement with him on many points) is writing in view of the failure of the life of Jesus movement of the nineteenth century. Sanday summarises methodically the results of the critical method as applied to the Bible and then asks the question concerning the doctrine of inspiration. Put in other terms: Sanday asks, How goes the authority of the Bible in view of the results of the critical method as applied to the Old Testament and the New Testament? 'Inspiration' is the concept he uses as the category for the investigation and assessment of the question.

Both Sanday and Kähler are agreed first, that the critical method is legitimate, second, that they should take the results on board, whether those results are negative or positive; third, that they must both reassess the question of the authority of the Bible; and fourth, that this is more than an academic concern. The Bible is the book of the church, and the church is to provide the context of the questions about its interpretation and its authority. Specifically the *function* of the Bible is in the context of the church. Both ask the question, How is the function of the Bible in the church affected by the academic work of critical, analytical scholars?

Kähler finds that the uniqueness of Scripture remains unaffected by the critical work of scholars. The Bible is witness to God's revelation. Hence there is a relationship between faith and the Bible, such as there is not between faith and other documents. There is risk, of course, in such questioning since the church is raising the question about its own foundation.

Kähler is quite deliberately presenting his view of the Bible as an alternative to the view that the origin of the writings and hence their inerrancy is guaranteed by verbal inspiration. However the alternative view Kähler also finds unsatisfactory, and with good reason. This view claims that the historical study can provide a basis for faith in God (rather than verbal inspiration) by demonstrating a '. . . historical connection between the biblical writings and those persons and events credited with the mediation of divine revelation. . . .'[4] This was unsatisfactory because it put the authority of the Bible at the mercy of historical research, 'documentary research.' The function of the Gospels is to 'awaken faith in Jesus through a clear proclamation of his saving activity'.[5] Historical research was unable to provide a definitive account of Jesus. If you cannot have a definitive historical reconstruction you cannot rest your faith upon any such attempt to reconstruct. Kähler's particular concern was with the historical Jesus. The purpose of the Gospels is not to provide a source for historical research, but to provide for faith in Jesus Christ. Scripture provides the ground for Christian proclamation, and it is through such proclamation that God reveals himself and that faith comes to be. 'That', says Kähler, 'should constitute sufficient theological justification for assigning a special authority to Scripture.'[6] It also rescues Christ from the scholars and makes him available to all Christians.[7]

2   Treat the Bible as any Other Book?

Jowett's essay[8] is about the interpretation of Scripture. He well understands that there is a connection between a theory of inspiration and the interpretation of Scripture.[9] The principles which he lays down for the interpretation of Scripture represent a departure from the traditionally and generally accepted principles of interpretation based as these were on a doctrine of plenary inspiration. For Jowett, the aim of the interpreter is 'to read Scripture like any other book, with a real interest and not merely a conventional one' (338).

The conventional way of reading Scripture regarded it as authority for the church's doctrine and practice. The term 'inspiration' had become a technical term. The practice of earlier days has now become a theory, a theory, moreover, which excluded genuine inquiry. Jowett specifies the principle of inerrancy. If you start with the assumption, 'There can be no error in the Word of God,' you won't find any, since the assumption serves as a directing principle. It directs you: 'Don't look for error!' Indeed it does more. It directs, you: 'Don't acknowledge what appears a discrepancy to be a discrepancy,' and 'Don't acknowledge what looks like a non-fulfilment of prophecy to be a non-fulfilment of prophecy!' and 'Don't acknowledge what is late to be evidence of a date later than that of the prophet' (342-3)!

If you interpret Scripture with the purpose of supporting doctrine, you cannot do so in an ad hoc way, as is endorsed by such a theory of inspiration. You must have a consistent method for getting from the biblical teaching to the doctrine. If the Bible is without error, then you can draw directly from it here a little, there a little. What will emerge will be true doctrine. Jowett directs us to a serious logical fallacy involved in the process of so interpreting Scripture. The fallacy follows from the acceptance of an unsatisfactory theory of inspiration, from which a misguided rule of procedure is drawn for interpreting Scripture. We must not approach the Bible under such restricting conditions.

The problem occurs when the Bible is used as a support for doctrine, without clarity as to the method to be employed for getting from the Bible to the doctrine. The understatement of the essay is that the relationship is a difficult one. Support for the construction of doctrine was found in the theory of the inspiration of Scripture, which it does not take Jowett too much effort to demolish.

All Christians, Jowett could write in 1861, agree in using the word 'inspiration,' and therefore seem to agree as to its meaning. But, since the term is used in different senses by different parties it has become a source of distrust and misunderstanding. The common use of the term cloaks a wide and bitter disagreement. We may divide Jowett's examples in different categories, and a threefold derivation of the term 'inspiration' emerges as we do so. The term 'inspiration' may be used to refer to:

(1) what happens to the 'writer' before he 'writes'.
(2) the process of 'writing'.
(3) the writing itself, what the 'writer' has produced, the thing written.

He does not pursue the matter further. After all it is not his intention to develop a theory of inspiration.[10] Suffice it to say that it is problematic to assert 'inspiration' in sense (3), when synonyms like 'inerrant,' 'authoritative' would serve.

He sets his principles of interpretation in relation to the traditional theory of inspiration and in doing shows that the traditional theory of inspiration is unacceptable. Here are four essential principles for the interpretation of Scripture:

(1) See Scripture as a whole. That will mean acknowledging the principle of progressive revelation.
(2) Acknowledge facts established by science and history.
(3) Do not ignore what any intelligent person is aware of, namely discrepancies and other problems.
(4) Treat Scripture as any other book. This fourth principle means (a) being aware of literary problems, e.g. the

sources of the synoptic materials, and (b) establishing the original meaning of the passage, what it would have been understood to mean by the writer and by his original readers. This is stressed over and over again in the essay.

If you interpret Scripture by following these principles you will have to revise the traditional doctrine of inspiration. That involves a revision of its meaning in each of the three senses distinguished above.

Emphasis on verbal inspiration implied inerrancy. The books it produced were inerrant. It also involved that the divine received undue emphasis in accounting for the process of 'writing.' It led to a neglect of the human. Theories of the accommodation of the divine to the human did not fulfil their intention of meeting this objection. That involved also the neglect of the historical, for example the question of the composition of the books. However 'inspiration' was defined on the three-fold scheme, unsatisfactory answers resulted.

Such a doctrine of inspiration could not survive and had to be abandoned. It was seen that the books sometimes erred; that they were not of a sort, as a 'flat' doctrine of inspiration required; that the relation of the particular writing in relation to the whole had to be assessed.

Jowett does not supply us with a revised doctrine of inspiration. He had no call to do so. The interpreter can, for all intents and purposes, ignore theories of inspiration. An authentic theory of inspiration will *follow from* rather than predetermine the interpreter's methods and results. Since the task of the interpreter is to get at and display the original meaning of what is written, he can readily do that without taking account of a theory of inspiration. It is anachronistic to read later interests back into the text. We must not come to the text with our own interests in mind and make the text conform to our understanding.

A case in point is the use of the word *theopneustos*,[11] translated 'inspiration' in the New Testament, where it qualifies 'all Scripture.' Jowett points out that a partisan approach assumes that this term applies to the New Testament, and so applies to the very passage in which it occurs. Of course, Jowett finds this dubious. He sees that to assume a particular doctrine leads one to find support for it in Scripture. In this case, to assume a particular doctrine of inspiration would distort the interpreter's approach to the text. His purpose in approaching the text should be, to say what the text meant, not to find support for a doctrine already assumed. When that happens words, phrases, and passages from Scripture are given meanings they did not have. That is not the interpreter's task.

So, for clarity's sake, we must distinguish between possible ways in which appeal can be made to Scripture. We will inevitably read Scripture with ideas in our heads. Such ideas will function as 'categories' for a certain kind of understanding of Scripture. Jowett recognizes a distinction between an exegetical and a theological interpretation of Scripture, but does not work it out in any detail. He recognizes in the understatement of the article, that it is not easy to prove a doctrine from Scripture (366), and repudiates two methods for constructing a doctrine from Scripture: (1) we must not demand logical equivalents for scriptural statements; and (2) we must not give words a technical meaning different from the original meaning, and then claim the authority of the text for what we have done. This is the point of his analogy of removing stones from an old building to put in a new one (367). The problem of working out what relationship exists between Scripture and doctrine remains. We might distinguish between Bible as text for analytic study and Bible as 'Scripture,' the former the object of historical and textual methods, and the latter as the basis for doctrinal construction within the context of the church. We would then develop separable but overlapping principles of interpretation.

Jowett must defend himself against the charge that he has put needless obstacles in the way of faith, that critical inquiry will undermine the authority or reduce the uniqueness of the Bible. He is concerned that there should be agreement concerning principles of interpretation, and assumes that the development of analytic methods will have positive results. He had no illusions as to the threat which criticism posed to the naïve and traditional mind. Consensus did finally emerge both in Germany and Britain and elsewhere that there was no going back. Critical methods had to be employed. Jowett, with some optimism about the results of the application of such methods to produce unity, insists that we must go forward.

He asserts this, even in view of his admission that extra-biblical sources were not available relating to the history or the setting of the Bible. But the ensuing century has changed all that. Jowett's call for a reassessment of the doctrine of inspiration and of the method of interpretation is of necessity a rather inchoate and tentative affair — very relevant for all its indeterminateness. Judging by the great stir which the book caused, Jowett's essay being one of the more important ones in *Essays and Reviews*, it was deemed a very important issue. To see rationally and to judge fairly were qualities which discussion of the issue demanded.

In the last section of the essay, he first warns that not everyone is suited to pursue the inquiries he has portrayed. Clearness of mind and a strong faith are two qualities which are needed for the quest and an ability 'to separate the truth from his own religious wants and experiences' (430). Those who renounce inquiry have no right to condemn others. Secondly, he points out that difficulties are not as great as may be imagined, given tact and prudence. Criticism may create difficulties, but it removes others. It is not only negative. Thirdly, we should not doubt the value of critical inquiries because of those who are suspicious or because of the difficulty. Considerations other than those that are appropriate influence opinions in these matters. It is difficult 'to regard these subjects with calmness and judgment because of jealousy . . . fear . . . reticence . . . terrorism' (432). Public opinion and church authority are not unquestionable guides to truth. That, of course, is a good Protestant principle.

3 AN INDUCTIVE VIEW?

William Sanday entitled his Bampton Lectures of 1893, 'Inspiration.' By doing so he indicated his concern to retain and to rehabilitate the idea of inspiration for theological purposes. He wished to produce a revised theory of inspiration that should take into account the historical analysis of the preceding half-century. His concern is with the authority of the Bible. His opening paragraph quite clearly expresses that concern. He says, 'I propose' 'to ask, and to do what in me lies to answer, the question, What is it which gives our Bible its hold and authority over us . . . .' He answers briefly that question two pages later. 'The authority of the Bible is derived from what is commonly called its 'inspiration'. This then is the subject for our more immediate consideration.' (1,3)[12]

He calls his theory the 'inductive' theory because it is based upon a careful consideration of the literary and historical evidence. That is why it is important, and that is what distinguishes it from the traditional theory. However, it is clear that the inductive theory is a modification of the 'traditional theory' (this is Sanday's own term). The older theory tended to make inspiration 'dead and mechanical.' The inductive view preserves its spontaneity. Inspiration, for Sanday, is not inherent in the Bible. He means that it is not a quality which can be spoken of with respect to the Bible as a whole and in general terms. Inspiration 'is present in different books and parts of books in different degrees' (400).

Here he rejects a 'flat' doctrine, one which indiscriminately speaks of inspiration as a property of the whole Bible, without discriminating one section, one book, one writing from another. The historical books interpret rather than narrate plain matter of fact. That much we get by way of explanation of the difference between the inspiration of the prophet and the inspiration of the historian. But what is this 'inspiration' which is present in different degrees in the different books? The answer he gives to that question is that it is a property of the different books. He can predicate a certain something, a quality, of the literature, which he calls 'inspiration.' He says of the writings that they possess a quality, namely inspiration, but not all to the same extent. He is emphatic about this and. does not differ from the older view in this respect. Both use the term *inspiration* to connote a quality, a property of the writings. Sanday does not question whether this is an appropriate way to use the term 'inspiration.' He refuses to apply the term 'inspiration' in any flat sense to the Bible, but still uses the term of the whole.

He also uses the term in a different sense. To use the term 'inspiration' to speak of the of the individual writer in the process of writing is a different meaning of the term *inspiration* than to apply it to the Bible to connote a property of the whole. Sanday uses the term in both senses. He distinguishes the inspiration of the individual from the inspiration of the whole. That is to say, he distinguishes the process from the product (402), and then claims that we shall have to move beyond the inspiration of the individual writers to a 'superintending Mind'. He recognizes that in doing so he is supplementing the inductive theory (391-2, 402). Thus he recognizes the limits of a theory of inspiration. It is limited to the empirical process and to the quality of the resultant text. To say that there is a superintending mind is to go beyond the bounds of the theory and to 'supplement' it.

In a moment of candour, Sanday emphasizes that the only question at issue between the two theories is the *extent* of the human element (423). The inductive theory cannot determine the extent of the human element in advance of the evidence. It examines the literature, asking careful historical questions, and then and then only draws conclusions about the form which the divine self-communication has taken. For Sanday there is no question about the divine activity and, it seems, no further problem with it. God reveals himself. A reasonable theory of inspiration takes account of the human element. It is by examining the evidence that we discover how the human element plays its part in the total process of revelation. The evidence makes clear how God's revelation (423) takes place, how the Bible came into being and is what it is.

Sanday does not use the term 'revelation' frequently. But when he does he uses it in two senses: of what is revealed (423) and of the activity of revealing (424).

The process by which the Bible came into being is in accordance with what we know about the world, about nature and history. When God works there is 'nothing violent, nothing mechanical, nothing really sudden, however much it may appear so, but a long concatenation and subtlest interweaving of causes, all knit together as if in a living organism' (423). In this process, weak human instruments carry forward the divine design (footnote p. 424).

In an earlier age, Sanday argues, the assertion of the authority of the Bible depended upon not discriminating between the operation of the divine and the operation of the human. It can no longer do so. The older theory held that God took control of the 'writer' and produced the words of Scripture. The human counted for little in the process. The older theory held that the whole of the Scriptures were divinely inspired so that the words of men were in fact the words of God. Thus the infallibility of the whole was a condition of the Scripture's authority. Inspiration described the process by which the words of men were the very words of God. In doing so the human element was neglected. Sanday insists that a recognition of the human element is essential for an adequate understanding of the status of the Bible. The human element is identifiable. The human element can be distinguished from the divine.

There are places where Sanday expresses his reluctance to pursue the implications of what he has proposed. So there is an incompleteness as well as a tentativeness about his statements on inspiration. But there is no tentativeness with his conviction about the validity and the fruitfulness of the critical, historical method of biblical study. In this he contrasts with Jowett, who, half a century earlier, felt called upon to defend the historical method and to commend, even plead for, openness of mind in accepting it and in giving sympathetic consideration to the conclusions it leads to.

Sanday does not feel called upon to provide a systematic theory of inspiration. He says so much, in connection with his assertion that the utterances of the prophets had an objective cause outside the prophet (146). Indeed his convictions were not worked out into a system in these lectures. Here is a list of those basic convictions:

(1) Prophetic inspiration is the type of all inspiration (128, 268).

(2) The utterances of the prophet (and so it would seem of those others of whom the prophet was a type) have a source outside of themselves (146). Hence we may say that the words were not merely their own inventions.'[13] Should we or should we not call this 'verbal inspiration'?

(3) The process over a long period of time is revelation. Revelation is progressive (164).

(4) The inspiration of the prophet, while often typical (cf. 1 above) is not *always* typical. For example, psalmists, wise men, historians had an inspiration 'of their own' (268). The inspiration of the prophet did not 'supersede' the ordinary use of historical materials.

(5) Specifically, inspiration did not prevent the possibility of error by 'interfering with' the 'ordinary use of historical materials' (269).

(6) In the New Testament, inspiration extends from the single truth to a system of truth, 'a body of connected truths, a system of theology' (353). This is 'the more sustained character of the apostolic inspiration' (354).

(7) The divine acts through the human, both through the reception by the individual and in the process of collection and presentation (355).

(8) The extent of the human activity is to be discovered through empirical investigation and not to be asserted *a priori*. This is a particular concern of the inductive theory (423).

(9) The authority of the Bible no longer depends upon an *a priori*, or a dogmatic, assertion of the divine origin of the

writings and upon a failure to distinguish the divine from the human. To assert the authority of the Bible does not depend upon its being infallible. The genuine humanity of the authors is taken into account. This means that we are now able to discriminate between the divine and the human elements in the process of inspiration (425).

(10) The process by which God reveals himself includes the human and has respect for the interrelation of natural causes and human causes. There is no gate crashing into history or into nature (423).

(11) The inspiration of the Bible is the basis for asserting the authority of the Bible (1,3).

4   INSPIRATION AND AUTHORITY

It is with this last claim that we now take issue. 'The Bible is inspired' does not mean 'The Bible has authority.' 'The Bible is the inspired Word of God' is the basic statement of any theory of inspiration. But it is ambiguous, and hence unclear. It is because it is unclear that it can support a particular theological viewpoint. In a word, the statement, 'The Bible is the inspired word of God' is often equated with the statement, 'The Bible has special authority.' But the statements, 'The Bible is inspired' and 'The Bible has authority' are not equivalent. Nor does it follow from 'The Bible is inspired' that 'The Bible has authority.' The claim that the Bible has authority does not depend upon the claim that the Bible is inspired. The claim that the Bible is inspired must be clearly defined before we even know what we are saying. We must look therefore carefully at precisely what the statement, 'The Bible is the inspired Word of God' means. There are, it seems, two alternatives. It might mean either: (1) The Bible is the having-been inspired word of God, or (2) The Bible is the now inspired word of God. (1) is a statement about a process in the past. (2) is a statement about a status in the present, when that process is complete.

The point of asserting inspiration is to show that the product the Bible has a unique history, to indicate the divine activity in the process of its production. It is, it is argued, a unique book because it has been brought into being in a special way, by the 'inspiration' of God upon the 'writer.' Once that has been asserted, claims about the product are then made on that basis. The argument runs: Because God has inspired the writer and the writing (past tense), the product of that process is unique, set apart, inerrant, etc. But if that is what is meant, when the claim is made, 'The Bible is inspired' (present tense), a quite different meaning is being attached to the term 'inspired.' 'Inspired' now means 'special,' 'inerrant,' 'authoritative.' That is *not* the same meaning as 'produced by a process in which the Spirit of God operated in a special way.' It is either a deduction from it or a separate assertion.

To say that the Bible *is* inspired, in contrast to saying that the 'writer' *was* inspired, or the process *was* inspired, is first, to attribute certain qualities to the book, and second, to recommend rules for its use. For the traditional theory to say the Bible *is* inspired means the following: (1) it discloses truths about God not available elsewhere, (2) it is authoritative, equally and in all its parts, (3) it is exempt from error. But if that is what one wants to say, why confuse the issue by using the term *inspiration*?

When used of the psychological state of the 'writer' the term 'inspiration' is appropriate and can express the conviction that the source of that state and of the writing that issued from it was unusual if not divine. It then suggests a parallel to other such phenomena, for example the mantic phenomena of Greek soothsayers and oracles.

But now, 'inspired' is given a quite different meaning. It is used to express the claim that the Bible is authoritative. But that is to assume that 'is inspired' and 'has authority' mean the same. That just cannot be assumed. One does not establish the authority of the Bible by giving an account of the process by which it came to be written. To say that the writer or the process *were* inspired is insufficient to establish the authority of the book. 'The writer and the process were inspired' can be given a reasonably clear meaning. 'The Bible (the product) is inspired' does not add anything to that meaning. It is rather difficult in fact to say clearly what it does mean. 'The Bible is inspired' *intends* to say something more than 'the writer was inspired.' The issue is *whether it does or does not say anything more.*

The traditional theory has to add other terms, to talk about inerrancy, infallibility, self-authentication. It has to invent new terms by putting qualifiers before 'inspiration.' So it spoke of *'plenary* inspiration,' *'verbal* inspiration,' *'thought* inspiration.' These terms are confusing since one is not sure whether they are intended to refer to the process or the product, whether they describe how the book came to be, or qualities of the book once it has been produced. Indeed they refer in different ways to both. What was produced in this way has a special character about it because it was so produced.[14] We are meant to understand by the expression 'The Bible is inspired' not simply how it came about but that it has a special status and authority. We are expected to accept the transition from the one to the other. But we must ask whether this is a verbal trick, which tries to make the term 'inspired' bear a meaning which it should not. Perhaps the theory is trading on an ambiguity it reads into the concept of 'inspiration,' 'being inspired.'

Consider the following argument:

(1) The Bible is having-been inspired, i.e. the process by which it came into being was inspired.
(2) Therefore, it is unique because of the inspiration process, i.e. it *is* inspired.
(3) Therefore, it has authority.

If you want to move from one assertion to the other you will have to establish the first assertion and provide convincing argument to justify the move from the first assertion to the second and also for the move from (2) to (3). For the fact of the matter is that the claim 'The Bible is inspired' does not have the same significance as, is not logically equivalent to, 'The Bible is authoritative'.

A doctrine about Scripture's "inspiration" is not
identical with a doctrine about its "authority."
"Authority" cannot *mean* "divinely inspired."
"Inspiration" is a property of texts, while "authority"
is a relational term . . . . Given a doctrine of Scripture's
"authority," i.e., how Scripture ought concretely to be
used and construed in the common life of the church
and in doing theology, a doctrine of "inspiration" gives
a theological explanation of why, when Scripture is
used in that way, certain results sometimes follow.[15]

What follows from this is quite simple:

(1) You can show that the Bible has authority without
developing (dubious) theories of inspiration.

(2) To establish the authority of a document for a
community in the present, you must ask what status it has
in the present and what it does in the present. You must
ask in relation to what and for whom it has the status it
has and does what it does.

(3) No account of how the book came to be what it is can
explain why it has authority now. All the books that have
been inspired might have been lost, or fallen into disuse,
or been forgotten. They would then be inspired and non-
authoritative. On the other hand books which were not
said to have been inspired might be exercising a quite real
authority in the present. So the question 'How does it
come to exercise authority?' 'Was it inspired or not?' are
two quite different questions. If there is some connection
between them it will have to be shown. We cannot assume
such a connection.[16] It would not be reasonable to do so.
'It surely cannot be supposed that to call Scripture
"authority" means that properly employed it could
"guarantee" the correctness of our proposals, if only we
could figure out how to employ it properly.'[17]

No doctrinal position is able to tell us how to use Scripture so
as to guarantee that God will be present to illumine and correct us.

To say so overlooks the essential importance of (1) the presence of the Holy Spirit. It also overlooks the fact that (2) the interpreter moves from the text of the Bible to the concrete situation of the church by using quite particular procedures of interpretation. He selects from the Bible and relates what he selects to the doctrinal or theological scheme he works out. He does not normally simply 'translate' the biblical language.

Reference to God, the Holy Spirit, reminds Christians that they are not dealing with only a text. With reference to Scripture it means that what authority the Bible has it has because God reveals himself through it.

We must relate the statement that the Bible is the final authority for the church to the further claim that God, as he manifests himself, is the absolute authority. God, through Christ, through the Holy Spirit is active in the life and activity of the church in the present. The two claims must be brought together.

It is therefore important to consider the question, 'In what sense exactly the Scriptures are the revelation of God and the standard of faith.'[18] So we have to go beyond accounts of the process by which the books of the Bible came to be produced and compiled. It is just naive to think you can simply move from claims about inspiration to claims about authority.

There is only one way in which one may appear to do this. That is to extend the meaning of inspiration to the event that happens when the writings become in the present the instrument of God's revelation in the church and in the world. One might then draw analogies or make comparisons between what happened when the writings came into being and what is happening with them as they function within the church in the present. If that procedure is followed, the meaning of the word 'inspiration' gets extended to cover the Bible's function as the medium of God's revelation in the present. But that very clearly is an extension of the meaning of the term, deliberately made to connect the idea of inspiration with that of authority. Since this cannot be done unless one speaks of God's revealing himself, through the Scriptures, in the present time, the key idea is that of revelation rather than inspiration.

An example of this procedure is to be found in the book on inspiration by Bruce Vawter. In setting out his own constructive statement he argues that we should extend the meaning of the concept of inspiration. So he writes (and we select just two extracts):

> Both Protestant and Catholic thinking have conspired to a growing recognition that biblical inspiration in the narrow sense, the sense in which it has generally been subjected to ecclesiastical pronouncements and the examination of theologians, is but one stage in the unfolding of a mystery of communication that encompasses earlier and later stages as well.
>
> Luther, it might appear, was posing the question as it ought to have been posed all along; in relation to a dynamic and living as opposed to a static and fossilized inspired word. That is to say, if the role of the word in the church was to be seen less as archival testimony and more as the continuing presence of the Spirit — the way, we have seen, that the Bible itself understood the word — then the inspirational process itself ought to be considered not as merely terminating in a literary text but as touching also the later reader and hearer of the word. For word is not properly word, not the means of communication and revelation, until it has been taken in, until the process of communicating is thereby completed. When we are dealing with an inspired word, then, inspiration should be regarded as proper to every stage of communication.[19]

Much in the viewpoint expressed here is constructive. The coming into being of the books is one stage in a complex process. The book is a living word and not a dead ('fossilised') letter. The process is not complete until the word has been received. The question is as to how best to express such important convictions. Vawter wishes to extend the reference of the term 'inspiration' to the later reception of the word, indeed to 'every stage of communication.' That is to place too wide a range of meanings on the term. It is more appropriate to use a related but more versatile conception. This is the conception of *revelation*. It can serve better the goals that Vawter has in mind, namely: (1) to point to a process of divine initiative in the composition of the books, (2) to indicate a divine presence in connection with the use of Scripture, (3) to insist on the importance of the receiving of the word, and to relate that receiving as the goal of the whole process to the activity of the Spirit.

In view of the ways in which the term 'inspiration' has been used in the past, it is unsuitable to attempt to extend its meaning in this way. One might try to utilize the term *theopneustia*, but again confusion and unclarity would result. The doctrine of inspiration had been in Protestant Theology 'for the most part a chapter of accidents'.[20] What happened was that it became a formalized doctrine, became abstracted from the most important data about the Bible — its instrumentality as the vehicle of God's revelation; its potential ineffectiveness as mere letter, isolated from the 'testimony of the Holy Spirit;' its genuine humanity and its errancy. The doctrine of inspiration focussed upon the letter and left no room for the reality which imparted to the letter the life it had within the church. In stressing the inspiration of the Bible, the doctrine gave short shrift to what it was that inspired the words and gave them life.

But it is essential in any serious account of Scripture that we reckon with this reality, the reality of God active in revealing and with the response which God's activity calls forth from the believer. Then we may rightly assess the place of Scripture as fulfilling an essential role in this total process. This is to be true to the heritage of the Reformers.

> . . . for the Reformers the question as to the inspired Word was as such always the question of that which inspires and controls the Word . . . . As Luther insisted in innumerable passages the word of Scripture given

by the Spirit can be recognised as God's word only because the work of the Spirit which has taken place in it takes place again and goes a step further, i.e., becomes an event for its hearers and readers.[21]

5 Verbal Inspiration

The Reformers used the language of dictation, but the Bible was not for them a body of propositions which had come as a result of a process of verbal inspiration, as the metaphors of God using men as his pen or his lyre had suggested.[22] What was important for both Luther and Calvin was the way in which the Bible actually functioned in the living process of witnessing to faith and creating faith in the church. So there was a reversion when the Protestant Scholastics made the Bible a book that was inspired down to the letter and said that it was therefore inerrant in the sense that whatever it said about whatever subject could not in fact be faulted. The stress upon the infallible church was met by an assertion of an infallible book, and this new doctrine of inspiration was designed to meet the situation in which objective certainty was required by a church which had no infallible teaching office and could not base its authority on tradition. Protestants could not appeal as the Catholic Church could to a father figure like the pope to make an authoritative pronouncement. The alternative was to appeal to the Bible and to say that the Bible was without error. That is the rationale behind the appeal of the Protestant to the Bible in this particular way. It was a radical development.

In the nineteenth century those who reasserted this teaching of the inerrancy of Scripture did so in face of a very different situation, the situation created by new sciences and by the influence of Enlightenment thinking. When they could least do so, because they lived in a very different cultural situation, some Christians simply asserted the older doctrine of verbal inspiration, and attempted to entrench behind older positions, as if the older doctrine could do service even when questions of a new sort were being pressed.

We have seen how Sanday attempted to re-habilitate the concept of inspiration but was unsuccessful at certain vulnerable points.

A doctrine of inspiration is not a crucial doctrine. The traditional doctrine of inspiration was one long detour in Christian theology. The following observations by Protestant scholars require little comment.

> To attempt to find the explanation of the phenomenon of biblical authority in the sphere of "inspiration" is to seek for understanding in a place where the Bible itself does not look for it. The attempt to "explain" the Bible in non-biblical categories is bound to fail, and such efforts have given rise in the past to most of the classical misinterpretations of biblical truth which have disturbed the life of the church. The very word "inspiration" is hardly a biblical word at all. . . . It has become clearer today that the authority of the Bible, as Christians have traditionally understood it, cannot be explained by means of the highly subjective categories of "inspiration" and "religious experience."[23]

> If the term "inspiration" were to fall into disuse, no fact of nature, or history, or language, no event in the life of man or of dealings of God with him, would be in any degree altered. The word itself is but of yesterday . . . . Therefore the question of inspiration, though in one sense important, is to the interpreter as though it were not important; he is in no way called upon to determine a matter with which he has nothing to do. . . .[24]

Warfield, an intelligent fundamentalist, was clear and honest in admitting that no other doctrines depended upon a doctrine of inspiration. He wrote: 'Were there no such thing as inspiration, Christianity would be true. . . . Inspiration is not the most fundamental of Christian doctrines.'[25]

Kelsey, commenting on Warfield wrote: '. . . no other doctrines hang on the doctrine of inspiration. It is logically dispensable. . . . If inspiration were dropped out, no other doctrine would go. It is logically dispensable.'[26]

But for Warfield, Scripture is inerrant and consists of the very words of God. What then is the status of a doctrine of inspiration if in Warfield's terms, 'we found the whole Christian system on the doctrine of plenary inspiration as little as we found it upon the doctrine of angelic existences?'[27]

His answer is that the doctrine of inspiration serves as a rule for approaching the Bible. It provides a paradigm. It directs the reader: Act as if Scripture is plenarily inspired. Do not allow anything to count against the hypothesis that Scripture is in all respects true. Where there appear to be errors or inconsistencies, treat them as if they were not. Here is a rule for procedure, a rule which is not to be questioned. It is a rule which leads to dogmatism. Because the Bible is inspired, treat it as without error of any kind. That is how the doctrine of inspiration operates. So the way then is open for the gathering together its 'doctrines' and setting them out. One *translates* their meaning for the present.[28] So this doctrine of plenary inspiration leads to a particular theological method. It is a priori, non-empirical. Indeed the attitude it engenders and represents refuses critical consideration of the biblical *writing*. In being thus non-contextual and non-historical it turns its back on the great progress in understanding available through the contextual and historical approaches to Scripture.

We may now put our finger on a central problem. If the doctrine of inspiration directs us to approach the Bible in certain ways, to treat it as inerrant, for example, it is asking something we cannot do. Therefore, by our being unable to do as it directs, it shows itself unworthy as a doctrine which gives an account of the Scriptures. Its fundamental inadequacy lies in the fact that it demands that one think and act in ways in which one cannot think and cannot act. This is in addition to the other inadequacies which we have now presented.

6 REVELATION

The alternative is to associate the concept of authority with that of revelation. It is to study the Scriptures contextually and historically, looking in each case at what the facts of the matter are. It is to relate the idea of Scripture to the belief that God acts in the world and to ask how God's activity shows up in relation to Scripture.

No one was more concerned with such problems than Karl Barth.[29] Two of Barth's early and continuing themes were that God is sovereign, which means that he takes the initiative and establishes his sovereignty within the church. He also insisted on the instrumentality of the Bible in the process of God's revealing of himself. He believed he was restoring, in a new context, the understanding of the Reformation concerning the Scriptures as the word of God. What one hears in Scripture, while it is human expression, is more than human expression. It is in fact the very word of God. But the authority of the Scripture is not constituted by being recognized as having authority. 'It is not for us or any man to constitute this or that writing as Holy Writ. . . . it has already been constituted and chosen. Its acceptance is only the discovery and acknowledgment of this fact.'[30]

The church does not give the canon to itself. What the church does is rather to confirm what has already been given to it. The point at issue here with reference to the canon is the quite simple one as to whether the church *constitutes* the authority of the Bible or whether it *recognizes* that the Bible performs certain distinctive functions, and on the basis of recognizing what it does then says that the Bible has authority.

The church does not control, does not have authority over, the revelation of God. The church does not constitute the Bible as authoritative. What the church does is to recognize and to confirm that these writings in particular do in fact have a place in the church which no other writings have. So the church is responding, in making its judgments, to what is in fact already given to it. It is through the Scriptures that God's presence, guidance, revelation is made a reality in the church. It is through the reading and the exposition of Scripture, and this of course includes its oral exposition and interpretation, that faith is created and nurtured and that the life of the church continues. Thus in stating that these books are the canon and therefore have authority, the church is not constituting the books as authoritative. It is simply recognizing that they are. And between these two alternatives there would seem to lie the issue between Protestantism and Catholicism — the radical and important distinction between constituting and recognizing something to be an authority. In the one case it seems to give the church autonomy to make judgments. The church gives status to a body of writings which they otherwise would not have had. In the other case, the church recognises the authority which the books have.

The question of the interpretation of Scripture is rather more complex than saying simply that in the catholic system tradition is set alongside of Scripture. If tradition says what Scripture means, then tradition is set over and above Scripture. Of course the Protestant also must say what Scripture means. The question of how to interpret Scripture is still a vital question for both Protestant and Catholic.

The main themes of Barth's doctrine of Holy Scripture are now well known. God is sovereign over his revelation. God makes himself known. In revealing himself he takes the initiative and the act of revelation evokes response, the response of faith and obedience. God has revealed himself in the past. He reveals himself in the present. It is the same sovereign God who makes himself known now as then. The decisive event of God's revelation is Jesus Christ, to which the Old Testament looks forward and to which the New Testament looks back. Each in its own order witnesses to that event, the one in anticipation, the other in fulfilment. The writings of Scripture are thus the written witness to the continuing event. They point in their particular form, to the event which lies behind them. The writings of human witnesses, they are prone to error, but in their role of witness they are irreplaceable. They are not identical with the revelation of God, but they are the instruments of that revelation. On the one hand, they point to God's activity in revealing himself in Jesus Christ in the past. On the other hand, they mediate God's revelation in the present. This is the activity of the same God, the same Spirit. Thus Scripture becomes the medium of God's word as God reveals himself through it. The Scripture is read and interpreted in the Church, and as it is read and interpreted it may become the vehicle for the act of God himself. Without such a sovereign act of God Scripture is a dead letter.

Any satisfactory doctrine of Scripture will take account of this dynamic instrumentality of the written word, the free action of God, the Holy Spirit, and the enabled response of the believer. No doctrine of Scripture will be at all adequate which fails to reckon with the total process. Hence the traditional teachings of inspiration are both formal and misleading. They distort because they focus on the writing as 'letter,' rather than upon God active through the words. Any account of the Bible must reckon with the contemporaneity of God's activity, through the witness based upon Scripture, and this means with the fact of response in faith and obedience to the spoken word, and this in effect means, to the reality of the sovereign God. Barth is carefully, but firmly, rejecting a theory of inspiration to express his doctrine of Holy Scripture. He knows that he must account for the humanity, the historicity and the error of the Scripture, while at the same time recognize the essential and irreplaceable position it has in the existence and witness of the church. Hence when he uses the term 'inspiration' he has accommodated it to his own theology (as Vawter did). Barth can thus say, 'Verbal inspiration does not mean the infallibility of the biblical word in its linguistic, historical and theological character as a human word. It means that the fallible and faulty human word is as such used by God and has to be received and heard in its human fallibility.'[31] It is the mystery of God and not the letter of the Scripture that is the subject of the *theopneustia*, self-disclosure of God in its totality.[32] Since nothing could be further from the Protestant scholastic's doctrine of inspiration, Barth dissociates himself from both that doctrine and its language. 'Revelation' is the key-category now. The concept of 'inspiration' can drop quietly away.

Theories of inspiration are not able to do justice to the claims in the name of which they were constructed and proposed. The limits imposed on us by the concept of inspiration, especially in its narrower definition, but also in its more liberal definition, and the direction in which it points us fail at crucial points in illuminating and explaining the Christian reality.

Chapter VI Notes

[1]II Peter 1:21. A few texts add the adjective holy before 'men'.

[2]W. Sanday, *Inspiration*, p. 430.

[3]Alan Richardson wrote: '. . . what the nineteenth century had not yet realized, if Sanday's work may be taken as its culminating point, was that the non-biblical category of inspiration . . . cannot provide a satisfactory basis for the re-statement of the truth concerning the authority of the Bible in the age of science.' *The Bible in the Age of Science*, pp. 75-6.

[4]*So-called Historical Jesus and the Historic Biblical Christ*, p. 107.

[5]*Ibid.*, p. 127.

[6]*Ibid.*, p. 129.

[7]*Ibid.*, p. 102.

[8]Benjamin Jowett, 'On the Interpretation of Scripture', in *Essays and Reviews*, seventh edition. London: Longman Green, Longman and Roberts, 1861, pp. 330-433. References in the text refer to these pages.

[9]He is ambiguous about it. He can point to the fallacy of accepting a theory of inspiration as providing rules for interpreting Scripture such as: any passage can be co-ordinated with any other passage of Scripture; take everything in the Bible as true; raise no 'critical' questions. Jowett denies that we can now rest doctrines on texts of Scriptures, simply co-ordinating passages which appear to contain similar words or ideas (421).

He can also say that a theory of inspiration has no relation to interpretation, so that the interpreter can for all intents and purposes ignore it. 'The question of inspiration . . . is to the interpreter as though it were not important' (351).

The fact is that he speaks of interpretation on two levels. In one case, the interpreter seeks to get at what the writer meant, to get at the author's intention. 'The true use of interpretation is to get rid of interpretation, and leave us alone in company with the author' (384). In the other case, there is the construction of doctrine in relation to Scripture. Jowett recognizes the difficulty of this latter task, but says no more about it. While he is concerned with the first level of interpretation, the problems about the second are always in his mind. He does not further discuss the method of doctrinal interpretation in relation to historical interpretation. The issues are complex.

Jowett was writing in 1860 in England, which had not yet experienced the full impact of the historical study of the Bible. Textual criticism was making great strides, the analytic study of The Pentateuch and the Synoptic Gospels was progressing in Germany. 'Lives' of Jesus were being produced. The painstaking work of the Cambridge trio, Lightfoot, Westcott and Hort was proceeding. In 1859 the *Origin of Species* appeared and Jowett is well aware of the 'problem' of science and the Bible.

[10]William Sanday, thirty-four years later, explicitly defends a theory of inspiration in his Bampton Lectures at Oxford He attempts in doing so to take full account the historical studies of the Bible of the latter half of the nineteenth century.

There is no *necessary* connection between the inspiration and the authority of the Bible. To have shown the inerrancy (inspiration sense 3) of the Bible is not to show its authority. To have authority the book has to be read and used. It has authority if it authorizes beliefs and practices in a community. If the inspired book was *never* used it would not have authority. There is a difficulty in using the term 'inspiration' in sense (3). It is noteworthy that Vawter, a knowledgeable Catholic theologian, in his treatise on inspiration, extends the meaning of the term to include its function in the church. But we can give a better account of that by using other terms. Then we do not confuse the issue.

[11]II Timothy 3: 16.

[12]References in the text are now to William Sanday, *Inspiration*.

[13]The words which they (the prophets) repeat and the visions of revelation which they describe are not merely their own inventions, but are suggested and brought home to them from without in such a way that they were irresistibly attributed to God, and given out as coming from him.' *Ibid.*, p. 147.

[14]The argument that is needed to establish this conclusion runs as follows: God indited the words, thoughts. So the product is true,

representative of God's will as no other document is. So it has unparalleled authority. So it must be followed, believed.

[15]David H. Kelsey, *The Uses of Scripture in Recent Theology*, pp. 210-211.

[16]People may come to acknowledge the authority of the Bible because they have accepted that it was inspired. What we have shown above is that that acknowledgment is questionable on the grounds of the traditional account of inspiration. It overlooks the important function of argument in the process, and does not clearly establish the unique *religious* authority which the Bible has for the believer.

[17]Kelsey, *op. cit.*, p. 215.

[18]H. H. Farmer, 'The Bible: Its Significance and Authority' in *The Interpreter's Bible*, *Vol.* I, New York and Nashville: Abingdon Press, 1952, pp. 3-31. The quotation is from p.3.

[19]Bruce Vawter, *Inspiration*, pp. 158, 78-79.

[20]K. Barth, *Church Dogmatics I/2*, p. 526.

[21]*Ibid.*, p. 521.

[22]These metaphors appeared in the early centuries of the church.

[23]Alan Richardson, *The Bible in the Age of Science*, p. 75.

[24]Benjamin Jowett., *op. cit.*, p 551.

[25]B.B. Warfield, *The Inspiration and Authority of the Bible*, p. 215.

[26]Kelsey, *op. cit.*, p. 21.

[27]Warfield, *loc. cit.*

[28]On this view the answer to the question, 'How does one relate the text of Scripture to the modern reader?' is, one *translates* the text. But is the idea of interpretation as 'translating the text' correct? There are many difficulties in thinking of this as the task of theology. What it suggests is that it is a relatively simple matter to provide the meaning of the text for the modern reader. But it is not always easy to move from what the text meant to what it may now mean. Serious problems arise in the course of interpreting an ancient text. Two later chapters in this book deal with some of these problems.

[29]Barth expounds a theology of Scripture in paragraph 19 of the *Church Dogmatics* II/2 pp. 457-537; and of authority, in 20, II/2, pp. 538-660.

[30]*Church Dogmatics, I/2*, p. 473.

[31]*Ibid.*, p. 533.

[32]*Ibid.*, p. 516. Cf. 'But the vulnerability of the Bible, i.e., its capacity for error, also extends to its religious or theological content. . . . Not only part but all that they (i.e. the biblical writings) say is historically related and conditioned.' *Ibid.*, p. 509.

SUMMARY OF CHAPTER VII

REVELATION: WHAT IT MEANS

Revelation means an unveiling, a making known. This demands initiative on the part of the one revealing, and receptiveness on the part of the one to whom the revelation may be made. The Old Testament speaks of the *knowledge* of God, the New Testament of the *mystery* now revealed. We examine the biblical understanding of revelation. Scripture is the product of revelation and the means by which the revelation of God continues. The community of faith bears witness to what it has known. It uses the Scriptures. These testify to and mediate the reality of God in the person of Jesus Christ. God continues to be active in history as the Christian bears witness to the event.

VII
REVELATION: WHAT IT MEANS

1 REMOVING THE VEIL

By starting with the simple proposition: 'God reveals himself
through Scripture', we can lay stress on the initiative of God and
the instrumentality of the Bible, the importance of the community,
the response of the believer and the resulting experience. While
we cannot within the limits of this writing develop a full-scale
theology of revelation, we may outline such a theology and show
how it can answer questions a theory of inspiration did not.

The word 'revelation' means unveiling. To reveal (Latin, *revelo*;
Greek, *apokalupto*) means 'to take away the veil, to remove what
hides something from view.' With the removing of the obstruction,
what was not known now comes to be known. It is a quite familiar
word. We use it in many types of context. The following are
examples.

> The picture was moved and revealed a hidden door.
> We may now reveal who the donor is.
> Former spy reveals all.
> She wore a revealing evening gown.
> He revealed his feelings in his letter.
> A slip of the tongue revealed his real intentions.
> A groan revealed that he was in pain.
> The X-ray pictures revealed that she was free of disease.

The clue to the problem was revealed to him by a chance incident.

By looking also at ways in which we do not use the term, ways which we feel are a misuse of the term, we can further clarify its meaning. We know there is something wrong with the following:

I revealed to myself who the culprit was.
He revealed himself in a book which no one ever read.

The term revelation: is used of coming to know something which one did not know before. That 'coming to know' depends on an activity by someone other than the person who comes to know. There must be response to that activity. Revelation is a relational term. To make something known to somebody someone takes the initiative, someone else responds to it. B must do something appropriate in response to what A does, e.g. keep awake, listen, interpret.

There is a clear difference between discovery and disclosure (a synonym for 'revelation'). I may find out many things about another person, by looking in the right places, asking the right questions of the right people. But I shall never be able to discover, that is find out by myself, what that other person alone can reveal to me. Unless that other takes the initiative, I shall never know what he alone could reveal. This means that he must intend, must purpose, to make known what he might keep to himself, and so not make accessible to me.

But even should someone intend to make known to me what I would otherwise never come to discover by myself, I shall not in fact know it unless I respond. The intention to reveal oneself, and the intention to know the other are not sufficient in themselves. Revelation takes place when there is giving *and* responding, an interaction between agents who are both free and purposive. Revelation is communication. Revelation takes place when what is 'provided' is grasped, what is 'offered' is 'taken', what is 'spoken' is 'heard.'

The metaphors of 'the word,' 'hearing the word,' 'speaking the word,' are familiar in the Bible. They point to the phenomenon we have been defining. The term *reveal* is used in Scripture with particular reference to Jesus Christ. He is to be 'revealed from heaven with his mighty angels in flaming fire' at the *parousia*.[1] Paul received the Gospel 'by the revelation of Jesus Christ.'[2] The seer of the Apocalypse speaks of his communication as 'the revelation of Jesus Christ which God gave him.'[3] From these passages it is clear that Jesus Christ is the subject of God's revelation, and that the term 'revelation' is characteristically used of the end-time, the eschaton. It is also used of present knowledge and experience of God in Jesus Christ.

2 Revelation in the Old Testament

We shall now look briefly at the way in which the Scripture speaks of God's revealing himself, contenting ourselves here with certain basic observations. We begin with the Old Testament.[4]

That God is living and active is a primary assumption of the Old Testament. The writers of the Old Testament teach that he has a purpose for the world, for individual nations and for persons in it, and that he is a creative God, ever and anew making His purpose known. The Old Testament makes no attempt to prove the existence of God nor to demonstrate the fact that he has revealed and continues to reveal himself. This it assumed. God's will and purpose lie behind the revealing act. The revelation of God is not the communication of abstract ideas, or eternal truth, or logical demonstration. Revelation is not of a piece with logical reasoning, as if being ignorant and lacking insight we need to learn new arguments.

Thus the prophets are not characteristically religious geniuses whose power of thinking is much more highly developed than that of ordinary people. The prophet is caught up in an event. The initiative is always with God. Revelation is an act of God's grace. He need not have continued to reveal his purpose to Israel. He did so. This is due to his grace. So a certain kind of receptivity is called for, not a rational plumbing the depths but a submissive willingness not only to hear the word of God but also to perform it and then to communicate it. Human sensitivity to the Word is not ruled out even if the message has its origin in God. 'The Lord hath spoken who can but prophesy.'[5] In the communication of the divine will a certain kind of receptivity is necessary all along, on the part of the prophet, on the part of the interpreter and on the part of those who later encounter the revelation and act upon it.

Revelation is possible for human beings because they are made for fellowship with God. Such encounters preserve the sovereignty and transcendence of God. He is still Lord of his going and of his coming, of his word and of his silence. Never does the revealing act of God detract from his supreme majesty, and never can man be on familiar terms with the deity. When God has revealed himself, an appreciation of his holiness is deepened and awe follows in the presence of the 'numinous.' Isaiah felt himself utterly unworthy, as did Moses and Jeremiah, when confronted by the divine reality. The revelation leads to a sense of unworthiness and sinfulness: 'Woe is me! For I am lost; for I am a man of unclean lips, and I dwell in the midst of a people of unclean lips; for my eyes have seen the King, the Lord of hosts.'[6]

The purpose of revelation is to enable men to live, to communicate the 'fear of the Lord' which is the 'beginning of wisdom.' In response to God's revelatory acts men are to be led to 'fear' him and this fear is to issue in ethical living, the health of soul and body. This then becomes the way to life. This life is found in relationship with God and of this relationship the term *yada* (to know) is used. It is no intellectual knowledge merely, but a profound personal relationship in which demands are made and acknowledged. It is not mysticism but leads to a healthy relationship with one's fellows. Thus the fool is one who does not 'know' God. What is in view here is a *practical* denial of God's existence, a life without relationship to God, unguided by God's revelation.

When the Hebrew spoke of knowing God, he was not referring to an intellectual exercise. That one knows God shows itself in one's behaviour. To know God was to be in relationship with God, to be in communion with God. The knowledge of God 'is a knowledge of the heart and demands man's love . . . (Deut. vi).'[7] Its vital demand is walking humbly in the ways of the Lord.[8] 'It is the recognition of God as God, total surrender to God as the Lord.' 'This knowledge of God is essentially a communion with God, and it is also religious faith. It is something altogether different from intellectual knowledge.'[9]

The Hebrew believed that his God, Yahweh, would go on revealing himself in the future. What he has revealed in the past will in turn provide the means for understanding what Yahweh will reveal of himself in the days to come. As the Hebrew understanding of Yahweh's revelation grew, one could look back on the *course* of Yahweh's dealings with the people and on a growth in understanding of that people. That course of revelation, response and development of understanding provided the means for the understanding of revelation yet to come. The Old Testament is incomplete, forward looking and hopeful. Take for example the portrait of the suffering servant.[10] Here was a 'word of Yahweh' to the prophet. Here is a series of oracles which could lead Israel to understanding as it applied the words to experiences yet to come. So event and continuing interpretation were inter-related. The 'word of Yahweh' from the past would serve as a means to understand the present and the future.

So the oracles of the prophets were preserved and highly valued. To study them meant that one had resources for interpreting the events Israel would experience in her ongoing history. Her faith represented the convergence of event and continuing interpretation of event, assisted by reflection on the former 'words' of Yahweh.

God revealed himself in different ways, sometimes but not prominently through outward ritual means. God revealed and continuously reveals himself in nature. This is not the 'natural religion' or the 'general revelation' of the theologians. There is here no attempt to argue God's existence from nature. God upholds nature in all its aspects and uses the forces of nature to accomplish his purposes.[11] Characteristically, natural elements become part of a great revelatory complex. Yahweh called Moses and gave him a revelation of his name. He directed him to lead the people from Egypt in the name of Yahweh, a God whom they did not know. Moses was to reveal Yahweh's purpose to the Israelites and at the same time actively engage the Pharaoh. An historical event involves the co-incidence of many forces, natural and personal. To say Yahweh reveals himself in the historical event of the Exodus means in this case the smiting of the first-born, the decision of the Pharaoh, the willingness of the Israelites to respond to the call of Moses, the opening up of the Red Sea and its subsequent closing, the coming into existence of a separate people and their formal adoption by Yahweh as his chosen people. It also means discerning that God is present in this complex of events. This complex of phenomena, personal and impersonal, makes revelation unique.

Such events must be interpreted as God's acts if they are to have religious significance. They must be recorded and transmitted if they are to exercise influence over Israel's understanding. Thus the initial act of revelation for Israel (the Exodus complex) is the basis for Israel's belief that Yahweh will go on revealing himself. That Yahweh had revealed his will in the past was the assurance that he would continue to reveal it, and the guarantee of his continued activity in time of crisis.

In the Old Testament understanding of revelation, the elect community is central. God comes to them in their concrete experience. The interpretation of a series of events as the activity of God is an intrinsic part of the revelation. The Hebrew sees the events from a particular perspective. He interprets the events of his history in a particular way. He 'sees' them as the revelation of a God who is progressively making himself known as his history unfolds. To see an event as an 'act of God' is itself an event. Through this process, God's many acts come to be seen to comprise a unity. The prophets of Israel saw Yahweh's acts as a unity, and a theology of history developed. Basic to this understanding of the continuity and unity of revelation is the Old Testament belief in corporate personality.[12] Israel was a unity through time. The individual was a member of the community. What God had revealed in the time past to one generation of Israel was relevant for all of Israel, because it was one people throughout its generations.

The events which provided the occasion for, or the substance of, revelation were many and varied. The event could be very complex, indeed for later writers, the whole of Israel's history was the revealing of God. The event could be extremely simple. Sometimes a casual experience or encounter on the part of the prophet was the occasion for an oracle. Amos plays on the word 'summer fruit' and Jeremiah on 'almond branch'.[13] Sometimes a deep personal experience provided the background for the message, e.g. Hosea's marital experience.[14] In due course the word of the prophet, i.e. the intermediary, came to have special significance. In Israel the word came to have importance as in some way embodiment of the revelation and the means to further revelation. Theologians have made a distinction between *revelatum*, the data, the deposit, and *revelatio*, the act of revelation. Israel considered the words themselves powerful agencies in *revelatio*. The word was not inert, not a dead letter. It was 'like a hammer that breaks the rock into pieces.'[15] The 'word' had a power quite unusual. They considered the prophetic 'word' as in some way powerful to effect the purpose for which it was intended. Once the word had been spoken it would, as an extension of the personality of its speaker or writer, exert a personal influence. Thus *God* spoke through the Word. The oft-repeated invitation, 'Hear the word of the Lord,' makes that clear. The right response was to 'hear,' i.e. to obey. The written word was thus a means for communicating the divine life and provided the means of entering into fellowship with the God it portrayed.

Various intermediaries are spoken of in connection with God's communication of his will. His *angel* is a mysterious being, albeit in the form of man. When three men appear to Abraham, one of them is the Lord, but which one? Reverence is thus called for each one and the mystery of God's being is preserved. He maintains his lordship over the revelation of that being. The term 'glory,' a more sophisticated and mysterious term than 'angel,' preserved the polarity between the elements of 'hiddenness' and 'revelation.' God reveals his 'glory' to Moses, but Moses does not see God. Rather he hears a recital of his character and attributes. This is his glory. God reveals his 'name.' The Old Testament always had a sense of mystery in connection with the name of God. God reveals himself and mystery remains. So, 'I am that I am' means 'I am the eternal one' or 'I am what I am,' i.e., 'it is a secret and so no concern of Moses.' At any rate Moses cannot have power over the name of God, for this would be to have power over God himself. God is sovereign over the revelation he initiates, and the mystery is not resolved in his act of revealing himself.

However and wherever he reveals himself, Yahweh is still sovereign over his revelation. God comes to men in many ways and at different times. He is to be seen by the receptive one in whose heart is a willingness to hear and an openness to see, even at the most unexpected times and in the most unexpected places. He reveals himself to the one who is ready to obey and to 'perform' the word he hears.

3 REVELATION IN THE NEW TESTAMENT

The Hebrew understanding of God's revelation to the covenant people in Old Testament times provides the background for the New Testament teaching concerning revelation and knowledge of God. We must read the New Testament in the light of all that went before in the revelatory history of Israel. The 'definitive revelatory events' of the New Testament 'are the climax of a history they presuppose.'[16] The decisive event is sometimes now called the 'Christ-event,' and focuses upon Jesus: what he said, what he did and what happened to him. The New Testament understands that the eternal God has chosen to make himself known decisively through Jesus. The relationship between Jesus and the Father was unique as was that between Jesus and human beings. He could thus be the means by which the knowledge of God became especially available to man.

This conviction that Jesus makes God known decisively and uniquely is expressed in many ways in the writings of the New Testament. Take, for example, the statement of the Gospel of Matthew: 'All things have been delivered to me by my Father; and no-one knows the Son except the Father, and no-one knows the Father except the Son and anyone to whom the Son chooses to reveal him.'[17]

The term 'all things' suggests a complete and crucial revelation of God. The term 'delivered' suggests that it is entrusted to, committed to, is the responsibility of, the Son. The aorist tense 'delivered' suggests that it was an activity that took place in the historical sphere. The relationship of Father and Son is, by the very choice of terms, portrayed as unique, and as historically displayed. The Son reveals God to those who come to know God. The Son is Jesus. It is Jesus whom Matthew reports as speaking these words.

The New Testament has christianised the Old Testament teaching that knowledge is personal.[18] For the Christian as for the Hebrew, there was no purely intellectual, no simply theoretical, knowledge. Knowing God is more like knowing persons than knowing facts. But some such knowledge is important. One hears the words about Jesus. Then one responds. One must understand the words one hears before one can respond appropriately. One must assent before one can trust. It is through Jesus' work that this kind of knowledge of God becomes available to humanity. The purpose of revelation is not simply to impart information, but to communicate the life of God. Hence the condition of reception is not intellectual acumen but trustful and obedient acceptance. This, the New Testament calls *faith*. An obedient will responding to the divine initiative leads a person to a knowledge of God. 'The primary thing is the doing of God's will. This makes possible a discrimination between teaching which is divine and that which is merely human. So the New Testament puts Jesus Christ at the very focal point of its understanding of God. To respond to Jesus Christ is to come to know God. It is in obedience to Jesus' commands that the believer comes to know that it is God who is revealing himself in him. To know God one must be obedient to his commandments. That means responding to Jesus Christ by trusting, obeying and loving him. 'By this we may be sure that we know him, if we keep his commandments.'[19] 'To know that Christ comes from God is possible only to those who know Christ personally in the subjective relation of loving trust and obedience.'[20]

Through revelation one comes to know what one did not know before. Jesus is the revelation of God in the sense that in him God is known to the believer, as he was not before known. In Jesus Christ, we know what *we* did not know before. But also, in Jesus Christ there is made known what *nobody* knew before, what was not known. The term 'mystery' (*mysterion*) does service in this connection. In the New Testament 'mystery' is something which was once not known, once hidden, but has *now* become known. The emphasis is upon the becoming known of what was up till now hidden, unknown. So it differs from the English word 'mystery' therefore, which signifies what is *not* known. The Gospel of Jesus Christ is a 'mystery.' What has become known was once hidden. What before was veiled has now been unveiled and opened to view. God has shown himself. What was 'kept secret for long ages . . . is now disclosed.' That is the mystery. That is the Gospel. That is Jesus Christ.[21] The God and Father of our Lord Jesus Christ has 'made known the mystery . . . set forth in Christ.'[22] This *mysterion* has been made known to Paul,[23] and he, in his turn, is the instrument through which it continues to be revealed to others. He makes 'the word of God fully known, the mystery hidden for ages and generations but now made manifest. . . .'[24] The task of the apostle is said to be 'to declare the mystery of Christ.'[25]

The writers of the New Testament claimed to know something which was before unknown. For the Christian the unveiling has taken place in Jesus Christ. It is now known that something decisive was heretofore unknown. The focal point, the source of this new knowledge, is Jesus Christ. The 'mystery' has been revealed in Jesus Christ. So Paul writes of the revelation of the mystery, the revelation of that which was hitherto hidden, 'which was not made known to other generations.'[26] This 'mystery,' this 'revelation,' is equated with 'the gospel' in the expression, 'the mystery of the gospel.'[27] The Gospel is the revelation of the righteousness of God to and through faith.[28] An examination of the Old Testament usage of the term 'righteousness' shows it to be a salvation word. God's righteousness is revealed when he acts for the salvation of his people.[29] It is then known that he is Lord. Here Paul claims that it is in the Gospel, in its content and proclamation, that the revelation has taken place, that God has decisively made himself known, that he has acted to bring salvation, once and for all. He who was veiled has now made himself known in Jesus Christ. 'In the Pauline terminology *mystery* is correlative with *revelation*.'[30] For Paul, 'mystery' meant that something *was* made known, that some thing *had been* disclosed. But at the same time, it could never be completely known or mastered. The mystery never becomes transparent. The knowledge of the mystery is not given to all. It is given only to faith. The Gospel is apprehended 'from faith to faith.'[31] The unique means by which the unique revelation is apprehended is faith. God acts to save. The metaphor of 'salvation' expresses the effectiveness of the revelation. Men are 'saved' as God's acting, God's revelation, is apprehended in faith. God is known only to genuine faith. God is revealed to those who have faith. The mystery is known to faith. Faith is obedience. 'Only he who believes is obedient, and only he who is obedient believes.'[32]

As we have seen, the biblical writers insist that to 'know' God was not identical with intellectual understanding. It was not simply to agree with certain assertions, to assent to certain propositions about God. To know God was to hear God. To hear was to obey. To obey was to identify oneself with God's activity. So one does not simply give assent to facts about Jesus. It is a matter of making a decision, of committing the will, of giving the resources of the self over. That is a very different matter. Assent there is. But assent is followed by trust.

What that meant for the earliest Christians and has meant ever since is that there takes place a reorientation of one's life. This is the meaning of the contrast made by the apostle between the new knowledge and the old knowledge.[33] The old knowledge is from a merely human point of view.[34] Between acquaintance with facts about a person and an intimate relation with a person there is all the difference in the world.

In summary then: God is revealed in Jesus Christ. The revelation of God in Jesus Christ demands a response of the whole person and issues in 'salvation.' God's revealing activity is apprehended by faith. It leads to relationship in which one makes the total response demanded. This demand of God accompanies the knowledge of Jesus Christ. Response to that demand completes the process of revelation.

4   GOD IS THE SUBJECT OF REVELATION

Having very briefly surveyed some of the main emphases of the biblical teachings about the knowledge of God, we shall now attempt a *systematic* statement of the Christian doctrine of revelation. This is in two parts.

God is the subject of revelation. Revelation is the making known of God, the infinite subject. In the process of 'making known,' he takes the initiative. In revelation he is himself made known and not simply truths about himself, injected into the mentality of the human recipient. A Christian doctrine of revelation presupposes an articulate movement of God toward the creature who stands in need of the revelation. The purpose is that the creature may attain complete existence, to come to completeness from an existence which has been broken and fragmented. The perversity of will, sinfulness, led the creature into a kind of captivity. In this state man cannot find God, cannot attain the knowledge of God. Revelation is not the story of how the creature alone, even at the pinnacle of his being or in the best representatives of his humanity, finds the deity. It is the story of the divine initiative. It is the story of how God comes to the creature.

That God is subject means that revelation is not discovery. Knowledge of God is not 'scientific' knowledge, nor is it conceived correctly on the analogy of the scientific method. When God is known, it is because he has moved toward the creature. For the creature in his helplessness cannot find God. Revelation is the movement of the infinite subject toward his creatures, in the here and now of their present existence. Knowledge of God is not the same as successful philosophical speculation regarding the ultimate. Through exercise of the great and wonderful gift of reason, the human cannot attain what only God can give — the knowledge of God and the knowledge of fellow human beings as God's creatures. 'What begins with the human self cannot end with the knowledge of God and of his will and purpose. Nor can it end with the knowledge of real man in his real situation.'[35]

So the suggestion that disclosure is an analogue of revelation is inadequate. John Baillie is quite right in using it as an analogue of the kind of process by means of which a subject makes himself known.[36] It does not comprehend, however, the fact that sometimes what someone has once disclosed may sometimes be discovered and sometimes not. Information may be discovered. Love may not. God is not 'discovered.' There is no revelation without the presence of God. When God is revealed it is God who is revealed whatever else is also revealed. Discovery of facts about God is not to be called revelation. When God is revealed, God is present. There is an ascending line of contrast: discovery, disclosure, revelation. Revelation is *sui generis*. To insist on this preserves the important conviction of the Christian that only what is beyond man's situation can reveal the nature of that situation.

It is not as if once God has made himself known the knowledge can then be easily passed on. You can pass on information about love but you cannot pass on the love of another person. He or she has to be involved in that event. Revelation is more like communicating love than communicating information. Hence for clarity's sake it is well to distinguish 'revelation' from 'disclosure.' For once a person has disclosed information, someone else can pass it on without that person being present. But a third party cannot communicate 'presence,' but can only speak words about it. That is why the Christian teaching of the 'testimony of the Holy Spirit' is essential for an adequate Christian doctrine of revelation. That teaching says that when God is known God is present. It insists that even when words are spoken about God they may be empty, formal and dead.

The relation between God and his creature which takes place when God reveals himself and his creature responds, is not to be thought of on the analogy of the way we know *things*, or learn facts about things or persons but on the analogy of the way we come to know *persons* and continue to be in personal relations with them. Revelation is not a possession but an event. The biblical understanding of 'know' and 'knowledge' is quite plain on this point, and is to be preserved in a theological statement of the doctrine.

God reveals himself through different means: other persons, the spoken word, the written word, through propositions, through ritual, through meditation, in historical event. In short, God reveals himself through human experience.[37] God speaks through means, but the revelation is always immediate. It is God who reveals himself. John Baillie suggested the idea of 'mediated immediacy.' This immediacy of person-to-person relation we can understand only in the experience of personal relationships. So, where God is not, revelation is not. Where God is and is known, whatever means he employs, there is revelation. There an event takes place. An event has taken place. 'Revelation is always a relational affair; the special occasions are the times when the divine presence is disclosed through a medium, but this presence has to be *received* in human experience.'[38]

This reception of the revelation of God is what both Scripture and theologians have called faith. Faith is that unique manner of apprehension, through which revelation is actualised. Faith does not produce revelation. Faith apprehends revelation. Faith responds to revelation.

The Christian revelation is not a gnosis, although there have been Gnostics in every generation of Christian faith — those intellectuals who put reason over faith. For them, the proposition replaces the commitment in trust. The syllogism and the system replace faith in the goodness of the heavenly Father. But God is not apprehended rationally, like an electric light bill or a Cartesian theorem. God is not captured in any of our propositions. God is God and God is sovereign over his revelation. To construct and to understand dogma rationally is one thing, and may be essential and important. To respond in faith to a revealing God is another. The rationality of the theology or the doctrine is that it represents *well* the revelation of God. There is no need to set faith and reason in opposition to one another on principle.

Theology is the understanding of God's revelation expressed in an appropriate logical form. When revelation is understood, the elaborations of an appropriate theology will correspond. So will an understanding of the authority of the Scriptures, and of the position of the creeds and formulations of the church. This leads to the second proposition.

5 REVELATION UNDERSTOOD WITHIN THE CONTEXT OF REVELATION

Revelation can only be understood within the context of revelation. In the very nature of the case one can only talk adequately of revelation after revelation has occurred. Before, one can talk about the *possibility* of revelation. But then you may not know what you are talking about.

But those who respond enjoy a fellowship between themselves which before was not and otherwise would not have been possible.

This is the fellowship of the church — the spiritual community, the community of revelation. The church is the creation of God. Were there no revelation, there would be no church. The Christian community finds this cause for celebration, in song and in festival. 'The church's one foundation is Jesus Christ her Lord.'[39]

The church is the locus of revelation. The Scriptures spring from the church's experience of revelation. The gift of apostleship, of ministry, indeed *all* the gifts, are given *to the church*. The church through which God reveals himself interprets the revelation and judges its validity. Thus, the individual is saved from subjectivity. The norms are to be found in the very context where the revelation has been operative. For revelation is an event.

Revelation leads to community and such community produces traditions. The individual within the community shares in those traditions and part of such participation involves giving account of the revelatory events which have established the community. In turn such accounts serve as the means for the continuing event of revelation. This is involved when we say that revelation takes place within the context of revelation.

Revelation as an event is illumination. Jesus Christ is the revelation of God to the individual, in that he becomes the centre of individual, personal history. He illuminates one's existence and shapes one's being. It makes a difference to the whole of one's life that God reveals himself. Thereafter you can give an account in historical, sociological and psychological terms of the difference that the revelation of God has made. That means tying one's present life to the past event of Jesus Christ and showing how that event has illuminative power for shaping existence in the present. That means showing how one can appropriate the resources which flow from the event of God's revelation in Jesus Christ, how one's history has been shaped by it. According to Christian theology, God who in the past revealed himself in Jesus Christ now reveals himself. It is in the act of remembering and interpreting the Christ event that that past event is of religious (and so theological) significance. The remembering and interpreting involves tradition.

6 SCRIPTURE AND REVELATION

We may state this principle quite specifically by reference to Scripture. Scripture is an account of certain historical events, a witness to revelation, a record of response to revelation in the past, and also a medium for the continuing revelation of God. In Scripture, some events are considered to be revelatory as others are not.

Consider nine introductory points.

(1) We may distinguish an event[40] and its significance. Of course having significance is itself also an event. (2) For an individual or a community some events have special significance. (3) That an event has significance is a present fact as one comes to understand it in a particular way. (4) That involves keeping the event in memory. (5) Hence communities develop and maintain traditions of interpretation. (6) We may speak of an event as revelatory as it has and maintains such present importance. (7) For the Christian community the decisive event is Jesus Christ. (8) The Christian speaks of the revelation of God in Jesus Christ through the Holy Spirit. (9) Such revelation of God is mediated through Scripture as the events it describes come to have significance for the hearer.

We can only adequately answer the question, 'What is the Bible?' as we understand it as the vehicle of God's revelation in the present. Revelation means the present activity of God. God acted in history and those to whom he revealed himself understood what he was doing. Coming to understand what is the meaning of God's activity is part of the revelatory activity. What is the point that there was an Exodus or an Easter morning if it is one among many other facts of past history, with no particular significance for one's present history, another fact one can learn and catalogue along with the others, and duly tuck away in the recesses of one's mind, and in due course forget?

Many events happen. Some are more significant than others in relation to persons or communities. A particular series of events may be significant for one and may not be for another. A community is a group, which shares meaning. Events come to have a common meaning within a particular community in which the members of that community share. Some events are of crucial significance. Members of that community then live their lives out of the significance they have experienced. Those significant events become the focus, the media, of the meaning they find. A nation finds meaning as it remembers certain events. So with the Christian community. They then live their lives out of the meaning which they have experienced. The church shares an experience and understanding of the revelatory event of Jesus Christ. Its members participate in the meaning of the life and death of Jesus as other communities and individuals are not able to. Jesus as the Christ is its centre of significance.

They understand how that event reflects the divine purpose. They then can say that that event is a revelation. Thus, there may be a gap (rational or temporal) between the event and its revelatory significance. The apprehension that God acted decisively in the past act takes place in the present. One *now* sees that the past act is God's act, that it has a place in God's purpose. That can only take place, i.e. revelation can only occur, as the same God who made himself known then, now reveals himself. God who acted then must now make known in the present what it means that he acted in the past. Without this, the past event is a piece of secular history, no more significant, as far as ultimate issues are concerned, than any other historical act or fact. That God is the subject of revelation means that only as he acts to bring about a knowledge of himself does revelation occur. This is the dynamism which must attach to any acceptable doctrine of revelation. God is active.

Words on a printed page are not revelation without a grasping of their significance. The believer then attributes that meaning to the God who was the source of the experience which gave rise to those words in the first instance. God is present in that understanding. Where God is absent no revelation occurs. God may be absent as works of theology, Church creeds, the Scripture, are produced, read, discussed and interpreted. Revelation occurs through Scripture only when God is present. Otherwise (as Paul remarked) there is a veil, which shrouds rather than unveils the meaning, when the Scripture is read.[41] That one speaks in the expectation that God reveals himself in the spoken word is the foundation for preaching: 'he who hears you hears me.'[42]

A central Christian doctrine is of God the Holy Spirit. What this means is twofold: (1) God is present when God is known. (2) There is a continuity between God's revelation in the past, and revelation occurring in the present. The acts of God in the past created relationship to him in the experiences of those who responded to them. Some of them left a record of their experience. Through this record, God may 'speak' today, in the here and now of contemporary existence. When God is present revelation occurs. An important avenue through which God makes his presence felt is the Scripture. The Christian doctrine of the Holy Spirit points to the fact that the 'God,' who 'was in Christ,' now 'speaks' through his chosen avenues to reveal himself in present existence. A Christian doctrine of revelation is thus inevitably trinitarian. God who revealed himself in Jesus Christ now reveals himself through the Spirit.

Thus, historical sympathy and response to revelation in reference to the Bible are two different things. As well as a record of past revelation the Bible may be an avenue of revelation in the present. That is one sense in which we may speak of 'progressive revelation.' The Scriptures are an avenue through which God may make himself known in the continuing life of the church. The words of Scripture are, on such an account, a means of revelation in another generation other than the one to which they testify. God may reveal himself in many ways.

The authority of Scripture is neither automatic, nor 'objective.' God is not captured by the mastery of facts about him. Revelation is primarily concerned not with words, nor even ideas, but with the very being of God. Concepts are used to give an account of revelation, to mediate revelation, but the communication of ideas or of information, while necessary to revelation, is neither sufficient for nor identical with revelation.

7 REVELATION AND JESUS CHRIST

For the Christian, all revelation centres in Jesus Christ. Jesus Christ means history. The Christian revelation has an historical anchorage.

The Christian claim is that God makes himself known in man at a point in time, not that he is an abstract ground of being. The revelation consists not in the communication of ideas, ultimate truths, even 'eternal truths of reason,' but in a human person. This is the 'scandal of particularity.' The ground of all that is made known within the reality which he created, in the form of a creature. That is very paradoxical. The assumption is that this realm of existence is revelatory in a special way. The rootage of the Christian claim is that the historical events in the first century are of primary importance. The Christian claim is that certain events within the historical reality are more important than others as media of revelation. The course of history as such is not uniformly revelatory. Some events rather than others provide us with the clue to the right understanding of God.

The Christian claim about Jesus is not a statement about 'objective' events of history. There are no such objective events. Events are always interpreted events. First, they are selected from the total series. Second, they are interpreted from the point of view of the observer. There is always an element of 'historical faith' which leads to certain emphases, to a particular kind of reconstruction of the data. The doctrine of Jesus as God-man is not a conclusion theoretically drawn from historical facts which objective historical research has established independently in its and their own right. It is not 'history from without' but 'history from within.' The documents at the basis of the Christian confession are records of the people, within the living community, who had been transformed in their existence by the Christ-event. They write out of their *living faith* in Jesus.

This is the primary historical datum: the living faith of the representatives of the church, which owed its very existence to the encounter with the Christ. Men of faith, whose faith had re-channelled their lives, wrote through the eyes of faith of the historical events that had made the difference. Their proclamation is therefore not 'objective history,' but *witness, kerygma*. 'That which we have seen and heard we proclaim also to you, so that you may have fellowship with us; and our fellowship is with the Father and with his Son Jesus Christ.'[43] They said that their convictions about the historical events which they had witnessed and in which they had participated had come to them from beyond history. They saw the Christ-event as the activity of God. Behind and through this man, Jesus, God had acted and was acting to reveal himself. The New Testament documents interpret Jesus, and the relations of the earliest believers with him, by speaking of the divine action. God was making himself known through Jesus. Through him they encountered the divine as well as the human reality. 'God was in Christ,' 'Behold the Man.' [44]

The New Testament documents are unique in being (1) the only extant records near-contemporary with the Jesus they portray; [45] (2) the only extant confessions representing the faith of the community that experienced the reality of God mediated through the human Jesus; (3) the primary means by which the encounter of the church in subsequent ages with the divine reality has taken place. The Bible is the instrument which has evoked and nourished a particular kind of faith and character. The crucial uniqueness of the New Testament witness is thus only open to faith, and mediated through the church.

8 KNOWLEDGE OF REVELATION

It may be known that the revelation is of God. Epistemological questions[46] inevitably arise. How do you know that the reality you are talking of as a Christian is actually God? How do you know that you are not projecting your desires, that your thinking of God is not some wish-fulfilment? How may you say that 'revelation' has occurred, and not illusion? What is the basis of your certainty?

How can you talk about God at all? And if you talk about God, how do you know that what you say is in any way related to reality?

One important issue arises which we may touch only briefly. There is no question of demonstrating either that God exists or that he has revealed himself in Jesus Christ. The Scriptures make no attempt at proof and we misconstrue them if we try to use them to demonstrate God's activity.

But the Christian is rational, and attempts to give a rational account of belief. He assumes (a philosophical term) or he knows (a confessional term) that in speaking about God he is making *claims*. He is *asserting* something about the way things are, about reality, however difficult it may be for him to do so. In however difficult ways he has to use language to do so, he is making cognitive statements about that which is beyond himself. His language is not simply expressive, or evocative or exclamatory. He is proposing to inform about reality. He is making proposals about the way things are.

The basic Christian proposals are about God and about man in relation to God. But there are other kinds of proposition as well, about historical events, and about nature for example.

Since theologians talk of revelation giving us knowledge of God, we shall have to evaluate the meaningfulness and truth or falsity of the propositions through which they attempt to express that knowledge in the same way and terms we consider to be generally normative. We shall assess statements for example for their scientific and historical accuracy, their consistency with everything we know, and with our values. When someone expresses their understanding about God in English, they can be criticised for using bad English. The canons of English grammar are just as appropriate, applied to my speech concerning the deity as concerning the little beast in the laboratory or the far distant galaxies, or the circle of relations in my family. So are the canons of logic and rationality. When anyone raises the question about the validity of language about God, *this means philosophy*. It means that all statements will be open to survey and criticism on rigorous philosophical grounds. If faith and revelation have genuine knowledge-giving power, the attempt to express this knowledge coherently means that the theological or doctrinal expression will be judged (1) as to whether it is coherent; (2) by its capacity to illuminate the whole of experience — scientific, historical, aesthetic, moral, social. As a claim to provide a reasonable explanation, it must stand alongside other secular explanations of the human experience, sometimes in opposition to alternative explanations of the world.

Some Christians — alas! — would decry the effort to engage in such attempts to present the meaning of faith. However, the irony of their situation is that they also must give reasons for their refusal, and if they do so with any determination they are engaging in the very process which they claim to be unnecessary.

The reasoned presentation of faith is necessary: first that the believer does not give the critic the approbation of silence; second, because a rational objection can lead to a change in interpretation of experience.

It is not a question of being able to demonstrate rationally that revelation has occurred. Hence one must talk of revelation in symbols, which point to the nature of a human experience. One may not demonstrate faith. But one can provide an interpretation of reality from the perspective of faith and propose it as an alternative to other and rival interpretations of reality. It will have to stand up to critical scrutiny.

CHAPTER VII NOTES

[1]II Thessalonians. 1:7. Cf. I Peter 1:13.

[2]Galatians. 1:12.

[3]Revelation. 1:1.

[4]For a simple account see Edward W H. Vick, *Speaking Well of God*. pp. 47-74.

[5]Amos 3:8.

[6]Isaiah 6:5.

[7]Th. C. Vriezen, *An Outline of Old Testament Theology*, p. 128.

[8]Micah 6:8.

[9]Th. C. Vriezen, *loc. cit.*

[10]Isaiah 42:1-4; 49:1-6; 59:44-9; 52:13-53:12. For an introductory account see Bernhard Anderson, *Understanding the Old Testament*, pp. 414-429.

[11]Job 38-39.

[12]H. Wheeler Robinson, *Corporate Personality in Ancient Israel.*

[13]Amos 8:l ,2, Jeremiah 1: 11, 12.

[14]Hosea l-3.

[15]Jeremiah. 23:29.

[16]Gordon Kaufman, *Systematic Theology: An Historicist Perspective*, p. 85.

[17]Cf. Mathew. 11:27. Cf. Luke 10:22.

[18]See Alan Richardson, *An Introduction to the Theology of the New Testament*, pp. 43-49.

[19]I John 2:3. Cf. John 7:17.

[20]A. Richardson, *op. cit.,* p. 46.

[21]Romans 16:25, 26.

[22]Ephesians.1:9.

[23]Ephesians 3:4-6; 6:19.

[24]Colossians 1: 26-28.

[25]Colossians 4:3.

[26]Ephesians 3: 3-6.

[27]Ephesians 6:19.

[28]Romans 1:16,17.

[29]Cf. C.H. Dodd, *Commentary on Romans, in loc.*

[30]A Richardson, *A Theological Wordbook of the Bible,* p. 156.

[31]Romans 1:17.

[32]D. Bonhoeffer, *The Cost of Discipleship,* p. 54.

[33]II Corinthian. 5:16.

[34]The Greek term is *kata sarka.*

[35]Karl Barth, *Church Dogmatics,* II/ 2, p. 541.

[36]Cf. John Baillie, *The Idea of Revelation in Recent Thought,* pp. 19-40.

[37]Cf. John E Smith, *Experience and God.* Chapter III, pp. 68-98.

[38]*Ibid.,* p. 71.

[39]Samuel J. Stone

[40]An event is something that happens, an occurrence, a taking place. An event may be very complex, or it may be quite simple. The apparently simplest event involves relationships which can lead us into discussion of matters apparently only remotely connected with it. Every event is contained within a web of antecedent and consequent influences. Some set it in motion. Others it sets in motion. No event is isolated. Every event takes place within a totality, call it 'world.' It is possible to abstract an event in thought, to hold up one particular happening out of the catena of antecedents and consequents. Thus it may be easy, but deceptive, to think that the event is isolated, and to talk of such an event apart from the relationships in which it stands.

[41]II Corinthians 3:14-16. 'Revelation' (Latin *re-vel-atio*) literally means 'removing the veil.' *Vel* is Latin for veil.

[42]Luke 10 16.

[43]I John 1:3.

[44]II Corinthians 5:19, John 19:5.

[45]There are two or three scattered references to Jesus in the Roman literature.

[46]Epistemology is that branch of philosophy which concerns itself with the problem of knowledge, addressing itself to the questions: What is knowledge? How is *knowledge* possible?

Summary of Chapter VIII

Revelation and the Knowledge Of God

Several terms are used to represent the different ideas of revelation and of faith. A satisfactory account will recognize that faith and revelation are not purely intellectual operations, and that here there can be no question of proof. So Scripture will be seen as part of a dynamic process and not as a set of propositions which can be grasped by an act of intellect.

VIII
REVELATION AND THE
KNOWLEDGE OF GOD

1 WHY WE DO NOT KNOW

Consider the question: why do we not know something? Answers are of three sorts. In suggesting them the present tense is used for convenience.

(1) Even though it can be known, we are not in a position to know it. We do not have the means to come to know it.
(2) It is not an object of knowledge. It, therefore, cannot be known.
(3) We do not have the capacity to know it. This lack of capacity is either (a) temporary or (b) permanent.

Examples may be either impersonal or personal. (1) Knowledge of what it is like on the other side of the moon or in the depths of the ocean was possible, but not until means were devised for actualising the potentiality was it known. (2) The square root of minus one, square circles are, by definition, excluded from knowledge. (3a) An English child's capacity for learning German literature may develop, assuming its intelligence. What it does not know, it may come to know. (3b) But an unintelligent English child will never come to know German literature

To turn to personal examples. Where there is personal knowledge[1] of one person by another, there has been both initiative on the part of one and response on the part of the other. (4) I did not know my great-grandfather, since he died before I was born. (5) A person cannot be an object of personal knowledge if he is not willing to take the initiative or to respond to initiative and make himself available. There can be no talk of response where such initiative is lacking A young infant does not have the capacity to sympathize understandingly (6a) with, let's say, a business man's failure or the troubles of a disappointed divorcee (6b). But he may, at some time as events take place in his life as he matures, come to develop such a capacity for sympathy

To speak of revelation is to claim that knowledge of God has been actualised. It is to claim that the conditions which make knowledge possible have in some way been met. This is to assert that the means are available (denial of 1); that God is an object of knowledge (denial of 2); and that the capacity to know God is present (denial of 3). To make the basic claim that God has revealed himself, involves also the following claims. God can be known. Even if man of himself is not in a position to come to know God, because he does not have the means or the capacity to know God, God may make himself known. God has made himself known.

Needless to say, theologians differ in respect of each of these claims. Karl Barth claimed that God reveals himself to man in spite of man's incapacity for that revelation, the capacity being created in the act of revelation. This led him to deny the relevance of any and all, including religious, culture to the revealing activity of God. God's act of revelation was unique. Other theologians have made different judgments regarding the extent to which human, natural capacity can proceed in giving meaning to the concept of God and to assertions about him. In this chapter we seek to examine the fundamental claim that God reveals himself and attempt to relate the concept of revelation to the concept of experience.

2   Revelation and Response

We all have had the experience of coming to know something we did not know before. We sometimes achieve new knowledge by inquiry, observation and intuition.[2] The term 'discovery' lays stress upon the success of personal initiative in the acquisition of knowledge. I find out something for myself, by dint of my effort.

The analogy upon which the Christian theist builds his teaching concerning revelation is not that of discovery, but of gaining personal knowledge. Knowledge of persons, depends upon the other person being willing to make known to me what I will never know unless he does. I would be liable to interpret the activities of the other wrongly. He may freely choose to let me have the opportunity to come to know something about himself, or indeed about something else which I would be unable to know unless he revealed it to me. No amount of initiative on my part would be able to achieve what he in his freedom can reveal to me. The *content* of revelation may be different in different instances, but in any case the process is the same. I cannot discover what can only be revealed.

Knowing that a proposition is true and experiencing personal encounter are two different things. If a philosophical knowledge of God were all that we had, we would never know whether we were right or not. Adherence to a creed is not to be confused with the attitude of responsive trust in God.

The conditions for attaining personal knowledge are that there should be an outgoing on the part of the one making available the knowledge and a reception on the part of the one receiving. Both are necessary before the process is completed. Response is essential to the complete process. When someone is prepared to reveal something to me, if I am to know, I must be awake, must be ready to listen, must actually listen, must have the capacity to understand and to feel appropriately. These are necessary conditions for coming to know. But of themselves they are not sufficient. There must be an actual initiation on the part of the one who wishes to communicate.

For example, someone may take the initiative and leave a sign for me to interpret: a smile, an unexpected gift, an enigmatic letter. For my part, I must be where the sign is, read it, and hopefully read it aright. Only when it becomes meaningful will I understand what it was intended to mediate.

The theist's claim concerning revelation is constituted by three complementary assertions.

(1) He has come to know what he did not know before.
(2) *God* has come to be known whatever else has come to be known.
(3) The initiative in the process is with God.

Knowledge of God is mediated through what is not God. The Bible assumes that God's revelation is mediated. The biblical viewpoint is not characteristically mystical. The mystic holds that there is nothing between God and men. One may still talk about the encounter but language is strained in doing so. Plotinus, for example, spoke of the 'flight of the alone to the Alone.' Others have spoken the language of void, of silence, of darkness, still others the language of love. In straining language, they attempt to indicate what encounter without means is like. But the Judaeo-Christian tradition has in the main turned decisively away from the mystical approach and emphasized the importance of a medium of revelation. Something mediates the revelation of God. God is mediated through symbols which may be words, words which have consistency, but which are strained to bear the new meaning they must carry in their new context. The question of their meaningfulness thus arises very seriously.

There is *something*, not nothing, *between* God and man. For the Hebrew it is the Law. Both Hebrew and Christian claim that individual historical events (some considered to be crucial), the interpretation of such events and the whole course of history, provide means for the knowledge of God. God reveals himself through that which is not God. God is known as historical events take place, as human beings speak and act, as human communities develop and interact.

Revelation for both the Hebrew and the Christian was and is experience of a community and of the individual within the community. This assumes that a community as well as an individual may be the subject of experience. Examples of community experience are to be found, for example, in the grief of a family, the success of a team, the will of a nation. Since there are communal ties, a common experience is possible.

Revelation continues to take place as the community reflects upon the events it experiences and as it remembers past experiences. As result of such reflection a tradition arises and provides categories for the shaping of new experiences. In this way the community maintains continuity between the present and the past. Understanding of God develops as the community thinks about past events and their interpretations and construes new events as the activity of God. The community sees the whole course of events and the interpretation of those events as the activity of God. It interprets those events in relation to his initiative. Both event and interpretation are considered divine acts. God reveals himself through the human understanding of events, diverse as at times that understanding proves to be and paradoxical as the claim may sound. For understanding develops as time passes.

We may distinguish two different meanings to the term 'revelation.' There is the event of revelation, in which God makes himself known. This involves the human response. There is also the content, the 'what' of revelation. The terms *revelatio* and *revelatum* serve to distinguish between the *process* of revelation and the *content* of revelation. *Revelatio* means the act of revelation. *Revelatum* means the content of revelation.[3]

3   PERSONAL AND NON-PERSONAL FACTORS

The Exodus of the slaves from Egypt is a complex event, a series of personal and non-personal factors being involved. Later, the Hebrew prophets reflected upon their fathers' experience under the leadership of Moses, and saw the whole complex as the activity of Yahweh, a God of purpose who was making his purpose known in the course of history as it unfolded. Revelation is a process and extends over a period of time. It is never context-less. It has its own history.

Christian belief takes up and extends this Hebrew perspective. Its crucial event is called the Christ-event. This term refers to a complex of historical events including both the fact of Jesus and his being accepted by those who came to believe in him. The creation of a community is integral to the event. For the Christian theist discerns the purpose of God in the life, death and resurrection of Jesus and in the coming into being of the Christian community which discerned such a purpose and believed in God as a result.

4   TWO DIFFERENT CONCEPTS OF REVELATION AND OF FAITH

Some Christians have thought of revelation as the communication of truths about God presented in propositional form. This view of revelation we shall call the propositional view. Others have spoken of revelation as the making known of God himself.[4] To each of these concepts of revelation, the view that revelation is in the form of propositions which are divinely authenticated and the view that God himself is revealed and that theological propositions are attempts to understand that revelation, corresponds a concept of faith.[5]

The view sometimes given the name of 'propositional revelation,' sees propositions as the stuff of revelation. These propositions constitute the content of revelation. They are grasped by an act of the intellect. The act of revelation, i.e. the revealing, the *revelatio*, consists in the communication of propositions. The revelation of God is contained in a series of true propositions. This theory holds that the becoming known and the acceptance of their truth constitutes the revelation of God. God has underwritten that truth. Grasping the meaning of the propositions and assenting to their truth constitutes the act of faith. Faith, on this view, is defined as assent (*assensus*).[6]

On this interpretation 'faith' means the intellectualistic grasping of the propositions. I 'see' that they are true. This does not mean that the propositions will be difficult to grasp. They are not 'intellectualistic' in that sense. It is intellect, rather than the whole person which responds. Such response is called *assent*. Assent may be given the name 'faith.' The 'believer' is then one who gives assent to a set of propositions. But assent is different in kind from the personal response to the initiative of another person. If you define the content of revelation as personal, the corresponding response is not an intellectual one but is rather a personal one, an affair of the whole being. Of course an intellectual act is involved in making a personal response. You have to understand what is being said. You have to interpret the signs rightly. You can parry the force of the initiative which demands a response by pretending not to understand it. If one does not understand the words in which it is expressed one just does not get the force of the demand. But one might take notice of what is said, understand it, and not make the appropriate response. *Understanding the meaning* of a demand, or a claim, is not identical with *responding appropriately* to it. Hence the older distinctions between noticing the truths expressed, the having them brought to the attention, *notitia*; and assenting to, accepting, these truths which have come to the attention, *assensus*. A third term referred to a further step: the act of commitment, of trust. This was called *fiducia*. These represent three stages in the complete process of coming to have faith.

From the point of view which understands faith as *fiducia*, as trust, an understanding of revelation as assent is quite inadequate. It substitutes belief for faith. Assent to the proposition is of quite a different order from faith. *Assensus* is not *fiducia*. One could acknowledge a set of propositions to be true, and not know anything about trust.

If revelation and faith are incorrectly analysed, misunderstanding of Christian theism will result. Instead of saying that God reveals himself *by means of* the propositions one believes, one speaks of believing the propositions, as if this were all there was to be said. These may be propositions of the Bible, or of a theological or ecclesiastical system. It may be a doctrinal system presented as based upon biblical propositions. But in any case the structure of the act is the same. Assent to the set of statements exhausts the meaning of faith. *Assensus* replaces *fiducia*. There may be psychological and sociological reasons for such an attitude. The theological or dogmatic tradition may be firmly fixed and the community demand assent as a condition of acceptance. Thus one may accept the truth of the propositions on authority. In such a case 'the believer' does not even have to understand them, nor how they were arrived at. One accepts them because an authority teaches them. That authority may be the Bible. It may be the church.

However, it is sometimes the case that the religious experience is better than the theology expressing it. The believer may have experienced the revelation of God through an act of *fiducia*, but accept an inadequate explanation, not knowing a more satisfactory way of understanding his experience. In such a case the structure of faith will be that of *fiducia*, but the (inadequate) theology will be that of *assensus*.

We cannot define faith as assent to propositions. Confusion results when the term 'faith' (*fides*: Latin) gets used both for 'assent' and for 'trust.' The terms *fides qua creditur*, and *fides quae creditur* point to the distinction we have already made between trust and assent.

Fides qua creditur means the 'faith by which one believes.' It means the obedient hearing of the word. It is a free act of decision, a real historical event, the experience of trust, which is at once act and effect. Once the event has occurred, there then follows the task of understanding it. It is the act of personal commitment and of trust which is also called *fiducia*.

Fides quae creditur means 'the faith which is believed.' It may refer to the content of what is believed, or to the act of assenting to what is believed. It is a system of teachings, a set of dogmas, something that can be known by investigation. It is assent to that teaching, which assent may be given because one accepts an authority that provides the teaching. One accepts what one may not understand because one has accepted an authority which says what it is one ought to give assent to. When that happens there is no room for real faith, *fiducia*. Faith is confused with assent, with the acceptance of a particular theology or dogmatic belief.

The theory of propositional revelation lends itself to two aberrations. The first mistake is to say that faith means acceptance on authority of what one may but need not understand. It may mean assenting to the truth of what one has not yet considered and so cannot judge. Such acceptance of what is believed on authority has been called 'implicit faith,' *fides implicita*. If faith means the formal acceptance of doctrines, one may think that by a deliberate act of will, one can resolve to accept the doctrine one does not understand. If Bible or church teaches it, even if I do not understand it, I will assent to it. I will 'believe' it. In each case the end result would be the same, namely assent to dogma without real understanding. That is if we assume that it is even possible to come to believe by an act of deciding to believe. It is very odd to talk of producing belief by an act of will. There is something Alice in Wonderland about it. 'Sometimes I've believed as many as six impossible things before breakfast.' 'I can't believe that!' might very well have been Alice's *response!* Can one produce assent by deciding and then willing to believe? What would it mean to assent to a doctrine one does not understand? What would it mean to be told what you *should* believe, to be told to believe what *we* believe, 'we' being the community, those in authority in the community, the interpreters of the authoritative writings.

The second mistake makes faith itself the object of theology. The object of faith is God and theology is about God. Because theology is concerned with God, it considers the means through which God is known. It therefore takes account of the act of faith, of the 'I believe' of the one who has faith. But faith grasps the reality of God. Faith is defined by the reality it grasps. Theistic faith is defined by the reality of God. One may however focus upon faith itself. For example one can analyse faith as a given, as a phenomenon. Then faith becomes an object of reflection. One studies faith as a human attitude, a mental state, or a social phenomenon, perhaps even as an accomplishment. Thus theology is reduced to a human science, dogma to a human construction. Theology becomes anthropology. Of course such studies are legitimate and profitable exercises. Psychological and sociological studies of individuals and communities enable us to understand them better. But such studies are not to be equated nor confused with theology.

In the one case revelation is the set of propositions guaranteed by their supernatural origin and argued for on the basis that the propositions are divinely guaranteed. The doctrines are assured, and warrants are provided for them. In the other case, revelation becomes a human experience, which takes place in a religious subject, an experience among experiences, albeit unique. Human experience replaces revelation.

There is a way between these two extremes. It is to give the tradition of understanding, the set of teachings, the theology, the Scriptures the role of *medium* of revelation, by speaking of experience and revelation as complementary and by taking experience as encounter with what is real, in this case the reality of God himself. Neither the 'propositions,' nor the traditions through which they are understood, nor the assent which grasps them, are ends in themselves. They are the means through which faith, *fiducia*, becomes possible. Nor are they simply incidental. They are necessary means through which God confronts man. The propositions are not merely the historical deposit of past responses to the divine initiative. They are both witness to what has happened *and* means through which God now reveals himself, through which revelation becomes a contemporary event. As the stories and convictions are handed down, heard again, interpreted and understood, there is provided the context for faith.

Faith, that is to say, trust in God, *fides qua creditur*, is made possible through such traditions of belief, through hearing and attending to the teachings, through preaching, through reading the Scriptures, in short through hearing the Christian recital. These are the means through which revelation takes place, through which faith, *fiducia*, comes to be.

Faith involves believing and knowing certain things but faith is not identical with that knowledge. Faith is not identical with historical knowledge or historical belief. The Christian theist believes that Jesus lived, loved, taught and died. To assent to that is not yet faith. Assenting to an historical claim, for example, that Jesus died, is not the same as having faith in God. Faith is coming to trust, and to express that trust in a new style of life.

5 COMMUNITY

Revelation takes place within a community. Faith is not an isolated act, even if it is highly individual and intensely personal, an act creative of personality. A new context becomes operative within which fundamental attitudes are reshaped. You pass from older presuppositions to new ones, and hence come to experience the world differently. The experience of faith has taken place as a result of passing from one context into another, from an old set of presuppositions to a new one.

You come to understand yourself differently. A change in presuppositions means a change in self-understanding. The old things pass away. The 'old man' becomes a 'new man.' All things become new. There is a new creation. These are ways in which the New Testament speaks of the change. The accomplished fact of revelation consists in effecting such a change of self-understanding, which we call faith. Since experience means encounter with reality, and revelation has its source in reality, there is no dichotomy between revelation and experience. Experience is the medium of revelation.

The total experience is different as the understanding of what is being experienced is different. The understanding is different as different presuppositions are employed to interpret the data. One is not always consciously aware of his presuppositions, nor of their sources. It is only upon careful reflection that one comes to realize that such presuppositions are the product of life within community, a product of one's history. They are culturally shaped. Culture is both a product of context and a creator of context. Since presuppositions vary, interpretations of the data vary and, as a consequence of seeing the world through such presuppositions and the interpretations they make possible, experience of the world varies.

So what the unbeliever experiences in one way, the believer experiences in another. It is a common experience for different people to experience the same events in different ways. The newspaper editor's response to the murder will be quite different from that of the bereaved family. At the signing of a surrender, the fact of putting pens to paper will mean something quite different for the victors than for the vanquished. The outcome of a successful prosecution has different meanings for the accused and for the prosecuting attorney. As there is difference in purposes, motives, expectations and attitudes, so there is a difference in experience.

Now the problem for the philosopher of religion or for the theologian is to clarify the claim that one of several possible ways of experiencing the world, the way of faith, is the revelation of God. In brief, it is not enough to point to the fact that the world is experienced differently, but to seek both to explain and if possible to justify the claim that in experiencing the world in a certain way, God has been revealed. Believers have certain convictions that enable them to experience the world as God's world. They view it as purposive, and not fortuitous. They see it as the expression of a good purpose and not as chaotic. The theologian addresses the questions: How does it come about that believers have the convictions they have? How is faith and revelation related to such convictions, specifically, how does it come about that believers interpret the events of their experience in such terms as that God is Creator and Lord of history? How does it come about that they experience the world and the events of human history as the revelation of God?

6 DIVERGENT INTERPRETATIONS

While, as we have seen earlier, the knowledge of God is mediated knowledge, that knowledge supervenes upon the believer's experience of the world. God is not identical with any of the means through which he is revealed. To make such an identification would, according to Christian belief, be idolatry. The sacred book is not divine, nor is the priest, nor the prophet, nor the place of revelation. History is not God. It is only in the case of Jesus that a careful qualification is made by the Christian theist. God is revealed in Jesus as he is revealed through no other means.

God is transcendent to any means through which he is revealed. When this or that historical event, or person, or community, or book, are the media of his revelation, they will have to be interpreted as such. Christians interpret certain experiences as revealing God, as experiences *of* God. How does that come about? What is the source of the interpretation which makes it possible for Christians to see this or that event, this or that experience as the means through which God reveals himself?

The argument seems circular. We can only interpret experience as experience of God, as the revealing activity of God, if we already have a certain framework of understanding. We only have the framework necessary if God has provided for the development of the particular convictions involved. Certainly, this scheme of convictions develops in a historical context. Thus, in this sense, revelation can be said to have a history. We may look then for the process in which the development of convictions of a certain kind has taken place, namely those convictions which make faith a possibility, that provide the preconditions for such faith. The Christian *theist* claims that such a process of development began to take place within the history of the Hebrew community, and was continued in the history of Jesus and within the Christian community, where Jesus emerged as a paradigm for the understanding of God. The Christian community claimed Jesus to be the decisive revelation of God.

7   GOD ACTIVE IN HISTORY

What then were these convictions? The Hebrews experienced their history as the act of God. They related a long series of historical events to one another and saw the whole as a unity. These events included the call of Abraham, the Exodus from Egypt, the succession of the prophets, the Exile and the Restoration of the Kingdom. So an expectation was raised that God would continue to act through the concrete events of history. An understanding of God as having a purpose, and as having created the world, opened the future for God's continuing acts. The Christian context was made possible by the acceptance of such convictions and they were given new content with the history of Jesus.

The Hebrews believed that God was at present active in their history. They also believed that God had been active in their history to enable them to confess that he had been active in their history. The belief that Yahweh had been active in their history was a product of Yahweh's activity within their history. To see events as Yahweh's act was itself Yahweh's act.

The difference between an historical, sociological or psychological account of the matter and a theological account is that the former describe in secular terms the way in which faith comes to be, the process from which theistic faith results, and through which the appropriate presuppositions emerge, without speaking about God. They analyse the confession of faith as a phenomenon that is given. The account thus given is a phenomenological one. A theological account takes responsibility for the claim thus analysed, that God reveals himself. It is to be hoped that it takes note of the phenomenological analysis, attempting to sift the arguments and to pronounce a judgment as to their reasonableness, but reckons with the fact that the statement about God is a confessional one. It claims that the convictions it accepts are reasonable and attempts to indicate their reasonableness.

But there is no question of *demonstrating* the truth of the convictions. They are taken to be true, but they are not proved. This is not at all frivolous or irrational. The taking of the convictions as true and their use as presuppositions makes it possible to explore meaning and to integrate the whole of experience. The process of integrating and of finding significance in the whole of experience is a rational process. The alternative is fragmentation, meaninglessness and irrationality of one sort or another.

How then does a change in fundamental attitude take place? The answer is that it is subject to change of context, to change of community. No one can decide to adopt a new set of attitudes, to alter his fundamental presuppositions, and as soon effect the change. You cannot decide to believe. But you can will to change your context. You can, like an emigrant, move from one community to another. You can, like a student changing his course, read new books, listen to a new vocabulary, think according to a new method and discuss new problems and think of old problems in a new way. You can seriously explore the possibilities inherent in supposing different assumptions than you had hitherto held. You might deliberately place yourself where reorientation might be encouraged. Or you might simply find yourself thrown into the midst of a new context. The conditions for experience, the interpretive categories, might then change and the experience of the world in turn change. It is through such a process of historical reorientation that changes in persons take place. It is in such a manner that one moves from faith to unfaith, from unfaith to faith, or from faith of one kind to faith of another.

The believer however recognizes that the cultural account of such reorientation of experience is valid, but does not accept it as it stands as a complete account. There is matter here not only for the sociologist but for the theologian. God is active, he claims, in the process of history. God is agent in the initiation of the process by which it comes to be known that God is agent. God is at work in providing the means by which he may be experienced to be at work. The process of coming to the appropriate presuppositions is an historical achievement, extended through time. God is active in this historical achievement, making available the presuppositions that lead to faith.

No subject has been more discussed in twentieth-century theology than that of revelation. How does God reveal himself? Does God reveal himself apart from Jesus Christ? Are there ways of coming to know God not related to the revelation in Jesus Christ? General revelation? Natural revelation? Is history rather than nature the primary realm of revelation? What does it mean to speak of revelation in history? And, what of the Bible? Is the Bible simply a record of God's revelation to his people, and others, in the past? A kind of documentary account of historical revelations? Or, is the Bible a means through which God continues to reveal himself in the present? Or, is it both? Is there some fundamental relationship between God's revelation in the past to which the writings of Scripture bear witness and the continuing revelation of God in the present time?

8   THE BIBLE AND THE PROCESS OF REVELATION

We now return to the question, In what way may we speak of the Bible as God's revelation of himself? To address this question we must make some preliminary theological assertions.

It is God who is revealed. God is the subject of revelation.

God takes the initiative in revealing himself.

God reveals himself by acting. God's revelation is an activity. God expresses himself.

Like coming to knowledge of another person, one must respond to God's initiative. Response is an intrinsic part of the revelatory process. God provides the occasion for revelation. Whether he reveals himself, depends upon the human response. Revelation is relational.

The Bible records what God has done, and it does so in the form of testimony. The Bible bears witness to his activity in the past: the Exodus, Conquest, rise of the prophets, Exile, Restoration, Jesus Christ, the faith and witness of the early church. These are God's revelations in the past. But a different kind of assertion is also possible, which does not refer simply to God's revelation in the past. The several occasions of God's revelation in the past constitute a unity which make up together a unitary process of revelation.

The Bible interprets many individual instances of history to be God's revelation of himself. As people are able to respond, to see in the events of history that there is special significance, so God is revealing himself. God reveals himself in and through the cross of Jesus when one sees, *understands* that is, perceives a significance in, the cross. Response depends upon understanding the historical event in a certain way. God reveals himself in the event as one comes to understand the event as the revelation of God. The response of faith in God is based on an apprehending that God reveals himself through the event.

The Bible presents revelation as a process. God acts in history. He causes events to take place. God guides history to an end. God expresses a purpose in the whole series of events which he initiates. God acts in history to give understanding that he has acted and that he is acting in history. God initiates the event of the coming to understand events as the revelation of God. It is a revelatory event to understand events (that may be interpreted very differently) as acts of God.

Where then has God acted to reveal himself? For the Christian theist God has acted and continues to act within Christian history. Christians live by and within a history. The claim is that Christian history reveals, is revelatory of, the meaning of life, of the past, of the future. One understands it as one lives within that history. It provides illumination for the whole of life. It provides for the life we live. It becomes our 'inner history' [7]

The Bible is the witness to what God did and was understood (in faith) to have done. It is the only, and so the primary, such witness. The God who revealed himself in the events to which the Bible testifies is the same God who now reveals himself through the reading and understanding of that testimony to his past revelation. The words of witness to God's past revelation are the instruments for his present revelation. Thus the Bible has a central and indispensable place in the life of the Christian, as an individual and within the community.

The Christian claim is that it does happen. It happens that God makes himself known now. It happens that the appeal of Jesus Christ takes place now. It happens that a recollection of what God has done in the past, as it is confessed and remembered, becomes the occasion for God's revealing of himself in the present.

Since Scripture is fundamental in all this, we can then, from this dynamic point of view, by recalling the current event of God's revelation in Jesus Christ, work out a theology of Scripture. Such a theology of Scripture, it scarcely needs to be said, will be more adequate than some of those which we have already considered. Moreover, in presenting such a theology of Scripture we do not now need to try to demonstrate the 'authority' of Scripture. In such a theology of Scripture we work out the implications of the events in which Scripture has played such an important role. Scripture has functioned to mediate the knowledge of God. Scripture *now* continues to function to mediate the knowledge of God. So things then drop into perspective. What older theories of inspiration so laboured to achieve now become irrelevant problems. That is a great gain.

There is no longer any need to labour the problem of the authority of the Bible. The older inspiration theory laboured to establish what it called the 'authority' of the Bible upon the inspiration of the Bible. By 'authority' it meant the right to demand a particular response, the right to exact a certain coercion. It was thought necessary to demonstrate that the Bible was inspired in order to assert the claim that the propositions of the Bible must be acceded to, followed, assented to, obeyed.

Now, an act of acknowledgment, an act of discipleship is a free act. It brings the person making it into a relation. When the believer says that God has revealed himself through the Bible, he has already acknowledged the fact of such a relationship. He has already acknowledged the place of the Bible in the process. He has therefore no need to try to demonstrate the 'authority' of the Bible. He testifies to that 'authority' as something which he knows for himself. He speaks of what has happened and may happen. His demand is no longer the rational, intellectualistic demand for an assent to the truth of the propositions of Scripture. There will of course be assent, and legitimate demands for such assent. But it will be put in its rightful place. Since the Scripture has functioned as it has, as the medium for the revealing of God, it has by virtue of that fact *a particular kind* of authority, call it a 'spiritual' authority if you will. That cannot be demonstrated. The authority of Scripture is the authority of the God who reveals himself through Scripture and without which revealing the Scripture would not be the book it sometimes is.

CHAPTER VIII NOTES

[1]It may appear clumsy to speak of personal knowledge of a person. But this expression satisfactorily differentiates this kind of knowledge from an impersonal knowledge. For example, I can learn a great deal about a person by going to the office of official records, even some information he might not be willing to impart to me. On the other hand, I can be invited to a personal relationship by his taking the initiative and providing the opportunity. The first results in non-personal, the second in personal, knowledge. The first is what we have earlier called 'intellectualistic.'

[2]John Stuart Mill's, *Methods of Experimental Inquiry* are found in elementary logic textbooks as the fundamental methods by which discovery may come to be made. The procedures of actual science are very much more complex than those 'methods' suggest. Cf. A. F. Chalmers, *What is This Thing Called Science?* But methodical inquiry does lead us to knowledge of a very complex and sophisticated kind. We all know that we can find things out if we go about it in the right way.

[3]To this distinction there is a corresponding distinction in the definition of belief, that between the content of belief, what is believed, and the act of believing.

[4]"Christian thought contains two very different understandings of the nature of revelation and, as a result, two very different conceptions of faith (as man's reception of revelation), of the Bible (as a medium of revelation), and of theology (as discourse based on revelation)' John Hick, *Philosophy of Religion*, p.51.

[5]*Ibid.*

[6]If the term 'proposition' is taken strictly, as it should be, to mean sentences which are either true or false, or verifiable or falsifiable, whole ranges of the biblical literature are excluded, sentences expressing demand, exclamations of praise, wonder and wish for example. That is very high price to pay for a theory.

[7]Cf. H. Richard Niebuhr, *The Meaning of Revelation*, New York: The Macmillan Company, 1960, for the classic exposition of this point.

SUMMARY OF CHAPTER IX

TRADITION AND SCRIPTURE

Tradition is something that has been handed down, a *content*. It is also the *process* of handing down something. Every Christian group hands on a body of teaching, of interpretation, as well as the Scripture. So Scripture is tradition. As well, the teachings of the particular community are tradition. Indeed the content of Scripture was handed down before being put into writing and before being recognized as Scripture. When it was put into writing it assumed a fixed form. So various traditions exist and have existed side by side. This the New Testament recognizes. So what is the issue between the Catholic who speaks of an unwritten tradition, and the Protestant with the principle of *sola scriptura*, the Bible and the Bible only? For the Catholic also asserts the primacy of the Scripture, and the Protestant interprets the Bible by producing doctrines and hands these on as tradition. To understand here, we must be clear as to what *sola scriptura* does not mean. It may then be evident that there is no necessary opposition between Scripture and tradition.

IX
TRADITION AND SCRIPTURE

1 MEANING OF TERM *TRADITION*

The term 'tradition' has several meanings. It may mean something that is handed on: a custom, teaching, or law, for example. It may also mean the act of handing some thing on, the passing on.

Within the Christian context there are several meanings.[1] The term 'tradition' may refer to Christianity, the Christian movement; to a particular section of Christianity; to a particular method of interpretation; and (in Roman Catholicism) to a specialized apostolic act of handing on and to the content of what is thus handed on.

We now take up these several meanings in rather more detail.

The term 'tradition' stands for what is held in common by Christians as an identifiable group, distinguishable from other groups. 'The Christian tradition' is, in this sense, a synonym for 'The Christian faith.' Whatever differences there are between Christians, there is something essential that is held in common, something of fundamental importance, so that for all the unlikeness in expression it is possible to speak of a Christian tradition. Since the term 'tradition' stands for what is held in common among Christians, it thus points to the contrast with the kinds of thinking and acting characteristic of other groups. So we speak of the Christian tradition in contrast to the humanist tradition or the Marxist tradition. There is no intention in so doing to overlook the many and important differences that exist between Christians.

2 PARTICULAR TRADITIONS

The 'church' is represented in many communions, many denominations. Each Christian communion expresses the Christian faith in a different way. Every Christian body has its traditions of teaching, of worship and of activity. These traditions distinguish Christians from one another. So we speak of the Catholic tradition, the Anglican tradition, the Methodist tradition. Now, some Christian bodies claim that they do not have a tradition, and think that they can exist without a tradition. But they do not succeed. Their tradition is that they dispense with tradition. In this sense, the term refers to the special character of the group, and suggests that what it is now by way of teachings, practices and worship is related to its past. In the present it has a particular character and this is, at least in part, a product of the past. It is what it now is because of what it has been. Particular Christian bodies appeal to particular events, decisions, teachers and leaders of the past. Some of these are of primary importance. The term 'tradition' points to the fact that all have their roots in the past. So the Catholic appeals to Thomas Aquinas, the Reformed to Calvin, the Methodist to Wesley, the Anglican to Hooker. These sources of teaching continue to influence the present outlook of each of these different churches. The term 'tradition' in this way points to the history of the group and emphasises that what a group now is has its roots in its history, and that its particular history is both unique and unrepeatable.

All churches, as well as making their special appeal to the significant figures of their particular tradition, also appeal to the Scriptures in one way or another. There are different traditions of the interpretation of Scripture. One group interprets Scriptures in one way. Another group interprets the same Scriptures in another way. But if the Scriptures do not mean the same thing for different communities how can we really say that they are the 'same' Scriptures? Every Christian community relates to the Scriptures, and teaches its adherents what Scripture means. Every Christian group has a *tradition of interpretation* it 'passes on' to its members. The term 'tradition' has reference to the particular methods of interpretation of the canonical Scriptures practised by and normative for this or that group, and which continue to be transmitted in the group through teaching, preaching and practice.

We can clearly see here the two meanings of 'tradition' as act and content. Each community employs and passes on a method or style of interpretation and beliefs which that method produces The tradition of interpretation is both an act of passing on and a set of determinate beliefs i.e. a content. The content has a history. The ambiguity of the term *tradition* points to this important fact. What any particular community does now, thinks now, believes now, has ties with its past.

3 UNWRITTEN TRADITION

It is regularly the case that what is orally transmitted very soon gets put into writing. The distinction sometimes made by Christians between written and unwritten tradition is of some importance. This is so because within the Christian community there is a body of writings it considers primary, namely the Bible. It thus distinguishes these written traditions from all others. As doctrines get developed, they in their turn are handed down. So the question arises concerning their status as compared to those primary written traditions, namely the Scriptures.

There is more than meets the eye in the claim about unwritten tradition. The adjective 'unwritten' in the expression 'unwritten tradition' thus gains a particular meaning. Whether the tradition is actually put in writing or not is not the point. It is a question of authority. This is evident when the Catholic claims that the unwritten tradition has been maintained within the church and goes back to Jesus. This unwritten tradition is a source of guidance and a means of revelation. The church has apostolic authority in exercising its teaching office, and this authority has its base in the apostolic succession of an 'unwritten' tradition. The question of the relation of such tradition with Scripture is thus inevitable and important.

The issue here is what the source of the church's teaching should be. Is there or is there not a primary source of the church's teaching outside and apart from the Scripture? Obviously the question of authority is in view here. Should one, can one, clearly distinguish between teachings and practices which are taught in Scripture, believed and practised in the church, and teachings and practices not taught in Scripture, believed and practised in the church?

Already at the end of the second century, Tertullian endorsed many practices for which there was no scriptural warrant.[2] For him, they were warranted by tradition and custom.

The Catholic church at the Council of Trent made a pronouncement which spoke of 'a second independent, original, authentic source of information and doctrine alongside of Scripture, capable of supplementing it, though never contradictory of it.[3] The original draft of the Tridentine decree (1546) stated that revelation is contained 'partly in written books, partly in unwritten traditions.'[4] There was some objection to the wording of this clause. As a result it was altered and the final version ran: 'The council is aware that this truth and teaching are contained in written books and in the unwritten traditions.'[5] The 'written' books are the books of Scripture. So how are these unwritten traditions related to Scripture? What is the relation between unwritten tradition and church? Is there or is there not unwritten tradition in the sense required? What is the nature of this tradition? Tradition not preserved in written form demands a community within which it is transmitted by word of mouth. If, in fact, such unwritten tradition has equal importance with the written, the canonical Scriptures, there will be within the community which passes it on a special authority on a par with Scripture. It guards, preserves and transmits the unwritten tradition and has importance in being the living voice which does so. This is part of the Catholic claim concerning unwritten tradition.

The unwritten tradition we are now discussing has, it is claimed, its origin in the apostles and has been passed on and preserved in the living voice of the church. It is thus a quite different sense of 'tradition' than the tradition of interpretation we have just briefly discussed. The Catholic claim is that such unwritten apostolic tradition is preserved and exercised in the church.

Trent insisted that such traditions must be in accordance with Scripture. There is to be no opposition between the unwritten tradition and the written Scripture. Within the Catholic church such unwritten tradition is formalized and thus recognized as having authority on a par with Scripture.

A representative Catholic article very clearly states that the Bible is not the first source of revelation; that Scripture is not superior to the apostolic traditions; that Scripture is not the total and complete source of revelation; and that Scripture as a source of revelation is not sufficient in itself. 'The sole judge in controverted matters is the living apostolic tradition, as it is embodied in the teaching of the apostles' lawful successors.'[6]

We can separate out different issues here: (1) whether in interpreting Scripture we 'go beyond' Scripture; (2) whether there are grounds for allowing authority to a 'living tradition' of interpretation, i.e. an office within the church which has the power to pronounce on doctrinal and other matters; (3) whether the claim to apostolicity is meaningful and defensible.

These distinctions will help us precisely to discern where the issue lies. For Protestants also interpret Scripture. They use new words. They develop forms of worship, and discipline. They give direction for the practical conduct of Christians. They adhere to methods of interpreting Scripture. They develop doctrines, none of which are simply a repetition or a 'translation' of the written Scriptures. The church then gives its backing to these, and the believers accept them. So the Protestant churches exercise authority by endorsing, indeed sometimes by enforcing, such traditions of interpretation and activity upon their members. Where then does the issue lie in the Protestant-Catholic discussion of the relation of Scripture and tradition?

4 TRADITION BEFORE THE NEW TESTAMENT

We will, in due course, embark on a discussion of such very interesting questions. First, we must notice that there is another meaning of the idea of unwritten tradition in relation to the Bible. I refer to the oral tradition which preceded the writing of our Gospels, our New Testament. The fact is that the story of Christian faith, of Christianity, does not begin with the New Testament. Indeed the telling of the story of Christian faith, the story about Jesus, and the interpretation of the meaning of faith does not begin with the New Testament. The writing down and the collecting together of the writings are later stages in the process. Between the event and the writing about it there is a period of preservation. They tell and retell the stories. It is remembrance through oral transmission. This is also true of the Old Testament as well. We shall content ourselves here with some simple statements about the New Testament writings.[7]

Look at the facts. Jesus died about A.D. 30. The first Gospel to be written, Mark, was produced about A.D. 65. The first letter, of Paul, was written in the fifties. So there is a gap, a bridge period, between the man whom the writers write about and the writing about him. But it was a period of intense activity on the part of Christians. There were many, many people who had seen and talked to Jesus, who had encountered him and who knew what he had said and done. They in their turn talked about him, year after year, and the best stories became widely circulated. There were very good reasons why such stories should not be lost and why they had to be preserved.

So the stories about Jesus which we find in our synoptic gospels circulated orally before they were written down. We have whatever teachings of Jesus are available to us now because the evangelists who compiled the Gospels preserved them in writing. These are our only literary sources for information about his life, teachings and death. The exception is that there are literally two or three oblique references to Jesus by Roman writers. We have only these sources. There are no others. The Gospels are the deposit in written form of the stories which had previously circulated by word of mouth. The oral traditions eventually took shape in written form. The first generation of witnesses died. Eventually the second generation of Christians died. No-one was then alive who had access to anyone who could *say*, that is speak for himself in his own voice, testify orally, that he had known Jesus or had been caught up in the events of the first Easter. *Actual* memories died with those two generations. What is passed on is a set of writings. Since these writings represented the early memories and experiences, the writings came to be valued, read widely and preserved.

Now writing has a permanence and so a fixity which the spoken word does not have. If due care is taken, writing can be handed down in a fixed form with relatively little change. What is written can then be given a status, receive a position of authority. The compilers and writers of the New Testament did not think themselves to be writing sacred Scripture. They were caught up in the task of witnessing. What they wrote represented an expression of their faith in Jesus. They drew on a fund of information which had come from many sources. What *Luke* says in the opening verses of his Gospel is true of each of the gospels. There is deliberate use of preceding sources. There is conscious selection from the materials available. As we move from the oral to the written stage, the writer exercises a control over the sources he uses and fixes the form of the resultant story for ever.

5   A Fixed Form in the New Testament

Once the writing is produced, it has a fixed form. Once the original witnesses die, the writers pass from the scene. Other written sources disappear. We are left with certain surviving products. These are our four Gospels.

We cannot interrogate written sources in the same way as we can speakers, living witnesses. There is a price to be paid for the permanence which writing brings. That the writings are fixed gives later generations two very important but rather different problems. The first is that we must try to get as accurate a text as we can, accurate in the sense that it does justice to what the original writer wrote. We must try to make sure, as far as we can, that the words we are reading are the same as those which were first written. This is the problem of textual analysis, sometimes called *lower criticism*. The other is the problem of saying what the text meant and what it means. This is the problem of *exegesis*, the problem of interpretation. It is sometimes called *hermeneutics*.[8] It is needed because there is a distance between the writer and the reader, a distance of time, of space, and in particular, of culture. His, the writer's, horizon is different from mine, the reader's.

The writing of the gospels, letters and other kinds of book now to be found in the New Testament represented a stage in the development of Christianity. As time passed the traditions about Jesus, the earliest interpretations of what he meant, and the stories and symbols of Christian activity and hope, assumed a permanent form and were passed on in that permanent form. This meant that copy after copy of the books was made and circulated. So you then quite literally handed something over to somebody. You passed on the scroll, or, later, the codex. The *tradition* was being handed down. The oral tradition became a written tradition and was passed on through the centuries into the church in very different circumstances. Tradition is a passing on. That is the literal meaning of the word.

Thus Scripture is a form of tradition. As such it holds a special place in the existence of the church. It is the primary tradition. This collection of writings and no others is primary; both in an historical sense and also in the life of the church.

6 THE PROBLEM OF SCRIPTURE AND TRADITION

All Christians would agree, both Catholics and Protestants, that the question of the relation of Scripture and tradition is an important one. We must be careful, in the first instance, to set out the problem adequately. This we shall attempt in the form of a series of questions.

(1) What is the relationship between what Scripture says and what the church teaches and does (both in worship and in practice), i.e. between the content of tradition and Scripture?

(2) How are the methods of interpreting Scripture related to Scripture itself? Do scriptural methods of interpretation (for example, the ways in which the writers of the New Testament use and interpret the Old Testament) become normative for the Christian's interpretation of these writings?

(3) What does the Council of Trent mean when it speaks of God's revelation being made through both Scripture and tradition? What is the content and the status of such unwritten traditions as are here assumed?

(4) How is the written tradition, the New Testament, related to the events which lie behind it? In particular does the authority of the written tradition depend upon accurate historical reconstruction (or on the possibility of it) of the events which produced the church? What role does the apostle play in the process?

(5) Just what primacy does Scripture, as written tradition, have over other sources and interpretations? And who determines whether it does and what it is?

7 COMING TO TERMS WITH THE PAST

One important general point remains to be made. It may be stated as a principle, since it applies in many different ways. It is quite simply that every religious community has, at some point, to come to terms with its past. Every individual and every community has a past. It achieves a degree of maturity as it consciously does so. What this means is that it recognises and then assesses the dependence in which it stands to others who have gone before it. Tradition is an instance of the principle of human dependence. Tradition 'is a particular instance of a law of human existence that men live in dependence on one another and by the processes of giving and receiving.'[9] A religious community is particularly concerned with its past since this involves the question of authority. 'The church also lives by tradition and history; it has a very special concern with the relation between the past and the present, with how the past is to become the present, and with the question of the authority under which men live.'[10]

Thus as the community comes face to face with new problems and new questions, it will attempt both to assess its past and to come to terms creatively with the resources it has inherited. It will attempt to deploy them in face of situations in the present. An emphatic, but ultimately unsatisfactory, way in which this has been done was by making an exclusive claim to particular traditions. This is illustrated from the case of Tertullian's exclusiveness.

Concern about heresy was without doubt an important factor in the church's interest to preserve a form of tradition. Already in the second century, with the rise of Gnosticism and the teachings of Marcion, Tertullian found it expedient to develop lines of argument against such doctrines. Both men appealed to the Scriptures and used them to suit their own purposes. Tertullian appeals both to Scripture *and* to tradition. He argues for the exclusive right of the true church to interpret Scripture. He will have no argument with the heretics on the basis of Scripture, since they have no right to use it.[11] Since the heretics have made innovations in practices and doctrines which cannot be established from those traditions, their claim to authority is thereby shown to be arbitrary and dogmatic. He presents his own summary of the teaching of Scripture, in a creedal-like statement.[12] Thus, at one stroke, there is no further conversation with the heretic. But what if the church itself thought and performed what was not contained in Scripture? How could it then defend itself? Obviously, it was urgent to define what Scripture was, what specific books it contained. You cannot appeal to a collection of books as your authority unless you can specify precisely what the limits of that literature are. Argument with Marcion, who produced his own 'canon,' had made that clear. But even if you have a carefully prescribed canon, what was to be said when there were practices, and so also teachings, which were not hinted at in Scripture?

Tertullian's answer is clear. For many of the practices in the church, e.g. rituals at baptism, fasting, offerings for the dead, the sign of the cross, there is precedent but no scriptural basis. 'If,' he writes, 'for these and other such rules, you insist upon having positive injunction in Scripture, you will find none. Tradition will be held out to you as their originator, custom as their strengthener, and faith as their observer.'[13] Written authority is not demanded. It is sufficient that the practice has been handed down. Appeal to precedent is sufficient.

Such tradition is unwritten. Appeal to such unwritten tradition is warrant for the current practice. A similar argument, namely that appeal to unwritten tradition is sufficient warrant for the church's practice, is made by an article in the *Catholic Encyclopaedia* which extends the warrant to sacramental rites, the liturgy, ecclesiastical discipline and the practical conduct of Christians. It instances in particular the obligation to worship on Sunday and annual Easter communion.[14]

8 RELATIVE IMPORTANCE OF GENERAL AND PARTICULAR TRADITION

The earliest Christian traditions, namely, the Scriptures and the oral sources behind it, are bound up with a particular history. Through such tradition Christians expressed the conviction that God had revealed himself through Jesus Christ. That written tradition, the Scripture, stands as a permanent point of reference, bringing the Christian back to the formative events of his history. Every Christian confesses his faith that a particular series of events in a specific place, Palestine, and at a particular time, the first century A.D., bear the revelation of God to men. All Christians, by definition, interpret these events in this way. It is this that leads them to give particular attention to those writings which have emerged from these events.

While all Christians give primary importance to the formative events of the first century and to the writings that emerged from those events, it may be the case that the distinctive formative events of the particular history of the denomination, the interpreter or interpreters that arose in the course of that particular history, and the literature that emerged from that particular history *in effect* assume the primary importance, become *effectively* more important than the biblical literature. More attention is given to them. They provide the point of reference when questions are to be raised and when activity is to be undertaken. They are explicitly, even if the fact is not acknowledged, as important as the biblical tradition, and more important than parts of the biblical tradition.

The Protestant should be quite honest at this point and see whether he recognises this to be the case. Should he examine the status and the structures of interpretation and their sources and find them functionally on a par with the Scripture, let him give that recognition due weight. There can then be frank discussion of the issues. What he may have to admit is that they have in fact become more important. The problem is not easily, and therefore not often, illuminated. Some other source may be of primary importance, while the group formally claims that Scripture holds the place of primacy.

Each Christian church has its own particular history. It confesses that God has guided it in and through those particular events which have brought it into being. Such events are of great importance for that community. When such events are discerned to be of such importance, a particular tradition of interpretation arises. The particular denomination may speak of a particular interpreter as the instrument of the divine guidance. The event of Luther for the Lutherans, Calvin for the Reformed, Wesley for the Methodists, Ellen White for the Adventists is of such importance. The event of the coming of an interpreter, or an interpretation, which can present a system of truths is in each instance confessed as God's revelation, or as the occasion of God's revelation. The interpretations the interpreter provides then become (in their distinctive ways) authoritative for that group and a particular tradition grows up. That tradition identifies the particular group.

9   ASSESSMENT AND ALTERNATION

Since the church is an historical entity, it is immersed in the historical process. It is, *in the present*, making decisions and putting them into effect, leaving 'footprints on the sands of time,' taking up particular attitudes to past positions and handing on such new decisions and attitudes. It has received. It also passes on. Generations to come will inherit the traditions it is now shaping, as it comes to terms with what in their turn previous generations have done. Once the traditions have become established and widely known, we can then examine them carefully, and assess their reasonableness and relevance.

As time passes and social conditions change, an alteration in the way in which events and teachings have been assessed in the past is almost inevitable.[15] The capacity to carry through such assessment demands and represents maturity on the part of the group which can accomplish it impartially, or even attempt it seriously. [16]

10 'TRADITION' IN SCRIPTURE

In this section and the next we will examine what Scripture teaches about tradition and Scripture, how the New Testament defines these ideas, with a view to asking whether and if so, to what extent, we may find and base a doctrine of tradition and of Scripture on Scripture itself. But would we not be arguing in a circle if we base a doctrine of Scripture upon the teaching of Scripture?

By the first Christian century the Jews had inherited a body of literature and a body of interpretation of that literature. The 'Torah' had been handed down from of old. The term does not simply mean 'law' in the strict legal sense, but *instruction, revelation.* Torah contained laws. It provided directives for life in all of its ranges. It was the task of the interpreter to indicate how such laws applied to the Jew as an individual and in his social and religious life in the community. He considered such traditions obligatory and binding. He thought that to follow such directives was the duty not of priests only, but of all pious Jews. To fail to keep the law is 'transgression,' a culpable passing beyond the boundary. The Jewish *torah,* handed down, elaborated, interpreted, argued over, is to be obeyed by everyone. If you do not, or cannot, or will not keep *torah,* you are accursed. If you did not know *torah,* you could not keep it. Those, on this official view, who know *torah* should have been better off then. For to know what *torah* demands would seem to be the first step to performing its demands.

Jesus came into conflict with the Jews, Pharisees and Scribes, over the issue of the meaning of *torah.* What had taken place was that a body of interpretation had grown up around the *law.* The interpreters made the attempt to interpret *torah* so as to apply it to every aspect of life, individual and corporate. So there grew up a great bulk of tradition: commentary on the books, and commentary on the commentary. The interpreter claimed authority for his interpretation. Was it not 'based upon' the words of Scripture, and were not the words of Scripture divinely inspired?

Jesus challenged the Jewish interpreters about their rendering of laws and *traditions,* ritual demands like the washing of hands and the cleaning of pots. The 'tradition' or oral teaching expounded in detail what was not precisely said in the written law. Often there was disagreement between interpreters.

Jesus' criticism is that the man-made law is wrong because it stands in the way of the commandment of God. It renders it of none effect. This commandment was about experience not the trappings of fussy ritual. It was about the religion of the heart. Jesus does not condemn it because it is tradition. He condemned it because it is the sort of tradition it is, and has the effect it has. That effect is to stand against real religion, real piety; to put people off real concerns, to substitute pseudo-concerns, and to invest those pseudo-concerns with authority and importance. Jesus saw it as a straightforward opposition. 'You leave the commandment of God, and hold fast the tradition of men. . . . You have a fine way of rejecting the commandment of God, in order to keep your tradition.'[17]

For their part the Jewish interpreters saw Jesus as a threat to their interpretation and to their authority. He was casting a slur on the traditions which they supported and in the support of which they had their status and the system had its stability. Hence both Jesus and the movement he had started must be put down as resolutely as possible. So when Stephen faces trial, his accusers charge him with innovation. His crime is that his teachings will lead to change. He 'will change the customs which Moses *delivered* (*paredoken*, the verbal form of the word for *paradosis, tradition*) to us'.[18] These were the traditions connected with the Temple and held sacrosanct by the 'elders and the scribes.'

Paul can also, sometimes, speak negatively of the traditions. He warned his people at Colosse against 'philosophy and empty deceit, according to human tradition, according to the elemental spirits of the universe, and not according to Christ.'[19] That this is not a general and wholesale negation of tradition and philosophy (more what we would call theosophy, as we learn from this letter) is clear from other passages where, as we shall see, tradition is given a place of first importance. It is not the handing down, but the *content* of the tradition, the actual teaching, that is in question.

Paul had received the teachings of the Gospel and was passing them on. He received the practices of the community and was passing them on too. He wanted the members of his churches to follow both the teachings and also the practices which he had received and was passing on. This was a particular concern of his in view of alternative beliefs and practices. So while he can condemn one set of traditions, he can commend another. There is no question of commendation or of condemnation because the teaching or the practice is traditional, that is to say, because of its having come from the past. The content of the tradition, what is handed down, may be commendable, indeed essential to the Christian community.

The Greek word for tradition is *paradosis*. It is translated into Latin as *traditio*, which, by transliteration, becomes in English 'tradition.' There is no verb 'to tradition' in English. So we cannot say, 'keep the traditions as I *traditioned* them to you.' But you *can* say that in Greek (as we shall illustrate in a moment). You can't translate word for word if you have not got a word. What you then have to do is to paraphrase rather than translate word for word. So we translate, 'I commend you because you remember me in everything and maintain the traditions even as I have delivered them to you.'[20] 'Delivered' would be more accurately rendered 'traditioned' if we had such a verb in English. We don't. So we miss the repetitiousness of the Greek text (*paradoseis . . . paredoka*).

The verbal form is used quite naturally of the communication of the Christian teaching. Apostles and other witnesses '*passed* it *on*.' That is what communication means. What they pass on, the actual content of their message, is the tradition. Also, the actual act of passing it on, is also tradition. The verbal form will obviously refer to the latter, the act of passing on. The noun is ambiguous, but usually refers to the content. To avoid such ambiguity, the Latin distinguished *traditum* (what was passed on) from *traditio* (the act of passing on). So *traditum* referred to the content, the actual teaching. Since we cannot make this distinction in English, we have to decide which meaning the term has in any given instance, and when we are using the word must make clear which meaning we intend.[21]

Paul advises believers to hold 'to the traditions which you were taught by us, either by word of mouth or by letter.'[22] They are to shun any teachers who depart from the tradition Paul had taught.[23] Here the reference is to a quite practical ethic that Paul had taught and exemplified. The Christian is to be diligent in his work and not sponge on other people, using the pretext, perhaps, that the Lord's coming was imminent. He commends those who are obedient to the form of teaching they received and to which they were committed.[24] Here the verbal form suggests that they 'handed themselves over' to the teaching — a derived meaning.

Elsewhere Paul speaks of two traditions, namely the practice of the Lord's Supper, and the content of an early statement of faith, a creed. He introduces his instructions about the Lord's Supper by using the words, 'For I received from the Lord what I also *delivered* to you. . . .'[25] 'Delivered,' as we have seen, is the verbal form of the word for 'tradition.' Paul was passing on, and by so doing endorsing, what had been passed on to him. The Lord's Supper was a firmly established part of the Christian tradition.

As he introduces his statement about the resurrection, he recalls a statement of faith which contains the threefold confession: that Jesus died, was buried, and on the third day rose from the dead.[26] He quotes it, prefacing it with the words, For I *delivered* (*paredoke*) to you as of first importance what I also received. . . .' Paul is repeating, and so passing on, the content of an early statement of faith. This brief statement of faith was a firmly established part of the Christian tradition. He knew it and his readers knew it.

Paul, on becoming Christian, had exchanged one set of traditions for another. He speaks of his zeal for 'the traditions of my fathers,'[27] such that he advanced in the Jewish religion further than his contemporaries. The term 'tradition' has the meaning here of a religion, a way of life. This is, of course, a familiar use of the term in our common language.

Luke, a very careful author, speaks of his acquaintance with the earlier stories of what had taken place in the life of Jesus. These stories 'were *delivered* to us by those who from the beginning were eye witnesses.'[28] Several traditions had grown up. Some were passed on by word of mouth, others were eventually written down. Luke seems here to be speaking of the verbal transmission of stories of Jesus. He had made an attempt to gather together as many of these stories he considered authentic. Those who knew them 'delivered' them to him. Such 'evangelists' as Luke committed these oral traditions to writing. What we learn from Luke is that such oral traditions take us back to the very origins of Christianity, and to those events which from the beginning the church has confessed as God's revelation.

What conclusions shall we draw from these simple observations?

(1) The term 'tradition' is used of both beliefs and practices, good and bad.

(2) The term 'tradition' (and its verbal equivalent) is in the New Testament used in a neutral sense. If the beliefs handed on are false, or the practices handed on are misguided, then the context indicates that this is the case.

(3) The term may be used as a synonym for the faith, in the sense of the Christian teachings, as for example in Jude 3-4: '. . . contend for the faith which was . . . *delivered* to the saints.'

(4) There is no suggestion here that the teachings are true or the practices commendable because they are old. Nor, conversely, are they to be rejected because they have been handed down. Whether they are the one or the other we must decide on other grounds.

(5) The term suggests a continuity through time. Later believers are one with earlier believers where the teachings and practices have been faithfully preserved.

(6) There is no suggestion of a secret teaching or practice. In fact Paul appeals to tradition in order to show that there is commonly accepted belief and worship. To 'deliver' a tradition to a congregation means to make it available to all of the members of that congregation, to publicize it.

(7) Historically, our earliest written traditions rely upon earlier traditions, written and oral. So we are taken back to

the time contemporary with the earliest events. The various techniques[29] developed by New Testament scholarship enable us to engage in careful, analytical reconstruction of those sources and provide us with the means for making considered judgments about the origins of Christianity.

(8) The New Testament sources now available to us represent a selective remembering of the events to which they refer.[30]

11 'SCRIPTURE' IN SCRIPTURE

We turn now to a similar analysis of the idea of Scripture. The term 'Scripture' means 'writing.' The word, like 'scribe,' 'script,' and cognates, comes into English through the Latin *scripto* (to write). The Greek term is *grapho*, from which all our compound words containing the root *graph* are derived. In English the word 'scripture' has a dignified and solemn meaning. We seem only to use it in a religious sense, of the 'sacred ' books of different religions: the Vedas, the Upanishads, the Gita, the Torah, the Koran, the Granth and, of course, the Bible, which word itself, *biblion* simply means 'book'.

In the New Testament the terms *graphe, graphai* are used in the way we use the terms 'writing,' 'writings.' Some works are singled out and are called 'the writing' or 'the writings,' these terms now being used with a special meaning. In that way the word 'scripture' comes to refer to an exclusive, limited, number of writings. It has become a proper noun, and in English is now spelt with a capital S.

We shall now look at some examples of the use of the words *graphe, graphai*, in the New Testament. We can see from their practice how the New Testament writers use the Old Testament. Examining how they use the term, we can get a clear idea of their attitude to the idea of 'Scripture.'

The New Testament writers think of the Old Testament writings as pointing beyond themselves, as having a fulfilment in the events of the recent past and in particular in relation to Jesus Christ and Christian faith. The emerging New Testament writings recognize the existing Old Testament writings as 'Scripture.' They refer to them as an authority for them for the understanding of God. So those who do not believe in resurrection go wrong, because they do not understand the Scriptures. (No particular passage is quoted).[31] The Scripture provides imagery for understanding the acts of God, e.g. of the stone which becomes the head of the corner.[32]

There are specific references to events which take place 'according to the Scriptures.' Indeed this often means for them that what happens is almost inevitable. Had Jesus called for legions of angels the Scripture would not have been fulfilled. Since Scripture must be fulfilled, he did not call for legions of angels.[33] The idea that what was written must find fulfilment is a very prevalent one in the New Testament. Several incidents in the story of Jesus and in the story of the early church are related to Old Testament passages. These incidents 'fulfil' these writings. For example, Jesus' presence in the synagogue at Nazareth,[34] his statement about the Temple,[35] about the traitor who lifted his 'heel against me,'[36] the dicing for the tunic,[37] Jesus' cry 'I thirst,'[38] the piercing of Jesus' side,[39] the death and resurrection,[40] the day of Pentecost.[41] In discussion with Jews the Christian's claim to understand and to provide evidence for the fulfilment of Jewish Scriptures was a powerful weapon [42] in the preaching of Jesus Christ.

Paul lived his Christian faith as a fulfilment of his Jewish hopes. Even a superficial reading of his great treatises, Romans and Galatians, makes one aware of his desire to give whatever authority he could to his claim that Jesus is the Christ, and that God's grace is manifest to the believer in him. He argues from the response of the Gentiles to Abraham,[43] from the fact of universal sin, so clearly portrayed in the Old Testament, to the grace of God in Jesus,[44] from Old Testament instances to the fact of freedom in Jesus Christ.[45] The Gospel was promised and now is fulfilled.[46] Where the writings are understood what was not known before has now been made known,. Before, they were hidden. Now the mystery is disclosed. Paul's principle in respect to the writings is clearly stated. 'For whatever was written in former days was written for our instruction, that by steadfastness and by the encouragement of the Scriptures we might have hope.'[47] It was for him to show that this was the case as he spoke to his Jewish audiences.

The writings however will be understood only if they are properly expounded. They must therefore be well taught, and well studied. Otherwise they will be distorted, their intention misconstrued, their meaning perverted. So the reader must approach them earnestly, seriously, desiring to understand, and being willing to be taught. He must be prepared to read them in the light of the coming of Jesus, of his death and resurrection and in view of the presence of God, the Holy Spirit, in the midst of the Christian community. Several passages of the New Testament make that quite clear, for example, the discourse on the road to Emmaus,[48] the encounter of Philip with Candace's official,[49] the case of Apollos the learned Alexandrian,[50] the commendation of the audience at Berea,[51] the warning from II Peter.[52]

The writings have a religious authority as they give grounds for Christian faith and Christian exposition. The authors of the New Testament adopt the attitude that the Hebrew writings are a source for the interpretation of Christian faith. They even go so far as to suggest that they were actually written for that purpose. They wrote for us, says I Peter: 'It was revealed to them that they (the prophets) were serving not themselves but you . . . .'[53]

The purpose of quoting passages which actually contain the word 'scripture' was to show that there was already a body of writings which the Christians were ready to take over as their own and to acknowledge as having a pre-eminent place in their thinking. How in the many particular cases the New Testament actually interprets the passages it alludes to or quotes is, of course, a very complex question, to which we have given some attention elsewhere in this book.[54] What we have illustrated is how Christian sources used the term 'Scripture' of the writings of the Old

Testament. In due course the church would have its own distinctive collection of books, call them the New Testament, and speak also of some of them as 'scripture.'[55]

12 SOLA SCRIPTURA: SELF-AUTHENTICATION AND CLARITY

The slogan, *sola scriptura*, expresses an important Reformation position. It states what is sometimes called the Scripture Principle. It does this in face of the Roman Catholic appeal to tradition, and via tradition to the authority of the church, the Catholic doubting the primary importance of Scripture. The point at issue is whether Scripture can establish its own authority, and if so what Scripture can do to show its own validity. Luther holds that Scripture validates itself. The Scripture is 'self-authenticating.' It is not authorized by the church. Scripture validates the church. Scripture has authority over the church. In providing its own validation, Scripture produces certainty. There is, therefore, no need for an appeal to another source, namely, the pronouncement of the church. So Luther's principle *sola scriptura* means that he will accept no ecclesiastical authority which does not have its ground in Scripture.

The Scripture principle also expresses what has been called the *clarity* of Scripture. Scripture is clear in itself. If it were obscure it would need an interpreter external to itself. When the Roman Church claimed that the teaching office of the church was needed before Scripture could be understood, that involved the judgment that Scripture is an obscure book. Luther took issue. The Spirit illuminates the Scripture and the heart of man. So Scripture is clear in itself, as it is proclaimed, and such 'external clarity' is matched by the attitude of the one who hears the word in faith, by an 'internal clarity.'[56]

The phrase *sola scriptura*, 'Scripture alone' or, as it is sometimes rendered, 'The Bible and the Bible only,' suggests that in some respects Scripture is set apart from all other sources and interests which occupy the Christian's attention. Scripture has a unique status setting it apart from experience, from reason, from tradition, from external authority of any kind, from other written sources. Nothing is on a par with Scripture. The slogan may be taken as a polemical watchword, as if to say, 'If anyone wishes to replace Scripture, to put something else in its place, we are already ready with our answer.'

13 The Issue Between Protestant and Catholic

As is the case with any slogan, there is much more than meets the eye. If we take account of its original intention, its ambiguity and its misuse we shall have plenty to occupy us. To understand it, we must see what it denies i.e. what the slogan 'Scripture and Tradition' has been taken to stand for. But we may ask whether, if we understand rightly, we may affirm what *both* of these slogans stand for. Can we affirm both *sola scriptura*, or 'the Bible and the Bible only,' *and* 'Scripture and Tradition'?

It will be clearer as we open up some of the problems involved if we allow ourselves certain representative questions from various sources. We will introduce these with only brief comment, and then discuss the issues raised. In the first Hans Küng simply asks whether the issue is rightly put as the contrast between the infallibility of the Bible and the infallibility of the church.

> The question we put to Protestants must be stated as follows: Is it sufficient to replace the infallibility of the teaching office with the infallibility of the Bible, to substitute for the infallibility of the Roman pontiffs or of ecumenical councils the infallibility of a "paper pope"?[57]

All Christian communities develop traditions of interpretation when they try to say what the Scripture means. Each therefore commends both the interpretation and with it a method of interpretation, along with the text it interprets. How then can anyone say *sola scriptura?* That is a particularly relevant question in view of the great multiplicity of interpretations.

> If the interpretation of Scripture is the Protestant her-
> meneutical principle, *whose* interpretation amidst the
> plethora of doctrinal and exegetical opinions should be
> accepted as binding for church praxis in a given
> historical situation? . . . There is a structural problem
> within Protestantism that is not solved by reiterating a
> thousand times that *sola scriptura* is the hermeneutical
> principle of Protestantism. There must be concrete
> structures within the church through which the
> hermeneutical process takes place from day to day. In
> Protestantism the structures have become shadowy, if
> not invisible. In Roman Catholicism they have become
> overdeveloped and divinised. The response of the
> Reformation to the Romanization of the church was
> not to dismantle but to disencumber the structures of
> the church.[58]

Maurice Wiles suggests that we must get on with the task of interpreting and take our stand on what we present as the truth, confessing the guidance of the Holy Spirit. He writes:

> . . . the concept of the Spirit's guidance *by itself* can be
> used to legitimate anything, which means that it can be
> used to legitimate nothing. But then the idea of the
> Spirit's guidance *by itself* is not a genuinely Christian
> notion. . . . If it is he who leads us into the truth of
> Jesus, then we need to recognize that while our
> attempts to discover true doctrine must always be
> related to Jesus, there cannot be any external tests by
> which we can know if we are doing the job rightly or
> not. . . . We will certainly be limited and may well be
> wrong, even in what seems to us as individuals most
> clearly to be true; we will certainly be limited, and may
> well be wrong, even in what seems to us at a formal

gathering of the church or of the churches most clearly to be true. The Spirit is sovereign and does not guarantee to underwrite even our most faithful and devoted undertakings.[59]

We have now quoted from a Lutheran, a Catholic and an Anglican. Karl Rahner, a leading Catholic theologian, warns against the perfunctory handing down and acceptance of tradition:

> No real achievement is ever lost to the Church. But theologians are never spared the task of prompt renewal. Anything that is merely conserved, or that is merely handed down without a fresh personal exertion beginning at the very sources of revelation, rots as the manna did. And the longer living Tradition is interrupted by mere mechanical handing down, the more difficult it may become to restore contact again. . . . But how many themes . . . remain unexamined! Over how many questions does there reign the graveyard calm of weariness and boredom![60]

Our final quotation will be a salutary reminder that what we do in the present is new, whether or not we turn to our advantage the resources of the past:

> The passage of time is irreversible. Every moment, every day, every week, every year is unique and unrepeatable. . . . The appeal to origins has great persuasive power, but as compelling as it may be, it loses its credibility when one takes seriously the historical character of Christianity. . . . If we believe we can restore apostolic practices, or reproduce Paul's teaching on grace and faith, or remodel our ministry on the primitive pattern, we delude ourselves; the past is past, and when we attempt to restore the past we always create something new — not necessarily something better — which was not there before.[61]

We are now ready to list a series of issues which arise when the question of Scripture is raised in connection with Tradition.

(1) Is it possible to steer our way through the different definitions so that we can consistently affirm both *Sola Scriptura* and 'Scripture and Tradition'?

(2) Is the problem to be put in terms of infallibility?

(3) Since interpretations of Scripture differ widely, what does *Sola Scripture* 'the Bible and the Bible only', mean? Since processes and structures of interpretation mediate the meaning of Scriptures, leading to such great differences, let us be explicit as to what those structures are.

(4) What does the guidance of the Spirit accomplish in the actual process of interpreting the Scripture?

(5) How may we speak of an authoritarian tradition if what is handed down is reshaped or reset on being reinterpreted?

(6) Conversely, if tradition determines the meaning of Scripture, how can we speak of the primacy of Scripture?

(7) How can we appeal to (e.g. apostolic) authority in regard to Scripture when it is *we* who select and shape the materials which we are interpreting when, in repeating the tradition, we are giving it a new context and a new meaning?

(8) What then is the issue between Protestant and Catholic?

Our procedure will be quite simple. We shall first consider statements of the Catholic viewpoint and see whether there is, in fact, more than one position on the question of Scripture and Tradition. We shall then consider the Protestant viewpoint, or viewpoints, as the case may be. We shall have our catalogue of issues in mind as we seek for some conclusions.

14 The Council of Trent and Catholic Teaching

The Council of Trent replied to the Reformation position by formally stating the principle of the joint appeal to Scripture and Tradition, in opposition to the principle of *sola scriptura*.

The Council of Trent was the historical occasion when the problem of correlating tradition and Scripture came to a head. The original draft of the Tridentine decree (April 8th, 1546) stated that revelation is contained "partly in written books, partly in unwritten traditions" (*partim . . . partim*). To appease a theological minority who objected to the phrasing, the decree was changed to read: "The council is aware that this truth and teaching are contained in written books and in the unwritten traditions." The final decree had what seemed to be an inoffensive "and" replacing the "partly . . . partly."[62]

'Unwritten tradition' has reference to the oral passing on within the church of apostolic teachings. Trent asserted the existence of such teachings but did not make a list of them.

Historically speaking, such traditions represent the sacramental rites, the liturgy, ecclesiastical discipline and practical conduct of Christians throughout the centuries. The historic form of one or another may have been of apostolic or even of divine origin. For example, the Sunday obligation to worship and the annual Easter Communion are ecclesiastical specifications of a divine or Apostolic law.[63]

Tradition, it is here being asserted, is an unwritten source of teaching which originated with the apostles, and so has apostolic authority, and which has been passed on within the church to the present. Such traditions, Trent proposed, have authority equal to that of the written, canonical Scripture.

The official Catholic position, as stated at Trent and reaffirmed at Vatican I, is that there are two sources of God's revelation to men.[64] Truths of salvation are contained in written books and unwritten traditions. This is in deliberate opposition to the Reformation claim that Scripture is the one and unique source of revelation. For Trent, the Bible is one of two sources of God's revelation to men.

The Bible is not, in order of time, the first source of revelation. Divine revelation preceded the Scriptures, which did not at first exist. The preaching of the Gospel to the Gentiles took place without the use of the written New Testament. The apostles' teaching preceded the New Testament writings. The Christian faith existed for several generations without the New Testament Scriptures as the main source of Christian instruction. It was the church which determined which books formed part of the canon of Scripture. Scripture is not the total and complete medium of revelation, since tradition is another source side by side with it. It is important to say this in the right way. The church is the guardian and interpreter of Scripture, and the possessor of the tradition. 'Tradition' is the wider term. Some of what the earliest tradition taught is contained in Scripture. Tradition continues along with Scripture.

Scripture is not sufficient of itself. It needs a living interpreter. The relevant doctrine and admonition which Scripture contains must be extracted from it and so the letter of Scripture is not conclusive where there is controversy. The right understanding of the Scriptures depends upon their being interpreted by the Church's teaching authority, which succeeds to the apostles. Scripture, however, maintains its authority. The church must keep and defend the Scripture, she may not neglect it nor deviate from it.

The Bible is one of the two sources of theological teaching. It is the chief source from which theologians derive arguments or proofs in support of theological conclusions. Argument from Scripture is indisputable. When the church endorses Scripture's teaching as revealed it is then obligatory. The Catholic is then 'obliged to accept it as of faith.' 'When the Church defines that such and such a scriptural text contains revealed dogma, the exact sense of this being determined, it is a strict duty for Catholic exegetes to accept an infallible definition of this kind.'[65]

However, an article of faith may be deduced from Scripture where it is contained therein implicitly. The catholic theologian may proceed on this principle, even where there is no formal definition of the doctrine by the church.

Scripture is a dead letter without a living interpreter. So, of itself, it is not sufficient. Doctrine needs to be extracted from Scripture. The assurance that this will be done well, i.e. that Scripture will be correctly interpreted, is that the church, in succession to the apostles, shall be judge in the matter. The Catholic teaching has no intention of reducing the importance or status of Scripture. It has a 'high' doctrine of Scripture. Vatican I affirmed the uniqueness of Scripture in no uncertain language. The writings are inerrant and are to be considered sacred, 'because having been written under the inspiration of the Holy Spirit they have God for their author, and as such have been handed down to the Church.'

The church is the instrument of tradition. Tradition is 'the communication by the living Church of the Christian reality and the expression, whether oral or written, of that reality.' To transmit that reality faithfully there must be an authentic organ or agent. That is the living church.[66] The church is the means by which the Christian message is mediated to the world. But how can one be sure that what is communicated is the authentic Christian message? The answer is that such authenticity is guaranteed by the church as the guardian of the tradition. The church has within it an official teaching body, and it is here that the church's message is endorsed and pronounced.

Christ endowed his church with an *official* teaching body, the magisterium composed of the Episcopal college united with the pope, who is the head of the Episcopal college as Peter was of the apostolic college. The magisterium's duty, as enunciated by Vatican Council I (1869-70) is to guard faithfully, judge authentically, and declare infallibly the content of the revealed deposit (Denz. 5020, 5069). The hierarchy and faithful form, corporately and organically, the one as the voice and the other as the echo, the authentic organ of tradition. Their first duty is to guard faithfully, that is, witness to, the revealed deposit.'[67]

The magisterium initiates doctrinal development, having regard to 'a sense of faith,' 'a consciousness steeped in tradition and Scripture.'[68] It is thus that progress in doctrine can take place. This is evident from the dogmatic definition which took place in the last two centuries, namely the immaculate conception (1854), papal infallibility (1870), and the assumption of Mary (1950).

Scripture was given a particular value with the production of the Canon. It was distinguished as of primary importance. But this does not mean that it is the only rule of faith.

> Tradition and Scripture are both wholly divine and wholly human. The church controls, verifies, proves and even criticizes her tradition by Scripture. She holds no truth on the basis of Scripture alone, independently of tradition, nor on the basis of tradition alone independently of Scripture.[69]

So there is room within the Catholic church for debate and discussion. At Trent two views were already in evidence. One spoke of two 'quasi-independent sources,' neither source containing the whole apostolic teaching. Since Scripture is insufficient in content, it requires to be supplemented by oral tradition. Only then does it represent the whole divine revelation.

The other view holds that divine revelation is contained wholly in Scripture *and* wholly in tradition. This does not mean that revealed truths are demonstrable from Scripture. It means that such truths are implicit in Scripture and can be derived from Scripture. Such truths are based upon Scripture. They can be deduced from Scripture. The process of interpretation draws out, makes explicit, what Scripture implies.

Some later discussion has sought for a compromise. Scripture and tradition are one, a harmony. They are correlative. Tradition interprets Scripture and expounds its content. Without such a tradition of interpretation, contradictory interpretations would proliferate. Tradition thus serves to determine, i.e. make determinate, the meaning of Scripture. As it interprets Scripture, tradition is a more complete expression of the life and teaching of the church.[70] Vatican II (November 24th, 1962) refused to endorse the phrase, 'two sources of revelation,' speaking rather of revelation presented to the church in two forms, oral and written.

15 Important Facts

In this matter we must avoid oversimplifications and stereotypes: in particular a stereotype of the opposition between the Protestant and Catholic positions. Certain important facts must be stressed:

(1) The Scripture principle, *sola scriptura*, has its setting in a particular historical context. It originated in a context in which the question of the locus of authority was all-important. It intended to provide a clear answer to the question: What is the source of authority in the church?

(2) The principle of *sola scriptura*, like the principle of Scripture and Tradition, needs to be interpreted with some care. Neither is unambiguous. Whether there is to be opposition between them, or whether each points to essential elements, and so must *together* stand as expressions of what is essential, will depend on the meaning which the principles are given.

(3) There has been and is considerable debate in Roman Catholic circles about the meaning of the formula 'Scripture and Tradition,' to the extent that one can say that it is an open question.[71]

(4) The interpretation one makes of Scripture determines the authority Scripture has in the church. The debate is about that authority.

(5) The Catholic claims that the church 'is in possession and command of both Scripture and tradition.'[72]

(6) From the seventeenth until the end of the nineteenth century the universally accepted view of the Scriptures on the part of both Protestants and Catholics was that the Scriptures were inerrant. The source of this infallibility is

in the fact that God inspired the writers, and the very words which they wrote. Today, with analytic and historical study of Scripture that viewpoint is widely questioned.

(7) Protestants also speak of the authority of the church, as the church interprets the reality of Jesus Christ, and expounds the Scriptures. There are thus elements of the Catholic view of the church which are unobjectionable. But 'the crux of the Protestant Catholic debate over tradition' is in 'the question of the interrelation of Scripture, tradition and the church.'[73]

The principle of Scripture was initially developed at the time of the Reformation to counter what Luther saw as an unwarranted claim to authority by the church. Since the Roman church claimed infallibility for the church, its councils and teaching office, the Reformers, in opposition to this, claimed infallibility for the Scriptures. Such infallibility provided the grounds for asserting the authority of doctrine which was directly opposed to Catholic teaching. The issue was that of the status of the church.

However, if the claim of the infallibility of Scripture is modified as it was in the Reformation teaching, and if as in modern Catholicism the claim that the church is infallible is dropped, then the question as to what is at issue will have to be reopened. If the issue is not that between two infallible authorities where there can be no compromise, then a redefinition of the problem will mean both convergence of views and the possibility of discussion.

But a further alternative remains. Within Protestant circles since the nineteenth century it has become generally accepted that Scripture is to be approached historically. This means that we must reassess and restate how the Bible is to be described. Given that the traditional manner of both Catholics and Protestants in speaking of the Bible as inerrant and inspired is misleading and inadequate, we must reopen the whole question about the relation of what *Sola Scriptura* means to what 'Scripture and Tradition' means. The point at which to start would be with the practical significance of the canon. Suffice it to say here that the acceptance of these and no other books as canonical has become a tradition in the churches. Another point would be to approach the question historically and show how a change of context has produced a decisive shift in the nature of the issues involved.

The original Reformation principle was altered in the movements that followed the Reformation, in Protestant scholasticism. The Reformers intended it to signify that Scripture could be understood, and so serve as the means of God's revelation, apart from the mediation of an ecclesiastical system. The Protestant scholastics formalized this principle and elaborated the doctrine of its verbal inspiration and inerrancy in order to maintain the clarity of Scripture. That was a high price to pay. What was forgotten in the process was the Reformers' emphasis on the living word, the witness of the Spirit and the centrality of Jesus Christ. Gerhard Ebeling clearly and eloquently expresses the radical shift of emphasis:

> Old Protestant orthodoxy has been accused, not without justice, of having misrepresented the Reformers' understanding of Scripture, and of being the cause of the later crisis in the understanding of Scripture which is still not entirely settled; it is, however, necessary to evaluate this accusation from the point of view of its positive intention. The doctrine of verbal inspiration, which embraced even the Massoretic pointing, was not so much an absurdly exaggerated claim to authority on behalf of *sola scriptura*, as the result of an anxiety to establish, in opposition to the authority of Tradition and Church, the hermeneutic significance of the *particula exclusiva* by demonstrating the complete absence of ambiguity in the substance and meaning of Scripture. Hence orthodox teaching about Scripture was specially concerned to maintain the *perspicuitas* of Scripture, and adopted the basic feature of the Reformers' *scriptura*,

the doctrine of the *claritas* of Scripture. Nevertheless the emphasis shifted from the clarity of the subject-matter to the inviolability of the actual words and letters of Scripture which might not be called in question; the difficulties thus created had to be concealed by an occasional resort to the mysterious obscurity of the subject matter. Another result of this was that the unity of Scripture was determined not by concentration upon the unity of the subject matter, but by the summation of its variety in a totality which was decreed to be indivisible. Furthermore, the unifying conception of the Word of God became to a great extent formalized, so that the inner connection between *sola scriptura* and the Reformers' fundamental insight of *solus Christus, solo verbo,* and *sola fide* was weakened, if not entirely lost, and at any rate no longer recognizable. Hence it now became necessary to safeguard the connection by treating the doctrinal tradition of the Reformers as, practically, a *regula* and *norma* for the interpretation of Scripture.[74]

16 WHAT *SOLA SCRIPTURA* DOES NOT MEAN

To clarify what the Protestant intends to express by the slogan, *Sola Scriptura*, we shall at the outset make a series of denials. Note that some of the following assertions taken with the opening sentence constitute double negatives.

Sola scriptura does *not* mean:

(1) that no other sources than the Bible are to be consulted for the nurture of faith,

(2) that only Bible words and language are to be used in the church,

(3) that one must deny tradition a place in the process of understanding Scripture,

(4) that one cannot read other books with a good conscience,

(5) that Scripture limits the range of our interests, that one cannot for example study science, history, psychology or literature with a good conscience,

(6) that Scripture is different *in kind* from other writings used in the church: specifically that Scripture is not itself a collection of traditions which came to be acknowledged as having a special function,[75] (It is).

(7) that Scripture is to be preserved from critical examination,

(8) that Christians are relieved of the task of asking how they may correctly interpret Scripture, namely of inquiring what structures they can profitably employ in deriving meaning from Scripture; of addressing themselves to the problem of *how* they co-ordinate one portion of Scripture with others, Scripture with other knowledge, Scripture with problems in the church and community,

(9) that no conversation with Catholics regarding their position on the question of Scripture and tradition is possible,

(10) that all portions of the Bible are of equal merit,

(11) that God does not manifest himself through other means than these written words, e.g. through sacraments; through other writings; and through preaching,

(12) that Scripture can be understood without the activity of the Holy Spirit.

17 NO NECESSARY OPPOSITION

The slogans *sola scriptura* and 'Scripture and tradition' are not in principle opposed to one another, except when each is narrowly interpreted in different directions.

Scripture, for the Protestant, is the special instrument of the activity of God. It has a certain priority over other instruments through which the Holy Spirit operates. This conviction has been expressed by speaking of the 'word of God.' God reveals himself as the word about Jesus Christ is spoken. Without the word of witness, which witness is the distinctive and defining activity of the church, Scripture is a dead letter. It is as Scripture is interpreted, as the living word is spoken that the church continues to exist. Without the living word there can be no church. *Sola Scriptura* lays stress on the historical fact that it is as a result of such witness that both church and Scripture came into being. Behind the Scripture and the church that interprets it there is the reality of the living Christ.

Now the reading and interpreting of the Scripture in the light of the present activity of the Holy Spirit continues to be the vocation and the task of the church. But in the performance of this task the church is not a static reality dealing with a dead letter, and repeating what it knows only too well. This produces the graveyard calm and boredom of which Karl Rahner spoke. It is because the living Christ manifests himself through Scripture that the church lives in expectation. It is to listen for and then be receptive of the message it may now freshly hear, at the time and place where it now is. It has been a feature of Protestant theology that it has concerned itself with the question of the reality of the word of God.[76] The church does not pass judgment from a point of vantage on the Bible. The Bible mediates the living reality of Christ, and the Christian receives it, hearing and obeying, or refusing and disobeying. This is a development of the Reformers' emphasis on the uniqueness of Scripture and the spoken word as 'bearing Christ.' The Scripture has authority as it bears Christ. Hence the affirmation *sola scriptura*. There is no necessary opposition between a faithful exegesis and proclamation which mediates the word of God and a critical study of the text. The contemporary interpreter faithful to his task will be aware of both these demands: to be open to receive the word of God, and to exercise critical methods to understand the text.

18 Argument Between Catholic and Protestant?

So, we now make a few summary and concluding observations.

First: Both of the expressions about Scripture, namely *sola scriptura* and *Scripture and tradition*, need considerable explanation if it is to be clear what they intend and what they do not intend to affirm and to deny.

Second: Without such clarification they may be made to stand in opposition to one another. It is when *sola scriptura* is given a particular meaning, and when the slogan *Scripture and Tradition* is given a particular meaning that they stand in conflict with one another.

Thirdly: The Reformers quite consciously interpreted Scripture by employing traditions of interpretation. Luther and Calvin quite readily, and in full knowledge of what they were doing, quoted both Augustine's doctrine of grace, and Anselm's doctrine of atonement. They read and interpreted Scripture within particular ecclesiastical traditions.

Fourth, the Roman Catholic formula does not intend to diminish or in any way question the special importance of the canonical Scriptures. We can agree that 'neither the unique authority of Holy Scripture (its canonicity), nor its claim to reverence as revelation, inseparable from its canonicity (its inspiration), are matters of controversy as between Catholicism and the Reformers.'[77]

Fifth, the respective interested parties have elaborated and debated these slogans, and the debate still continues between them. Thus the concepts may stand for complementary rather than opposed positions, according to the definitions given. Whether there is an issue will depend on those definitions.

Finally there are points of agreement between Protestants and Catholics.

(1) In the earliest days of the church there was no Christian Scripture. There was a period before books of the New

Testament had been produced. Oral transmission has historical priority.[78] 'The early church got on without Scripture alone.'[79] It did, of course, begin to read the Hebrew Scriptures with Christian eyes.

(2) The decision about the canon of Scripture was made by the church, and was duly endorsed by the practice of the whole church, a practice which has continued in all sections of the church up to and in the present. The Christian church in its many parts assumes the canonicity of Scripture.[80]

(3) Earlier unsatisfactory modes of expression have been debated and often seriously revised. In particular the concepts of infallibility and inerrancy have now been largely dropped. That is a condition for further fruitful discussion.

(4) The revelation of God, the Spirit, takes forms other than that of the written word: sacramental acts, on the one hand, and the act of proclamation on the other. It is the responsibility of the church to encourage, to recognize and to interpret such acts. It is not for the church to try to exercise control over the activity of the Holy Spirit.

(5) Scripture must be interpreted. When interpreted a pattern emerges. Principles of interpretation become established. In short, a tradition of hermeneutic gets established. Understood in this way, what is meant by 'Scripture and Tradition' complements what is meant by *sola scriptura*. The particular church endorses one method of interpreting Scripture and the doctrinal results it produces.

(6) The acceptance of the critical-historical method and its application to Scripture provides an instrument for reassessing traditional positions. It makes such a reassessment urgent. There is no opposition between the attitudes of receptivity to the revelation of God through the text and careful critical analysis of the text. One approach to Scripture may serve to reinforce the other.

CHAPTER IX NOTES

[1]Cf. R.P.C. Hanson, 'Tradition,' in A. Richardson, *A Dictionary of Christian Theology.* pp. 341-343.

[2]Tertullian, *On the Soldier's Crown*, 3,4. Stephenson, p. 183.

[3]*Denz,* 1510.

[4]Hanson, *op. cit.,* p. 342.

[5]Denz, 1501.

[6]Cf. the article, 'Bible, Use of, in Theology', *A Catholic Dictionary of Theology*, pp. 266-268.

[7]We cannot here go into this in detail. There is a whole range of literature on the topic.

[8]Cf. *Hermeneuo* is the Greek word for 'to interpret.' It means both to translate (from one language to another) and to render the meaning of a passage.

[9]C. Evans, *Is Holy Scripture Christian?* p. 1.

[10]*Ibid.*, p. 2.

[11]Tertullian, *On the Prescription of Heretics*, 37. Stephenson, p. 181.

[12]*Ibid.*

[13]Tertullian, *On the Soldier's Crown*, 3,4. Stephenson, p. 183.

[14]*Catholic Encyclopedia.* Vol. 14, p. 226.

[15]The form of words may be the same on two occasions, but the changed context may mean that these have a different, even an opposite, significance. Doctrine has meaning within particular social and ecclesiastical contexts. Its context is in a form of life.

[16]Cf. Peter Berger, *Invitation to Sociology*, pp. 68-80.

[17]The particular issues on this occasion, as recorded in *Mark* 7: 1-13 (cf. *Matthew* 15; 1-9), were (1) ritual washing of hands, (2) ritual washing of cups etc., and (3) the practice of 'Corban' by which a son could avoid supporting his parents by declaring his goods 'dedicated!'

[18]Acts 6: 14.

[19]Colossians 2: 8.

[20]I Corinthians 11: 2.

[21]There is thus a double ambiguity in the English versions of the New Testament. 'Tradition' may mean either act of passing on

or the content of what is passed on. 'Tradition' may be commended or condemned. Our point here is that commendation or condemnation is on the basis of the content and its influence.

[22]II Thesalonians 2: 15.

[23]II Thessalonians 3: 6.

[24]Romans 6:17.

[25]I Corinthians 11: 23.

[26]I Corinthians 15: 3,4.

[27]Galatians 1: 14.

[28]Luke 1: 2.

[29]E.g. such techniques as source criticism, form criticism, redaction criticism.

[30]See the present author's *Jesus, the Man* Chapter 2, 'They Remembered Him,' pp. 22-27.

[31]Matthew 22:29.

[32]Matthew 21:42.

[33]Matthew 26:54.

[34]Luke 4: 21.

[35]John 2: 22.

[36]John 13:18.

[37]John 19 :24.

[38]John 19:28.

[39]John 19:36,37.

[40]John 20:9, Acts 2:25-36, 8:32-35.

[41]Acts 2:14-22.

[42]Acts17:2-3,18:28. Jewish Christian writers used the Old Testament as in the first instance they addressed Jewish audiences. They therefore found passages that they could apply to their new experiences. These had had a first application in the Old Testament. Now they could be re-applied and used to make the new teachings fulfilments of prophecy from the Old Testament writers.

[43]Galatians 3:8, Romans 4.

[44]Galatians 3:22.

[45]Galatians 4:21-31.

[46]Romans 1:1-4.

[47]Romans 15:4.

[48]Luke 24.

[49]Acts 8:26-38.

[50]Acts 18: 24 - 19:7.

[51]Acts 17: 10, 11.

[52]II Peter 3:16.

[53]I Peter 1: 12.

[54]Cf. Chapter XI. 7-8.

[55]Cf. our survey in Chapter I of how the canon came into being and why the question of the Canon is important.

[56]Cf. G. Ebeling, *The Word of God and Tradition*, pp. 126-157. Paul Althaus, *The Theology of Martin Luther*, pp. 74-78. The quoted phrases occur on p. 78.

[57]Hans Küng, *Infallible?*, p. 171.

[58]Carl Braaten, *History and Hermeneutics*, p. 151.

[59]Maurice Wiles, *The Remaking of Christian Doctrine*, p. 13.

[60]Karl Rahner, *Theological Investigations, Vol. I*, pp. 10-11.

[61]Robert L Wilken, *The Myth of Christian Beginnings*, pp. 156-157.

[62]*Cf.* 'Tradition (in Theology)' in *The New Catholic Encyclopaedia* Vol. 14, p. 227. Quoting Denzigen 1501 and supplying italics.

[63]*Ibid.*, p. 226.

[64]Cf. the following source: 'Bible, Use of, In Theology', in *A Catholic Dictionary of Theology*, pp. 266-268.

[65]*Ibid.*, p. 267.

[66]*Catholic Encyclopedia*, 14, p. 225.

[67]*Ibid.*, p. 227.

[68]*Ibid.*

[69]*Ibid.*

[70]*Ibid.*, p. 228.

[71]*Ibid.*, pp. 225-229.

[72]*Ibid.*, p. 225.

[73]*Ibid.*, p. 228.

[74]Gerhard Ebeling, *The Word of God and Tradition*, p. 139.

[75]Cf. above: our discussion of the relation between authority and function in Chapter III.

[76]Karl Barth's, *Epistle of Paul to the Romans* insisted that we must listen to what Scripture says to us in our time; that where we perform faithful, as well as critical, exegesis of the biblical text there will be a recognition of the dynamic reality of the revealing God. Rudolf Bultmann's concern was to make sure that the words of Scripture should not be a stumbling-block to the hearer's reception of the revelation of God. The forms of thought of the New Testament must not be a barrier to the hearing and the reception of the God of the living Christ. The 'New Hermeneutic,' as it came to be called, had a similar concern. We do not determine what the text may say. We must subject ourselves to it and then we shall discover the significance it can bear to us in our present situation. Through the spoken word, linked to the written word, the living word is manifest in the witness of the Christian community.

[77]G. Ebeling, *op. cit*., p. 122.

[78]*Ibid.*, p. 13.

[79]*Catholic Encyclopaedia.* 14, p. 228.

[80]See the discussion in Chapter II.

[81]Cf. Hans Küng, *Infallible?* and our earlier discussion of Inspiration.

Summary of Chapter X.

Interpreting the Bible:
A. Figure, Form and Content

Not only must we make a clear distinction between literal and figurative language, but also distinguish the different ways in which language can be figurative. For example, there are such types as the allegorical, the typological, the parabolic. We examine these, with the question in mind, 'In what senses, if at all, do these respective methods enable us to interpret the text, rather than give the text a preferred meaning?' Such types may have an historical form, being cast in the form of a story. But they are not historical. So when we are faced with a passage that is historical *in form*, we must ask, Is it or is it not in fact historical? This becomes of particular interest when cosmological convictions are expressed in such historical form.

X

INTERPRETING THE BIBLE: FIGURE, FORM AND CONTENT

1 LITERAL AND NON-LITERAL

Language is a sensitive and very varied instrument. It has many, many uses. It can be used very precisely, with exact definition, as with mathematical and legal terminology. It can be used suggestively, as with poetry, where the language chosen can lead the reader to make many and different associations. Most of our language for most of the time lies somewhere between the poles of exact precision and wide suggestiveness.

The distinction between literal and non-literal language is easy to recognize but rather more difficult to define. Non-literal language is of many kinds. We put it under the general head of 'figurative,' sometimes using other terms, calling it 'metaphorical,' 'symbolic,' 'oblique.' For example, we say that the sun sets and rises, that electricity flows and prices fall, that a machine works and that John is a mule. Because so much of our language is non-literal, when pressed, we find it difficult to say exactly what makes literal language differ from non-literal language. One way we can make the distinction is by saying that we do not have to think so much about the meaning of a literal statement as we do about the meaning of a figurative statement. One handbook on religious language suggests 'the less figurative a statement, the less reflecting on it we must do, before we can extract the information it contains and check its credentials.'[1]

Two points are worth noting here. The first is that figurative language may provide information. The second is that whether we understand the figure easily will depend on whether in our culture it is familiar and has an accepted meaning. Some figures of speech are readily understood. Some are, in fact, so readily understood, even taken for granted, that we do not have to think much about them at all. The ones we noticed above fall into that category. Moreover, some people have more imagination than others and are able to cope with metaphorical language more adequately. Some people are pedantic and literal-minded to the extent that unfamiliar metaphor is either taken literally or is not understood for the subtlety it has. It is then a barrier for communication. But we tend to become pedantic about conventional metaphor. We are no longer struck with its suggestiveness (for example: 'the suggestion is brilliant'). It becomes monotonous. We would more likely than not be impressed by such metaphors as: 'If you don't buck up you'll get fired,' 'John loves Bonzo with all his heart.' In a religious context, it is easy to take for granted such metaphors as 'word,' 'hear,' 'speak,' when Scripture 'speaks' of the believer 'hearing' the 'word' of God or of the prophet speaking God's 'word' So the suggestiveness of metaphor is stifled by custom

Figurative language may 'speak to' the emotions, may call forth from us certain emotional responses. For example, a well-told story may evoke an emotional response from us that may have little to do with whether it is or is not true. Figurative language may also serve to spike the will, to urge to action, as when (for example) a writer or speaker likens life to a contest and urges the hearer to exert effort.

But religious language claims to convey information, indeed to convey very important information, information with unique significance. Religious language that is metaphorical not only speaks to the emotions. It often makes claims. It intends to refer to what really is the case. The same truth can be expressed in different forms: in literal language and in metaphor. The difference is that metaphorical language does the job of informing in an oblique way and while requiring thought may also more readily evoke an emotional response.

To call God 'Father' is to use a metaphor. Through the use of metaphor it also makes a claim about God. But we can also tell a story about a father, and while telling the story not mention God at all. If we are unimaginative, we may take the story literally to be about something that happened. But if we take the story as figurative we shall try to discover what it tells us about God. The details may not be literally true, but the story intends to convey a meaning. It intends to teach us something true about God. The story of the Prodigal Son, or the waiting Father (as Thielicke called it) is thus an extended metaphor in narrative form.

The story of the lost sheep is not about sheep.[2] Its purpose is to suggest something about God. To say 'God is Father' does not mean that he has a female consort, who produces offspring. But it *claims* something. It claims that *in some respects* God is more like human fathers than not. We then have to go and think about it. As we do, we shall make some decisions as to what the term 'Father' suggests we may truthfully say about God. Figurative language often invites us to assess the claims it makes. Because it is figurative it often makes a more lasting impact upon us than literal language.

There are many kinds of figurative language: metaphor, simile, proverb, parable, allegory, type — to mention a few.

2 TYPES OF FIGURATIVE LANGUAGE: ALLEGORICAL

We shall concern ourselves now to distinguish parable, allegory and type, and provide biblical examples and ask how we may constructively interpret these different forms of expression.

The most puzzling form is probably the allegorical. The term 'allegory' is not a biblical term. In biblical terms it is not possible clearly to distinguish allegory, parable and type since the words used of metaphor in the Bible are less precise than our English terms. But we can use the term 'allegory' consistently. It refers to a story which uses a series of symbols, some of which it is difficult to fit together with the others. The details of the story are often complex, and each detail has a meaning. We cannot overlook any of them. The allegory, unlike the parable, is often not taken from the happenings and situations of ordinary life, but is fabricated, an imaginative setting together of often confusing symbols. The meaning of the symbols has to be grasped before the significance of the allegory as a whole is understood. In an allegory you may deliberately hide your meaning. The purpose here would be to convey your message only to those who understand the meaning of the symbols and to conceal it from everyone else. To indicate one thing you say another. You may be referring to Rome, but you use the term 'Babylon.'[3] You refer to the revival of Israel, but you talk about dead bones on a battlefield coming together to form living bodies.[4] You refer to the church, but you talk about Jerusalem.[5] Often the author puts individual references together with other such symbols and joins the whole up in a narrative form.

Now as far as Scripture is concerned we should make a distinction between different instances of allegory. For it has happened that passages not originally allegorical have been interpreted as allegorical. 'Allegorical interpretation' entails that the interpreter assumes that the terms in the passage are to be taken as symbols and he then sets about finding meanings for them taken as such. This method of interpretation, if the term 'method' is not too complimentary of it, has sometimes been used of texts not originally intended as allegories and not obviously to be taken as such, with often unusual and bizarre results. We usually need have little doubt whether the writing is allegorical or not.

So we must distinguish between (1) passages of Scripture which are allegorical in intention, are intended by the writer to be allegorical, and (2) passages of Scripture not obviously allegorical but taken as such and interpreted in another than the original sense.

In both cases the reader will have to figure out the meaning hidden in the figurative language (1), or the language which he takes as figurative (2). This may well require imagination and ingenuity. In the process the interpreter is likely to impose a meaning on the text very remote from what the author intended.

To make clear our distinction, we shall take some typical examples.

The first is Ezekiel's story, his 'riddle.' It is about seeds and trees, leaves and eagles and east winds. But at the same time it is not about seeds and trees and leaves and eagles and east winds. That is clear, first, from the story itself (17:3-10, 22-24) and second, from the words Ezekiel uses of the story. It is 'a riddle' or 'an allegory' (v. 2). The Hebrew terms connote metaphor but do not exactly correspond to the English term 'allegory.' Third, it is clear because the prophet provides an interpretation which renders the meaning he intended. This meaning is concerned with Judah's relations with Babylon and with Egypt and the dire consequences of failing to accede to the supremacy of Babylon, from whose capital city the prophet is writing, as a captive in exile with his people.

Here then is the story,[6] but without the interpretation.

> 'A great eagle with great wings and long pinions, rich in plumage of many colours, came to Lebanon and took the top of the cedar; he broke off the topmost of its young twigs and carried it to a land of trade, and set it in a city of merchants. Then he took of the seed of the land and planted it in fertile soil; he placed it beside abundant waters. He set it like a willow twig, and it sprouted and became a low spreading vine, and its branches turned toward him, and its roots remained where it stood. So it became a vine, and brought forth branches and put forth foliage.

> But there was another great eagle with great wings and much plumage; and behold, this vine bent its roots toward him, and shot forth its branches toward him that he might water it. From the bed where it was planted he transplanted it to good soil by abundant

waters, that it might bring forth branches, and bear fruit, and become a noble vine. Say, Thus says the Lord God: "Will it thrive? Will he not pull up its roots and cut off its branches, so that all its fresh sprouting leaves wither? It will not take a strong arm or many people to pull it from its roots. Behold, when it is transplanted, will it thrive? Will it not utterly wither when the east wind strikes it — wither away on the bed where it grew?"

Thus says the Lord God: "I myself will take a sprig from the lofty top of the cedar and will set it out; I will break off from the topmost of its young twigs a tender one, and I myself will plant it upon a high and lofty mountain; on the mountain height of Israel will I plant it, that it may bring forth boughs and bear fruit, and become a noble cedar; and under it will dwell all kinds of beasts; in the shade of its branches birds of every sort will nest. And all the trees of the field shall know that I the Lord bring low the high tree, and make high the low tree, dry up the green tree, and make the dry tree flourish. I the Lord have spoken, and I will do it."

The prophet spoke in the symbols which his hearers, rural and captive, readily understood, symbols very different from those which would appeal to an industrial urban dweller, free to pursue his own interests. As originally delivered, the story may well have stood by itself. The hearers would readily feel its impact and understand the message of the prophet. It was not about trees and animals but about the political situation and sane relations with superpowers, and the dire consequences of foolhardy attitudes and moves.

However, setting aside this cultural difference, the allegory of Ezekiel is very impressive. It does not strike one as being far-fetched. We know the historical situation and are able without too much difficulty to read ourselves into it. The symbols are maintained with consistency and strike us as being appropriate. This leads to an interpretation which strikes us as being historically pertinent. So the impression overall is of a highly successful employment of symbolism, with a directness of application which satisfies us.

The second kind is that of a text not intended as allegory, but allegorically interpreted, the interpreter giving a different meaning to the text than what it originally had. An instructive, but extreme, example of this is the story of the Good Samaritan, as interpreted by Augustine. We shall follow this with a further allegorical interpretation of the words of Genesis as it appears in the Epistle of Barnabas. 'And Abraham circumcised of his household eighteen males and three hundred.' In both of these cases an allegorical interpretation is *imposed* upon the text, since the text is not allegorical to begin with. And there is no saying what sort of interpretation that will be. There is no control over the interpretation and often the reader remains bewildered, even astonished, that anyone could lead the original text on such a dance. (See below).

There is, of course, no need to interpret the text in this way. There is no fit between text and meaning. In contrast to the example we have just considered there is lacking any sense of pertinence or appropriateness. We just wonder how the interpreter arrived where he did from where he started. Where the text is allegorical, an allegorical interpretation is *necessary* in order to render its meaning. But where the text is literal or parabolic, then the historical meaning or a simple application of the meaning of the whole, rather than a pressing of a meaning into every detail of the story, is required. To go beyond this is to do violence to the text. But when an interpreter is determined to extract a meaning which he considers important from a text, the lengths to which such a one is prepared to go are often quite surprising. If he is determined to make the obscure text meaningful he has here an instrument to hand. The attractiveness of the allegorical method of interpretation is in its capacity to extract some meaning from a text, however obscure that text might be. By means of allegory a meaning can be got from the text having no relation at all to the original meaning, but congenial for whatever reason to the interpreter.

Three alternatives emerge. The aim of the interpreter might be to discover the meaning the original writer had in mind; or, it might be to find a meaning in the text for oneself and one's own context. The alternatives then are: (1) to discover the original meaning; (2) to find meaning related to that original meaning, over which the original meaning exercised a control; (3) to find a meaning without regard to what the original meaning may have been.

The weakness of the allegorical method of interpretation is that it makes the third of these alternatives a *real* temptation. It provides us with a striking example of the ways open to an interpreter in handling the text, since (1)-(3) are alternatives for any interpretation and not only the allegorical interpretation.

Our first illustration is Augustine's treatment of the Good Samaritan.[7]

> '*A certain man went down from Jerusalem to Jericho*; Adam himself is meant; *Jerusalem* is the heavenly city of peace, from whose blessedness Adam fell; *Jericho* means the moon, and signifies our mortality, because it is born, waxes, wanes, and dies. *Thieves* are the devil and his angels. *Who stripped him*, namely, of his immortality; and beat him, by persuading him to sin; *and left him* half-dead because in so far as man can understand and know God he lives, but in so far as he is wasted and oppressed by sin, he is dead; he is therefore called half-dead. *The priest and Levite* who saw him and passed by, signify the priesthood and ministry of the Old Testament, which could profit nothing for salvation. *Samaritan* means Guardian, and therefore the Lord himself is signified by this name. The *binding* of the wounds is the restraint of sin. *Oil* is the comfort of good hope; wine the exhortation to work with fervent

spirit. The beast is the flesh in which He designed to come to us. The being *set upon the beast* is belief in the incarnation of Christ. The *inn* is the Church, where travellers returning to their heavenly country are refreshed after pilgrimage. The *morrow* is after the resurrection of the Lord. The *two pence* are either the two precepts of love or the promise of this life and of that which is to come. The *innkeeper* is the apostle (Paul). The supererogatory payment is either the counsel of celibacy or the fact that he worked with his own hands lest he should be a burden to any of the weaker brethren when the Gospel was new, though it was lawful for him 'to live by the Gospel.'[8]

The second illustration is taken from the *Epistle of Barnabas* and is his allegorical treatment of the statement in Genesis: 'Abraham circumcised of his household eighteen males and three hundred.'[9]

'Learn therefore, children. of love, concerning all things abundantly, that Abraham, who first appointed circumcision, looked forward in the spirit unto Jesus when he circumcised 'having received the ordinances of three letters. For the Scripture saith; *And Abraham circumcised of his household eighteen males and three hundred.* What then was the knowledge given unto him? Understand ye that He saith *the eighteen* first and then after an interval *three hundred.* In the eighteen I stands for ten, H for eight. Here thou hast JESUS (*IESOUS*). And because the cross in the T was to have grace, He saith also *three hundred.* So he revealeth Jesus in the two letters, and in the remaining one the cross. He who placed within us the innate gift of His covenant knoweth; no man hath ever learnt from me a more genuine word; but I know that ye are worthy.'[10]

It so happens that both the Greek and the English expressions for 300 begin with 'T.' The Greek is *triakosious.* The English is 'three hundred.' No doubt Barnabas is using the Septuagint, the Greek version. But there is not the slightest possibility of drawing out such a meaning from the Hebrew text. 'Ten' in Hebrew begins with *a* (*ayin*), 'eight' begins with *s* (*sin*) and 'three hundred' also begins with *s* (*sin*).

Using these exerpts as illustration we may now notice certain interesting features of allegorical interpretation.

(1) Each feature in the text, in the narrative, is given meaning. In this respect an allegory (that is a text which is allegorical in intention) differs from a parable which has one basic meaning. So Augustine has allegorized the parable of the Good Samaritan by finding meanings in each detail of the narrative. Barnabas has also made each term in the text, in the narrative, to have a meaning.[11]

(2) The meanings provided by the interpreter may be quite arbitrary. There is no control over them. A later writer, allegorizing the same parable, finds quite different meanings in them than Augustine did. By taking the original text as allegory, different meanings can be got out of it. At one time by the allegorical method one meaning is arrived at. At another time by the allegorical method another meaning is arrived at. That is why the allegorical method cannot simply be written off, since by using it an interpreter can make the Bible contemporary, could ensure that the Bible became a living book.

(3) We cannot specify consistent principles by which meaning is derived from the text. Who could tell by reading half of Augustine's interpretation how he will interpret the other half of the parable. We can hardly speak here of 'principles' of interpretation.

(4) Allegorical interpretation is rigidly attached to the text, indeed to the very letter of the text. The text is taken very seriously indeed. The text *must* be significant. It *must* have a meaning. The allegorical method ensures that it will get one (or more)! The allegorical method is based upon the words of Scripture. It is quite compatible with literalism.

In fact it supports literalism. There would be little point in emphasising the importance of the words of Scripture if, in the event, those words were found not to have meaning. Allegorical interpretation ensures that they have meaning.

(5) The two texts we selected are very different. Texts to which an allegorical interpretation is applied may be of many different kinds. They may, for example, be legal texts ('You shall not muzzle the ox when it is treading the grain'), love poetry (Song of Solomon), parable (The Good Samaritan), prediction ('out of Egypt will I call my Son'), historical or quasi-historical narrative (Abraham circumcised his male servants), apocalyptic vision (women in white and scarlet, destructive beasts).

The text may be allegorical to start with. As such it demands as its meaning a reference to something literal: an historical event, a personage, a contemporary state of affairs. But if, instead of making such an application of the text, one approaches it with certain presuppositions, a quite different course is possible — of allegorizing the original allegory.

An illustration — one among many we might take — may be found in the thirteenth chapter of the book of Revelation. Should one take the hints in the book literally that the expression 'the time is near'[12] means that the message of the book had contemporary importance, then the text will have a relevance to the situation of Christians of the first and second centuries. In that case the beasts of the chapter, which provide the allegory, would refer to Roman emperors who persecute and threaten the life and existence of the church. Should one approach the passage, as the book, with the presupposition that its message refers solely to the future, the distant future in particular, to a time when one might plausibly say that the Lord is coming 'quickly,' then other interpretations of its symbols will be sought. The beasts now become the ecclesiastical tyrant, or the oppressive modern state, or both in combination.

So one very serious question with regard to allegory arises, which calls for an answer: How shall one exercise a control over the process of interpretation? For it is a fact that 'certain Protestant minorities have turned to the allegorical method to substantiate doctrines that are not otherwise well grounded in Scripture.'[13]

So the use of the allegorical method may lead to an interpretation which is a metamorphosis of the text? 'After all 'in many instances, to interpret is to transform. . . .'[14] 'The possibilities of the text may be limited only by the interpreter's imagination unless the original meaning of the text or, for example, a contemporary set of doctrines, exercises control over those possibilities. If it is possible that an original meaning can exercise such control over subsequent meanings, we will first of all have to establish the literal and fundamental meaning.' That demands that we have an acceptable means of doing so. But the point in question is as to the appropriate method of interpretation. Should we establish the original meaning of the text in non-allegorical fashion, and then another meaning in allegorical fashion, how shall we justify using both methods, and how shall we defend the results which may be very different from one another?

It is obvious that if the allegorical method of interpretation is to be used with profit there must be some control over it.[15]

One normally hears two suggestions in this connection. First, the principles of interpretation must be consistently applied. Second, the resultant system must be consistent. Any method of interpretation must be consistent. So an allegorical method (i.e. a use of allegorical interpretation that is rather more than incidental) will have worked out certain principles and applied them consistently. Otherwise it will be arbitrary.

Moreover any resulting system of doctrine will have to be both intelligible and consistent. Allegorical interpretation may serve to produce components or support for a doctrinal system. Examples of this are Christian theories of atonement based upon allegorizing the priesthood and temple service of the Hebrews, or further, eschatological schemes based on the symbolism of the apocalyptic sections of the Bible and proposing to forecast literal events of the end-time. When this happens there is a two-way traffic.

Allegorical interpretation makes possible and lends support to the system. The system provides categories and sets limits to the process of interpretation. The system demands the allegorical method of interpretation. The allegorical interpretation supports the system. This system may be a doctrinal system comprehending the whole range of Christian doctrines and not simply an eschatological system. An allegorical method of interpretation may be used to support these teachings. So, if one has already worked out a system one will fit the particular passage into that system. So 'the beast,' or 'the thousand years' or 'the priestly work of Jesus' can look different in different doctrinal systems. Supporters of those different systems may well employ (at least in part) the allegorical methods of interpretation to sustain them. By means of the allegorical method support can be found which otherwise would be lacking.

Since allegorical interpretation assumes that what is *meant* is something other than what is *said* in the text, such support (once the process has started) is not difficult to find. It is found along certain lines as the system demands. A system of doctrine has a certain momentum of its own. The end product must be consistent. Any interpretation which does not fit the system is rejected and the limits of possible interpretations are thereby controlled. While there might be many possible plausible interpretations of say, the thirteenth chapter of Revelation, the system already constructed will largely determine how the particular allegories used there will be interpreted. To take another example, If one allegorizes the Temple Service of ancient Israel, that is, provides an allegorical interpretation of it, one may find a complete system of doctrine implicit: Jesus, the atonement, remission of guilt by death, the church, the believer, the sinner, the judgment, God the judge, the Mediator, the cross, forgiveness, final rewards and punishments. Provided that the resultant system is consistent, plausibility appears to be given to the method of interpretation by which such a system is reached. After all it is the biblical text which is the source of the exposition, and that in itself is crucial for the claims of this kind of interpreter.

The allegorical method of interpretation makes it possible for passages of Scripture which might otherwise be embarrassing or obscure to receive a meaning congenial to Christian interpreters. But we face a real difficulty if we cannot use such a method of interpretation.

One form in which the question concerning our use of Scripture arises is as follows: Having taken over the Jewish books as a whole what is the Christian interpreter going to make of its very different components? With some the Christian interpreter will have no difficulty whatever. With others he will have to make up his mind if he is serious. If we simply choose to be indifferent and overlook whole chunks of the Old Testament, let us recognize our practice in doing so, and put our practice into theory, and produce an honest doctrine of Scripture. We are not particularly concerned, let alone inspired, by knowing how ancient farmers treated their oxen. And *we*, even if Paul did, cannot allegorize the passage. So we let it alone. We don't like the Jehu story. So we leave it alone. We are embarrassed by the Song of Solomon. So we leave it alone. In this way we overlook whole portions of Scripture.

It was because the Old Testament was in places problematic, and because certain Christian interpreters were very serious about getting a meaning for themselves out of the Old Testament that they used the allegorical method of interpreting it. In this way a spiritual meaning could be extracted from Scripture One great benefit was gained by the allegorical method of interpretation. It permitted one to recognize that there were real difficulties in the historical accounts, and it enabled one to be quite explicit that some things in Scripture could not be taken literally. To allegorize Scripture meant that one was taking it in all earnestness. It had to be made to render its meaning, however difficult that was. The allegorical method ensured that the interpreter who used it arrived at a meaning. Moreover, one admitted the ultimate mystery of Scripture, finding in it both the literal and the non-literal. An ancient theologian made the crucial distinction. So, the exact reader must carefully ascertain in how far the literal meaning is true, and in how far impossible; and so far as he can, trace out, by means of similar statements, the meaning everywhere scattered through Scripture of that which cannot be understood in a literal signification.[16]

Origen distinguished between the simple believer who could only understand the 'literal' meaning and the spiritual believer who appreciated and found edification in the spiritual or allegorical meaning, which the simple believer could not attain.

What the 'spiritual' believer attained was a rendering of difficult, embarrassing, and misleading passages of Scripture. But should we call it an *interpretation* of the text? Has allegory made so free with the text that it is like someone sitting at the piano with the score of Beethoven's Moonlight Sonata in front of him and producing something like 'Oh! What a beautiful morning'? If we ask how it is possible to connect the meaning which such an interpreter gives to a text with the meaning which the author of the text intended, the answer is that there is no reason why we should. By using the allegorical method of interpretation the text could be given a 'nose of wax' (Luther's expression) which could be turned in any direction. By allegorizing a text, one could read into a biblical passage a meaning which its author did not intend and would not have understood.[17] If that is so, can we say that we are *interpreting* the text? Is it 'interpreting' a text to make it render whatever one will?

Allegorization provides a method of handling the text for those who desire to take it seriously. The fact is that the allegorical method 'was not opposed to literalism, but was a necessary complement of it. . . . Allegorism presented an acceptable method of dealing with the scandals created by a literalist theory of biblical inspiration.'[18] The Bible is to be taken as the authoritative word of God. An allegorical interpretation renders a divine meaning to passages which otherwise could not bear it. Take the Song of Solomon as a love poem and it has no divine authority, interpret it allegorically, and it assumes a quite different status. It is now made to teach lessons about God's care for the church. It is no wonder that the allegorical method was sometimes called the spiritual method of interpreting Scripture. It is no wonder that Origen, astute, devoted and imaginative, quite explicitly embraced the allegorical method as a way out of his difficulties.

That a writing is interpreted allegorically is not simply a sign of the seriousness with which it is taken. It is a sign that one considers that writing to be especially important. 'Only in a book which is regarded as possessing peculiar sacredness and authority is the attempt made to elicit another sense from the words than the obvious and literal one.' 'The use of allegory implies a sacred text.'[19] The text is *so* important. Because it was so important, set apart from all other writings, there had to be a way of rendering it meaningful. One invested the text with meaning. One then professed to have rendered the appropriate meaning of the text. No wonder the allegorical method was attractive. No wonder it produced contradictory and unpredictable results.

It is obviously not satisfactory to claim that Scripture is inspired and authoritative in all its parts and then to ignore much of it because it is offensive or incomprehensible. So one tries to gain some sort of moral edification from the accounts of the sins, crimes and weaknesses of the characters of the Bible. At least one did not just pass over the stories. Instead of ignoring them, one drew spiritual lessons from the stories of sin — for example the sins of the patriarchs. Augustine wrote:

> If he reads of the sins of great men, even though he can see and verify in them figures of future things, he may put the nature of things done to this use, that he will never hear himself boast of his own virtuous deeds and condemn others. . . .[20]

The gist of Augustine's answer is that the immoralities of the Bible characters are allowed so that we may be spiritually edified, and educated, by coming to recognise that we have no reason for boasting. That is an odd theory indeed, but one which provided a galaxy of spiritual meanings for those puzzled by obvious difficulties in the stories which were an offence to their moral sensibility.

It was not until the coming of the historical method that the nineteenth century produced a more satisfactory alternative to allegorization as a method. Before this development the allegorical method provided an escape route from embarrassing problems.

3 TYPES OF FIGURATIVE LANGUAGE: TYPOLOGICAL

The *typological* has often been considered distinct from the allegorical method, on the following grounds.

Two situations, occasions, events are related to one another in such a way that a resemblance can be drawn between them. One historical occasion bears a striking resemblance to another historical occasion so that for some purpose, they can be matched. For example, Abraham's having faith and leaving everything is a type of the Christian's faith (Romans 4). Moses on Sinai is a type of Jesus on the Mount (Matthew 5). The Israelites return to Canaan is a type of the Christians' reward (Hebrews 4).[21]

One may then quite simply define typology as '. . . a way of seeing events of the Old Testament as forerunners and anticipations of definitive events in the New.'[22] The former can be taken as an anticipation of the latter, even a pre-figuring of the latter. A double selection takes place. The later situation or event will be selected and then related to the former event, which has also been selected. The latter is seen as fulfilment of the former. What 'fulfilment' means has then to be explained. Does it mean 'completion,' or 'explication of what was implicit,' 'a rendering otiose of it'?

The typological method of interpretation may be extended to refer to persons and to places, but, so it is held, the historical connection is evident in all instances. To speak of *prefiguring* suggests the historical connection, in contrast to *signifying*, which does not.[23] The experiences of Israel in the desert prefigure

Christian sacraments. That is typology. The rock is Christ. That is allegory.[24]

For a Christian typologist, the typology serves a Christological purpose. From a Christological point of view the events, persons and places so selected foreshadow Jesus Christ. The following is a clear statement of this principle. 'The same God who revealed himself in Christ has also left his footprints in the history of the Old Testament covenant people . . . we have to do with *one* divine discourse, here to the fathers through the prophets, there to us through Jesus Christ' (Hebrews 1:1).[25] We need the Old Testament witness so that we can understand Christ. 'Christ is given to us only through the double witness of those who await and those who remember.' To understand Christian faith one must think about God's saving acts in the past. One then sees that the pattern of God's saving activity repeats itself. Two sets of events are connected.

Typology is tied to history, whereas allegory is not. History is seen as a unity. God is seen as one. The one God reveals himself throughout the whole course of history. One event through which God reveals himself can be related to another such event and both can be illuminated in the relationship.

The conviction of the New Testament is that God acted in the history of the Hebrew people and that their history as a whole and events within that history found fulfilment in the coming of Jesus and the event of the coming to be of the church. So Old Testament history is seen as prophetic, not in the sense of the particular of specific oracles spoken by the prophet, but as a whole history. God's promise as he dealt with the people of the Old Covenant is now fulfilled in Jesus' coming. So 'history itself becomes prophetic.'[26] The deliverance from Egypt becomes a prototype, finding fulfilment in the events of the New Testament.

The possibility thus opens up of seeing events in the life of Jesus as fulfilment of the prototypes in the Old Testament. Jesus' cry from the Cross reflects the words of the Psalmist (Matthew 27:34-39, Psalm 22). The feeding of the five thousand echoes the experience of Elisha (John 6:9-15, II Kings 4:42-44). Jacob's dream of a ladder between heaven and earth features in Jesus' reply to Nathanael (John 1:51, Genesis 28:12). Moses' forty days of fasting while receiving the Tablets of the Law is a prototype of Jesus forty days in the wilderness (Mark 1:12, Exodus 34:28). 'The time is fulfilled', *peplerotai ho kairos* (Mark 1:15) The Greek verb suggests completion, accomplishment, fulfilment, and not just passage of time. So, 'The time has come' is not a satisfactory translation.

Because the New Testament writers discerned the fulfilment of the whole covenant history of the Old Testament in the events of their time they could find in those writings and events significant prototypes of particular incidents in the history of Jesus Christ and the emergence of the Christian communities. This is clearly evident in the Gospels and in Paul.

Typology is not bound to the letter of Scripture. In that respect, it is free. But it is 'bound to a much greater degree by the historical sense' of the passage. Gerhard von Rad contrasts typology to the 'rigid attachment to the text' and the 'unbridled freedom in matters of spiritual interpretation'[27] in the case of allegory. We have seen that it is because the letter of the text is taken so seriously that, when it is impossible to interpret it literally, the text is allegorized.

Bruce Vawter makes the same contrast as does von Rad. 'Typology's main presupposition is simply that there is a providential connection between the persons and events who have been bound together in a common salvific history.' 'Allegorism on the other hand, is always unhistorical and usually anti-historical. It approaches its Scriptures not for the purposes of discerning in them a pattern of historical revelation; but rather as a source of absolutely normative words that can be fitted to any present requirement.'[28]

But the contrast may not be as clear-cut as these quotations suggest. James Barr is more cautious and warns against such categorical definitions. He asserts: 'Allegory cannot be *categorically* described as anti-historical,' 'we cannot make this into an ultimate distinction from typology.'[29]

Several issues have come to light in the course of our discussion.

(1) It may well be that we cannot make a strict division between allegory and typology But as a general guide to different methods of interpretation the distinction is useful and should be allowed to stand. We can make without difficulty whatever qualifications are necessary, to take account of instances which do not neatly fit the one or the other.

(2) We may find the distinction between allegory and typology useful in making a general contrast between certain distinguishable types of interpretation, both of biblical and non-biblical sources. Perhaps we should think of the distinction as between two ideal types to which now some usages will rather well approximate and now some other usages.

(3) The third issue concerns the subjectivity of the allegorical interpretation. It is commonly claimed that the allegorical method of interpretation is subjective. There are several reasons for this. First, the allegorical method cannot be concerned about and so cannot do proper justice to the original text, and so to the understanding of the original readers.[30] Second, such interpretation reduces the originator, i.e. the author, to an anonymous instrument and hence has no respect for his genuine humanity and historicity. Third, by a meeting of opposites, allegorical interpretation combines an undue emphasis on the letter of the text with an unwarrantable freedom in handling it, a freedom leading to license. In the sense that it does not respect the original meaning and intention it is non-historical. Finally, for allegorical interpretation the goal and purpose of the interpreter are more important than the text. So the text is interpreted to support a doctrinal or an eschatological system without due regard for the text itself. That represents a failure of respect which ill accords with respect for Scripture and with a 'high'

doctrine of the inspiration of Scripture and of its authority. This is paradoxical since the traditional theory of inspiration laid great emphasis on the importance of the actual text.

4 TYPES OF FIGURATIVE LANGUAGE: PARABOLIC

Another form of figurative language which features in the Bible is the parable. A parable is a story. The meaning is presented in narrative form. The truth which the parable conveys is not the literal truth of the narrative. The story may be literally true. It may not. It does not matter. There may have been a prodigal son and a waiting father.[31] There may not. The point of the parable does not depend on whether there was or was not. There was no rich man who roasted in hell and called for water.[32] That story is an imaginative construction. So one has to ask, 'What is the meaning of the story of the roaming and returning 'unclean spirit,'[33] or of the sower and his seed,[34] or of the binding of the strong man?'[35]

The form of the parable is relatively simple. Two things are put beside one another, and one point is drawn from or intended by, the comparison. The term *para-bole* means literally '(something) set, cast or put beside (something else'). Two things are put side by side so that, when compared, a feature or features of the one illuminates the other and understanding results. The mustard seed is 'put beside' the Kingdom of God. The waiting father is 'put beside' God. If you think about the stories, you will perceive something about the meaning of the 'Kingdom of God' or of the nature of God.

The parable differs from the allegory in that the meaning it conveys is neither difficult nor complicated. Normally the parable has one meaning, making one point, or several closely related points. Once you see the meaning of the parable you can make up your mind about it. Sometimes the meaning is so clear that no explanation is needed. In this respect it contrasts to the obscurity of the allegory. In order to get the meaning of the parable it is essential to understand the context and the relations it implies, since some one feature of the parable may give the clue as to the meaning of the whole, as for example the amount of dough in the parable of the leaven.[36]

Since something in the story, or the story as a whole, corresponds to and illuminates something in the situation or the situation as a whole, you must think both about the situation and about the story. In that respect it is like seeing the point of a cartoon You have to have eyes to see and ears to hear. Otherwise the meaning will elude you.[37] The story may entertain you because it is interesting. But you are also supposed to get the point it is trying to make.

It should be clear that the contextual question arises with the parable as with other symbolic forms of expression. So there was a situation when Jesus originally spoke his parables, around A.D. 30. A new eschatological prophet arises and speaks about the Kingdom of God andd the 'Son of Man'. There is another kind of situation a generation or so later. Jesus has died. The new community called the church has come into being. It must now face a whole range of problems living in the Roman Empire as a threatened minority. One of these is that the Second Advent it had expected did not happen. We contemporarty readers have our own situation. So the parable then has its third context, remote from either of the others.

So we may and must ask different questions of the parable. What does it *say*? What *did* it mean? What *does* it mean? In answering the question of meaning, we must have a sense of what is appropriate in each of the three settings we have mentioned, and try to maintain a harmony between them.

5 HISTORICAL NARRATIVE

Historical narrative is literal not metaphorical. The episodes and persons in the narrative are taken at face value. Allegory and parable have a narrative form. But their intention is not to inform us of facts as does historical narrative. So the *historical narrative* is crucially different from allegory, parable and myth, although each of these, too, has a narrative form.

An initial decision has to be taken then when we are faced with a passage in Scripture whose form is narrative. It is a matter of deciding about the intention of the author who writes in the narrative form. By 'narrative' we mean that it is put in the form of a story. One form of narrative is historical. But the writing is not necessarily historical because it is put in narrative form. The question, 'What does the narrative mean?' may lead to different answers. It is only literary ignorance that would wish to dispute that. The subject matter of the narrative form is very varied.

Many narrative passages in Scripture can be assessed as historical accounts of what happened in the past. They give us information about the past. So they are to be evaluated according to the rules of historical research.

Other passages may be historically informative and also point to a meaning beyond their historical information. A typological approach finds a meaning in selected historical episodes, as we have seen.

Other passages in narrative form are not literally true. We must ask of these, 'What did they mean? What do they mean?' and use the right methods to give a reasonable answer to these two different questions.

The following subject matter is put in narrative form in the Bible:

(1)   the doings of men and women: for example, the story of Jesus' trial in Jerusalem under Pilate; the story of Paul's trial at Caesarea and his voyage to Rome.

(2)   the acts of God: for example, God's creating the physical universe, the 'heaven and the earth.'

(3)   the doings of supernatural beings in relation to men and women: for example, the story of God, Satan and Job; and of the annunciation to the Virgin Mary.

(4) the doings of God, angels, demons, men and women at the end time: for example, the apocalyptic narrative of the resurrection and the Holy City.

In each case the text is in story form. Only in the first case is the narrative historical i.e. 'appropriate subject matter for historical inquiry.' The historian just has no way of handling the other kinds of narrative, since their significance is theological. To make this distinction different writers use different terms. What is important is that the distinction between (1) and (2) - (4) should be quite clear.

What is put in the form of (historical) narrative may refer to what is beyond the limits of human history. A narrative form portrays the divine and superhuman both at the beginning time and at the end time. History has limits. Because of this we must distinguish between narrative which portrays what is beyond history, and narrative which portrays what is within history. That is an elementary but vital distinction. By definition, history means human beings in relation with nature and in interaction with one another. Historical events and relations are such as can be reconstructed from evidence. The term 'history' has two meanings. History is (1) what the historian studies, human events and (2) what he writes, reports and interpretations of (1).

Narrative which portrays what is beyond history is not *historical* narrative. That is a simple matter of definition. To be clear we may give different terms to these two literary forms. We might call the one 'narrative symbol' or 'symbolic narrative' (The terms 'saga' and 'myth' have also been used.) and the other 'historical narrative.' There would be one ambiguity here. For, as we pointed out above, an historical episode might be taken as also symbolic, for example, the Exodus of the slave people from Egypt or the return of the exiles to their homeland. The narrative is then both historically true and symbolically meaningful, as it can be taken as allegory, parable or type. A narrative form which takes us beyond the limits of history cannot be literally true: for example, the myths of the gods in the Babylonian creation and flood stories. But they can be profoundly meaningful.

So the questions the interpreter, that is, anyone who reads the biblical literature with any serious intention of understanding it, will ask with regard to the stories of the Bible, those passages cast in a narrative form, are as follows: Is the story literally true? That means: Is it to be taken as historical, giving information about what happened in the past in a straightforward way? Or, does the story indicate a meaning but is not literally true? If so, the reader will seek to find the meaning and then be led to ask: Is the meaning true? Does it have theological meaning and if so what is it? Can I appropriate that theological meaning? A further question arises when the narrative *is* historical and also is given a symbolic meaning. Is the proposed meaning appropriate?

6 PREDICTION AND FULFILMENT

Some interpretations of the Bible emphasize the predictive elements in Scripture. The interpreter explains that they are related to later events, and claims these events as 'fulfilments.' So *Matthew* sees the passage 'Out of Egypt I have called my son' not as a reminiscence of a past event, but as a prediction of a future event. He then correlates the passage *taken as a prediction* (as it was not in its original context) with the event of the journey of the infant Jesus and his parents into Egypt.[38] He performs this interpretive feat for a particular purpose, namely, to indicate the divine guidance in the events of Jesus' life, and to display those events as the fulfilment, the culmination of Jewish history and of Jewish expectation. The passage from *Hosea* (11:1) is one of many which assist him in his purpose.

The activity of the Hebrew prophet *whatever he did*, and of course he performed a great many activities, was primarily (and by means of his many activities) to mediate an understanding of the purpose of God to his people. He did this in a different way from the priest and the king who were also mediating figures. The prophet spoke God's word. He interpreted the will of God to the people by speaking and by acting. He interpreted events in the light of his understanding of God's will, which he often claimed had been revealed to him in particular. He saw himself as the instrument of God's revelation. He speaks 'on behalf of' ('pro') God. Prediction, when and if it occurred, was just one aspect, one function, of the prophet's total activity. In some cases, it was a relatively minor part. To equate prophecy with prediction is a grave mistake.

To speak then of the 'fulfilment of prophecy,' is to construe prophecy as prediction. That is not at all the obvious thing to do. Before speaking of prophecy as being fulfilled, the interpreter has to take the passage he is interpreting as a prediction. We saw how Matthew did that to a passage which was not predictive. The interpreter would then if we showed interest have to persuade us that what he is doing is a right and proper procedure, and not simply arbitrary. So if the interpreter sees a particular passage as predictive, or predictive in a certain way we must ask, What is the justification for his taking the passage in that way? On what basis does one judge that a passage is predictive? What constitutes a relationship of prediction and fulfilment and what grounds can be provided for claiming such a relationship? Those are important questions. Passages in the Old Testament, not having any particular and obvious predictive reference, have often been taken by later interpreters to be predictive. Such interpreters often claimed that the predictive reference was the primary one and this led to a neglect of the contextual meaning and reference of such passages.

When passages were taken as predictive by the earliest Christian writers and related to the events of Jesus and of Christian faith, that refleced Christian conviction, not the intention of the passages quoted so frequently. 'The interpretation of Hebrew prophecy as prediction of Christ's coming is a misleading method of presenting in popular form one of Christianity's basic beliefs.'[39] That was the belief that God had brought about the fulfilment of his age-old purpose in the coming of Jesus Christ.

The prophets are not fatalistic. That is to say they do not believe that the future is pre-determined. Prediction implies that it is. But the prophets were not so much concerned 'to predict the future but to shape it.'[40] That does not mean that the prophets had no concern for the future. They had a very real concern. It led them to attempt to set in train events which would lead to a different future than would come without their intervention. They were creative. They were often the real power, rather than the kings, behind the initiation of events in Judah and in Israel. Their conviction was that God was the Lord of history, and that they were his agents in the fulfilment of his purposes. 'The characteristic contribution of prophecy to knowledge of the future is not the revelation of any detailed sequence of events (which is *never* to be found), but the insight which sees the master-plan of the living and purposeful God within the complexity of events.'[41] It was that purpose which the writers of the New Testament discerned had come to its fulfilment in Jesus Christ.

The prophet may sometimes have intended his words as predictive. He may not. Where he did not, the interpreter will have to make out a case for taking them as prediction. He cannot simply assume that he can take that for granted. The interpreter must begin in each case by inquiring into the meaning of the text for the original authors and audience. Every writing comes out of and therefore reflects a particular historical situation. The interpreter fails in his responsibility if he neglects such particularity. This is so fundamental that it scarcely needs mentioning. But within certain church contexts people are so keen to interpret texts in a certain pattern that they neglect it or deliberately refuse to examine that historical particularity.

Where the interpreter must justify his taking passages as predictive he may do so in two main ways. He must show that the oracle can be connected with the event or events which he claims to be fulfilment. There are degrees of clarity here. Some events clearly fulfil the prediction. Some may be said to fulfil them. With others it demands some imagination to propose a fulfilment. One must 'see' that there is a 'fit' between the passage taken as prediction and the event taken as fulfilment. One ought also to reflect upon how one makes the connection. That means arguing the case, perhaps working out a system. It is not a simple, to-be-taken-for-granted procedure. There is nothing inevitable about it. It is a construction.

A second main way is rather different. The interpreters appeal to the traditions and experience of their community, which community claims that it is itself an example of the fulfilment of prediction. A 'prophetic movement,' in its basic meaning, is a community which 'speaks the word of the Lord.' But a group may take itself to be one which has come about in 'fulfilment of prophecy.' That is an interesting claim, since there is nothing inevitable or mechanical about the occurrence of historical events. Historical events are probable and contingent, not necessary. When a religious group claims that its existence fulfils prophecy, it relates passages of Scripture it takes as predictive to its teaching, to its origins, to its continuing existence and to its future. Such a group must reflect upon its existence and upon particular passages of Scripture, which it finds it can interpret in relation to itself. As it does so it grows in self-confidence, not to say in pride. The argument (and it must not be forgotten that it is an argument) is that the very existence of the community is confirmation of the predictions to which it refers, and of the interpretation which sees the writings as predictions.

7 A CASE STUDY

To illustrate we shall take a brief case study.

The Seventh-day Adventist claims that the church came into being as a fulfilment of prophecy. Therefore it is divinely appointed and was and is divinely guided in its teachings and in its organisation. Its existence and success is no accident and its future is assured. Its apocalyptic scheme is to be taken as a literal account of future end events.[42]

A brief general comment, then, about apocalyptic should be helpful in putting things in perspective.

Apocalyptic is to be distinguished from prophecy in several ways. It succeeded classical prophecy in the Hebrew community. It was, that is to say, late in the Hebrew tradition. The New

Testament book called the Revelation, the Latin translation of the Greek word *apokalupsis*, is modelled on the Hebrew apocalypses. To read these and other apocalyptic writings is to understand that this represents a unique form of writing, one especially suitable for particular circumstances: times of persecution for example, when the 'powers that be,' i.e. the Roman state, that were the cause of suffering, could not be explicitly named. The continuous use of symbols ensured that those in the know would, if they applied themselves, get the message and that nobody else would.

Apocalyptic has an eschatological interest. It is concerned with the time of the end. The community to which the coded messages are directed is living in crisis. The end is near. Response is urgent. What the prophets, on those occasions when they looked forward, placed at some time in the future, the apocalyptists say is now taking place, or is imminent. Eschatological meaning is given to prophetic passages. So the groups to whom the writers addressed their apocalypses saw themselves as living on the knife-edge, at the very last frontiers of history, at the moment just before God will take his final step and close the human story. Apocalyptic, one writer says,

> created an atmosphere in which reformist sects were encouraged to see themselves, along with their own constitutions, practices, leaders, vicissitudes, enemies and persecutors, as representing a final stage in the great world drama which could under apocalyptic conditions, be surveyed from beginning to end.[43]

Apocalyptic groups are unique when compared to non-apocalyptic groups. They are not unique when compared to one another.

We have suggested two ways in which the interpreter might seek to justify taking texts as prediction and interpret them in terms of a fulfilment about which he is certain. We may now suggest two further ways. He may appeal to the consistency of his eschatological scheme. He may, also, appeal to authorities which endorse the interpretation and the method of interpretation. Where available, these should be independent of the sources and the tradition of interpretation.[44]

The second way is to claim divine authority *within* the group of such a kind that claims to put the correctness of intepretation beyond question. If there is a particular manifestation of divine guidance which guarantees the truth of doctrinal proposition the the propositions are, it is argued, put beyond question.[45]

We return to the point at which we began this discussion of fulfilment. Where events are said to fulfil predictions, the Christian theist claims that the connection of the events is not simply fortuitous. That is a theological assertion and is not to be taken for granted. Why should we not think of history as just one series of events after another series of events, after another, after another? Celebrated historians have done so. It is not to be taken for granted that history is meaningful. We may find a meaning, a pattern in history if we see historical events from a point of view. But then we recognise that *that* perspective is *our* perspective. There are alternatives. The theist's perspective, which results from the very revelation which it claims to represent,[46] is that God has acted within human history. So, history has a unity which it otherwise would not have. The argument from prophecy[47] puts this conviction in a particular way by saying: Only God could have done it. Only God could have known it. Only God could have revealed it. Therefore the propositions of the Bible are true. Behind this argument there lies the important insight that historical events are not accidental, and for the reason that God is active in the whole course of events. It is a good question whether this is an assumption made or a conclusion drawn by the Christian theist. At any rate it means that he will have to make clear what he means when he speaks of God 'acting.'

8 MYTH

We shall now discuss the question of myth, since in a serious book about the understanding of the Bible it is unavoidable.

Moreover it is interesting. But we immediately face a difficult problem. Albert Schweitzer said that he did not find the term offensive.[48] But many people have and still do. We might question whether the term would ever come into general use in popular Christian circles.[49] The problem is that the term suggests meanings which are rejected by Christians in reference to the Bible. For many people the term 'myth' not only suggests (1) something that is not literally true, but also (2) delusion, falsehood, imposture. They can accommodate the first of these, for they are aware of the importance of metaphor in the Bible. They are quite familiar with the parable and know that the story does not have to be factually true to convey an important meaning. They are aware of the non-literalness of the allegory and neither of these offends them. But there hangs on to the term 'myth' the suggestion of fanciful unreality and here they baulk at the suggestion of myth in the Scriptures. The term has other meanings: (3) ideas, including ideas about God, expressed in narrative form; and (4) doctrines also expressed in narrative form. Let us first deny (2) as a necessary part of the meaning of the term, 'myth.' We may then let the term suggest that narrative may be symbolic of meaning. We shall then understand such symbolic narrative when we probe more significant and important questions, than 'Did it happen that way?' We shall ask 'What understanding, what meaning is the writer trying to convey to us through this narrative expression? What meaning does the narrative have for us in our day and age?'

The problem is that even when someone has defined his understanding of the term 'myth' with some precision, the popular response to the term is based on those elements which one may have excluded by definition. So perhaps the term will never become serviceable as a neutral word for a particular kind of narrative symbol. That, of course, does not mean that there are no such narrative symbols, distinguishable from the parable, and the allegory.

'Myth' means a certain kind of narrative symbolism. Myth provides a framework which enables one to present one's symbols as a unity, and hence to evoke a response to the series of symbols taken as a whole. One might, for example, draw a contrast between the manner in which the scientist or the historian talks about beginnings in answering the question, 'What happened at the beginning?' with the way the theologian addresses himself to what appears to be the same question,[50] since the words in the sentence are the same. How does one, how *can* one speak of what is beyond the limits of our scientific and historical knowledge? We can ask about what lies at the limits of our knowledge and our experience. Such transcendence obliges us to speak in symbols. Genesis does so by telling a story about the creation.

But to understand the symbols we must examine our experience. Symbols have meaning as they have reference to our experience, personal or corporate. They are cashed in our experience. The narrative symbol, myth, like other forms of symbolism is cashed in our experience. We find that a story 'rings true' as we say. It finds a response in our experience. It shows itself to be appropriate as we relate it to our experience.

We have seen that our experience is very different from the experience of ancient people. So we may have a real problem: to get into their world. Their experience provided the context of the original symbols they used. Their form of expression is so different from ours.

Myth is in certain respects like allegory. Both have a narrative form. The narrative form is not to be interpreted literally but as providing a framework within which the writer suggests meanings. The narrative is not to be taken as historical, even if there are ties with historical events. We have to find an appropriate method of rendering the ideas behind the narrative, before we ask about its meaning, its truth, or its appropriateness.

D.F. Strauss, whose work on the Gospels in 1855-6, introduced the idea of myth into biblical theology in a comprehensive way, drew out the similarity between allegory and myth. He wrote:

> The mythical and the allegorical view (as also the moral) equally allow that the historian apparently relates that which is historical, but they suppose him,

under the influence of a higher inspiration known or unbeknown to himself, to have made use of this historical semblance merely as the shell of an *idea* — of a religious conception (65).[51]

Both the mythical and the allegorical use a narrative form, but the narrative is not to be taken *au pied de la lettre*. The form is the means to express an idea. You have to penetrate behind the form to the idea being expressed through it, have to penetrate the shell (which resembles an historical account) to the kernel.

The difference between allegory and myth, for Strauss, is that in allegory the narrative has a supernatural source, whereas in myth it does not. There is a natural, that is a cultural, process in which myths are originated and developed. In that respect myth is like legend. He can in principle therefore give an historical account of the process which produces a myth. We focus on the human creativity which produces the story. The myth was like the legend in this respect, in that it was produced by the community and expressed the spirit, the ethos, of that community. It was different from the legend in that the myth expressed an abstract idea, an eternal truth.

D.F. Strauss devoted his attention to the Gospels and his inquiries led to two lines of questioning. (1) If the stories of the Gospels are *not* to be taken literally, what is the meaning they intended to convey? Whether they are historically grounded (or not) is a matter of historical judgment. At any rate they have the function of enshrining a meaning. One understands the point of the story when one grasps the meaning which that story enshrines. (2) The suggestion that the narratives were contextual products led to new questions about the New Testament, about the composition of the individual stories and of the Gospels in which such stories were put together. The introduction on the grand scale of the concept of myth (in a rather carefully defined sense) had important theological and historical consequences.

Often there *is* an historical element in myth. That statement means first, that the narrative may point to an event and second, that the myth functions to enable a community to understand its present. There is no call to deny on principle that the events which feature in the story actually took place. It is an historical task to provide evidence of the truth of such statements and, where possible, to make a judgment about it.

Strauss, for his part, recognised three kinds of myth. The first he called *historical myths*. These are narratives of real events in which the divine and the human, the natural and the supernatural are not distinguished. *Philosophical myths* express thoughts and ideas in historical garb. *Poetical myths* are a blending of the two. In any case 'sensible imagery' is used, language drawn from the senses (seeing, hearing etc.) The language of myth is drawn from the concrete world rather than from the realm of abstract ideas. Often there is an historical foundation (54). In any case one has to get inside the 'shell,' to the 'kernel,' not assuming that the point of the narrative is to provide us with a straightforward historical account. One has to ask what 'higher meaning,' what 'divine significance' the narrative may disclose.

Before Strauss, others had written 'Lives' of Jesus. These were of two kinds. There were those who assumed that the historical form always indicated actual historical events. Such writers were quite content to take the text as historical and ask nothing further. For these it was as if the possibility that an historical form might serve to convey meaning were not to be considered. Such people produced the 'supernaturalistic' *Lives*. On the other hand there were the 'rationalist' *Lives*. Their writers assumed that all the stories had a natural explanation. Where the story told of a miracle it could be explained rationally. In each case the miracles were explained as natural events. What the Gospels presented as extraordinary events, could be explained in non-supernatural terms. The Gospels presented them as extraordinary events which in fact they were not, since one could provide an alternative explanation, one which showed that a quite straightforward event was at the back of the miracle story. Reference to natural causes was all that was required for explanation.

Strauss takes those who hold the former of these attitudes to task, because they overlook the depth that there is to the story. For such supernaturalism, it is enough to know that the event happened the way it is set down in the text. Such a naively historical attitude has no desire to press further and ask what meaning the story intends to convey. Such a person, he writes, 'clings with childlike fondness to the empty husk of historical semblance, though void of divine significance, and estimates it higher than the most valuable kernel divested of its variegated covering' (66).

Strauss, contrary to the assessment people made of him in the aftermath of the publication of his book, was not determined to be sceptical about the Gospels. In this respect, he was no different from other scholars of his time, in that he raised historical questions about the Gospels. He quite obviously wishes to shield himself from the charge of methodological scepticism. We must, he asserts, make a distinction between saying that we do not know what happened, and saying (what is very different) that nothing happened. We must try to distinguish the historical from the non-historical in the Gospels, and must be content with something less than a final solution to such historical questions (91).

We have spent a little time with Strauss so as to get the feel of the discussion about myth and to get a brief acquaintance with the kind of questions under consideration that provide the context for discussing it. We have seen that to take narrative as a form of expression leads to questions both about historicity and about the meaning of the narrative symbolism. Strauss presses these two problems and provides in his book the carefully considered answers he gave to them: (1) What is and what is not historical? (2) What is the meaning of the stories?

He insists that the interpreter can understand the Gospels only if he has sympathy with their attitudes, places himself in 'conformity with the spirit and modes of thought of the people and of the age' (65).

It was Rudolf Bultmann who in the mid-twentieth century raised the problem of myth, or mythology (as he preferred to say) for the understanding of the New Testament. He learned, to his surprise, from the chaplains to the German armed forces that the message of the Gospel of Jesus Christ, what Bultmann and others were calling the *kerygma*,[52] was not getting through to the men they served because they took offence at the framework in which the kerygma was set. They never got around to hearing the real message because they had stumbled over the form in which it had been set. They could not believe the Gospel because they never really heard it. They did not, could not, accept the worldview the New Testament writers assumed. So Bultmann addressed himself to this practical problem of communicating the Gospel. Something must be suggested that would prevent the offence and make possible the hearing of the Gospel of God's revelation in Jesus Christ in a contemporary world. Bultmann suggested that you do not have to accept the worldview literally before you can understand the essential message of the New Testament. What you must do is to understand the reality the original writers were presenting, — the act of God in Jesus Christ and the call for response of faith — in such a framework that does not now give offence but which makes contact with modern people.

That should not be disturbing, but should be welcome. In calling for such understanding there should be no offence. The task of the Christian preacher and witness from the very beginning has been to present the Gospel in an intelligible manner, having regard for the audience to which one is addressing oneself. In doing so the preacher should not cause needless barriers to understanding by the manner of his presentation. So we have to distinguish between the message and its setting, between its meaning and the manner of its expression. We must preserve the message, the meaning. That will involve us in removing the immediate occasion for offence, so that the real offence of the Gospel can clearly come to light.

Bultmann used the term 'mythological.' In English it was intended as a theological term, not loaded as is the term 'mythical.' Whereas 'mythical' suggests delusion, fantasy, untruth, unreality, the term 'mythological' should not. The process which he advocated so as to render the message of the New Testament a meaningful option for modern readers and hearers and which we have now briefly summarized, he labelled 'demythologizing.' That means, quite simply, that the myth, i.e. the narrative form of expression which assumed the three-storied universe, the interrelation of supernatural and natural, and of the supernatural and the human, can be replaced. The New Testament presents an understanding of God in relation to human creativeness and dependence in the form of myth, *in cosmic terms*. It expresses an understanding of human existence. 'The real question is whether this understanding of existence is true. Faith claims that it is, and faith ought not to be tied down to the imagery of New Testament mythology.'[53]

The term 'myth' refers to the 'worldview' of the New Testament writers,[54] one which they shared with others in the first century. There are two basic elements in this world-view. First, the universe is a three-storied structure: heavens above; flat earth; *sheol* under the flat earth. Second, the supernatural and the natural are interwoven. God, Satan, demons and angels influence human history and cause events in nature and in human life.

This worldview, this mythological form of understanding, is the form in which the Gospel is expressed. To understand the Gospel, you have to go behind the form and ask, What is it that comes to expression in this mythological form? That is a question anyone can ask. It is a question which does not involve the questioner in accepting the worldview in terms of which the Gospel expressed as his own. Modern man cannot do that, nor can he make a pretence that he is. But he does not need to.

The message of the Gospel is 'cashed' in experience. The message of the Gospel is that new life, new vision, new self-understanding is available, and that this comes as God acts in human life. God reveals himself now and a change occurs.

CHAPTER X NOTES

[1]Peter Donovan, *Religious Language,* p. 13.

[2]The two stories are to be found in *Luke* 15.

[3]I Peter 5: 13, Revelation 18.

[4]Ezekiel 37.

[5]Galatians 4:25-26.

[6]Ezekiel 17: 3-10, 22-24.

[7]Luke 10: 25-37.

[8]Augustine, *Quaestiones Evangeliorum,* II, 19 — slightly abridged, as quoted in C.H. Dodd, *The Parables of the Kingdom,* pp. 13-14.

[9]This represents a putting together of two passages, namely Genesis 14:4 where the number is given, and 17:23, where the act is done.

[10]The Epistle of Barnabas, 9.

[11]They were certainly not the first to have done so. If we may assume that the parables of Jesus were simple stories and that the interpretation of the parables is somewhat later, we already have in our Gospels evidence that the parables were taken as allegories, according to Joachim Jeremias, *Rediscovering the Parables,* pp. 54-71.

[12]*Revelation* 1:3.

[13]David Stacey, *Interpreting the Bible,* p. 71.

[14]Samuel Beckett, *En Attendant Godot,* p. xxvi.

[15]Thomas Aquinas held that allegory must be controlled by such original meaning of the text.

[16]Origen *De Principiis,* IV. i. 19. in the Eerdmans edition of the *Ante-Nicene Fathers,* Vol. IV, p. 369. In the Butterworth edition, Origen, *On the Principles,* the same passage is IV. iii. 5, p. 296. Origen presented a quite conscious justification for the use of allegory as a commendable method of interpretation. Such interpretation was quite explicit and, for him, quite defensible, even indispensable, for a mature understanding of Scripture.

[17]Alan Richardson, *Christian Apologetics,* p. 180.

[18]*Ibid.,* p. 182.

[19]Sanday, *op. cit.,* pp. 39, 79.

[20]Augustine, *On Christian Doctrine*, III, 22-23. Translated by *D.W.* Robertson, Jr., Indianapolis: Bobbs-Merrill, 1978, pp. 98-99.

[21]Other examples are the two sons of Abraham (*Galatians* 4), the manna, and Moses' smiting of the rock (I Corinthians 10).

[22]David Stacey, *op. cit.*, p. 67.

[23]*Ibid.*

[24]I Corinthians. 10:1-5.

[25]Gerhard von Rad, in C. Westermann (ed.). *Essays on Old Testament Hermeneutic*, p. 36.

[26]Alan Richardson, *The Bible in the Age of Science.* p. 177. Cf .G. Ernest Wright, *God Who Acts.*

[27]von Rad, *op cit.*, pp. 39. 21.

[28]Vawter, *op.cit.*, pp. 31-32.

[29]James Barr, *Old and New in Interpretation*, p. 106. Cf. 'distinguishing it strictly,' p. 146.

[30]See below, XI. 4.

[31]Luke 15.

[32]Luke 16.

[33]Matthew 12:43-46, cf. Luke11:24-26.

[34]Mark 4:3-8, Matthew 13: 3-8, Luke 8:5-8.

[35]Luke 11:21-22, Matthew 12:29.

[36]Mathewt 13:33, Luke 13:20-21. Cf. J. Jeremias, *The Parables of Jesus,* p.117.

[37]Mark 8:18, Matthew 13:15-16.

[38]Matthew 2:15, Hosea 11:1, Exodus 4:22-23.

[39]E.W. Heaton, *The Old Testament Prophets*, p. 124.

[40]*Ibid.*, p. 126.

[41]*Ibid.*, pp. 129-130.

[42]There is no question that, among other arguments, this particular argument strengthens the confidence of believers within the community. While in Adventist exegesis quite particular texts are pointed to, the overall function of the argument is to secure the Adventist's confidence in the group as a whole and in general. That secured, the details will fall into place, even if they seem to be falling out of place. This happens when fulfilments are specified

and do not take place. The divine authority is, in a quite specific sense, behind the 'movement.' Its leadership, its doctrines and its organisation are divinely appointed. That is a very sweeping claim indeed. Confidence in the group, the 'movement' in turn becomes justification for the grounds on which that group's confidence is based, the interpretation of texts as predictive, and as being fulfilled in the existence and experience of that group. If the group is divinely guided, the interpretation which led to the formation of the group is *ipso facto* divinely guided.

The Adventist claims that the existence of the church is itself a fulfilment of biblical predictions. A further conclusion follows. Extend now the interpretation of the texts which has yielded that confidence to the future and a system of last-day events can be worked out, an apocalyptic time-table. So an eschatological scheme comes into being. That, in particular, has been derived in the main from exegesis of the book of *Revelation*. Confidence that the scheme is valid is grounded in the very existence of the church, which is interpreted as evidence for the correctness of the method of interpretation.

The appeal of the system and of the method of interpretation lies, without question, in indicating the uniqueness of the Adventist movement to the Adventist. Very frequently in the literature and preaching of the church this point is stressed. This movement is God's last movement, with a unique message to give to the world. In this way the status and function of the church is clearly justified, provided of course the church gets on with the job of doing what it believes that it has been predicted it will do. Its role is to do and to teach what no other religious body is doing or is teaching.

[43] James Barr, *Old and New in Interpretation*, p. 126.

[44] Adventists have done this in different ways, for example, by producing historical works which trace the story of 'prophetic interpretation' in the past. L.E. Froom's *Prophetic Faith of our Fathers* is the most ambitious effort of this kind. It seeks to display figures in the history of the Christian church whose principles of interpretation are the same as or similar to those used by

Adventists. Gathering together a significant number of such interpreters, the case for the validity of the method of interpretation, it is argued, is strengthened. Because interpreters in the past have pursued such an interest and used such an interpretation, it cannot be that those who now use it are isolated cranks.

The argument has a certain non-logical appeal. One cannot of course, argue from the number of believers to the truth of what is believed. That is the fallacy of the argument, the fallacy of *consensus*. But there is the psychological appeal which we might call that of 'safety in numbers'!

[45]Adventists have traditionally claimed that quite specific guidance has been present in the prophet, Ellen White and have characteristically taken all her propositions as true. That claim, parallel to the fundamentalist claim about the Bible, is expressed in the language of inspiration. It provides an interesting example of a further fundamentalism within fundamentalism.

[46]Cf. above 4.14: The Concept of Revelation.

[47]Cf. above 3.12: The Argument from Prophecy.

[48]A. Schweitzer, *The Quest of the Historical Jesus*, p. 79.

[49]Cf. Maurice Wiles in J. Hick (editor), *The Myth of God Incarnate*, p. 164: 'the term may remain unusable in the general life of the church.'

[50]Readers are referred to the chapter 'The Question of Beginnings' in my book *Quest, An Exploration of Some Problems in Science and Religion*.

[51]References are to D.F. Strauss, *The Life of Jesus Critically Considered*, 1972.

[52]For Bultmann, the term referred to the *content* of the proclamation. *Kerygma* means proclamation and is used in the New Testament of the apostolic preaching. Others e.g. C. H. Dodd, stressed the *act* of proclamation.

[53]Rudolf Bultmann, 'New Testament and Mythology' in Hans-Werner Bartsch, *Kerygma and Myth*, p. 11. Bultmann's essay was written in 1941.

[54]Bultmann, *op. cit.*, pp. 1-3.

Summary of Chapter XI

Interpreting the Bible: Text and Revelation.

Interpreting is the process of finding or rendering meaning. A text needs interpreting when its meaning may be made clear, or made clearer. When we feel a distance from a text, find its way of thinking different from ours, we need to interpret in order to understand. We need to go beyond the form to the content. We may have to put the content in a different form. Different interpretations lead us to see things in different ways. Some texts lend themselves readily to different interpretations. This may be particularly the case when a text is translated from another language. The Scriptures we use are translations. We have two problems: to say what the writer intended, and to say what the text now means, i.e. to provide a relevant and contemporary meaning. This involves more than simply repeating what the Scripture says. The New Testament provides examples of interpreting the Old Testament. Often the resulting meaning is far different from the original. Do we take the New Testament procedures as models for our own interpretation of Scripture? If not, why not? The interpreter has different goals: to discover what happened; to come to a decision as to which is the best possible text; to say what the writer meant; to say what the word from the past can *now* mean. The Christian interpreter can approach the Scriptures with different goals in mind, but may not forget that it is through Scripture that God reveals himself.

XI

INTERPRETING THE BIBLE: TEXT AND REVELATION

1 DEVOTIONAL READING OF THE BIBLE ASSUMES INTERPRETATION

Even if one reads the Bible only for devotional purposes, one is interpreting. The idea is to arrive at a meaning in some way related to the living of one's day-to-day life. Most Christians most often read the Bible for the help and guidance it gives them in their daily lives, and not to inform themselves about ancient history, nor to 'prove' some dogmatic position, nor to enjoy it as literature. Reading the Bible devotionally is for the majority of Christians more important than doctrinal reading, even if doctrinal positions are implicit in all reading of Scripture. 'The Bible, after all, is not read simply because of the information it conveys about ancient Israel or the early Church. It is read because the readers believe that in it they find expressed something of God's acts and intentions and demands.'[1]

The Bible 'speaks' to the individual or to the church here and now. That is sufficient grounds for reading it. Whether there was a place called Ezion-geber; who the son of Japheth was; or when and where Quirinius lived does not really matter. Quirinius never comes to prominence in the Christmas meditations. The place names of ancient battles are of little importance when one wants help in living one's daily life. Nor does one hope for such help from chronologies and ancient laws, let alone passages where the technical terms prove difficult.

This means that the Christian understands what he reads. If there are difficulties, he is often quite prepared to overlook them, or to postpone considering them. Perhaps he will, at some time, give attention to them, with a view to understanding them better. Meanwhile he understands to a certain extent and in a certain way. Meanwhile he will gain practical benefit and spiritual help. That does not depend on the reader's linguistic, historical or literary competence. It demands that he be receptive to what God may reveal, here and now. That is the attitude with which the Christian undertakes a devotional reading of Scripture.

But, to get help from a passage means that you have some understanding of it. If it is puzzling you will have to try to arrive at an understanding. You cannot be helped by a text you read but do not understand at all. Whether your understanding is appropriate or adequate is not now the point. You have to have some understanding of the text. A New Testament story (Acts 8) tells of the official who was reading a passage but did not understand it. He was puzzled by it and desired to know what it meant. Philip the evangelist who was passing by provided an explanation and so led him to an understanding. The process of coming to understand a text we call interpretation. There are right and wrong ways of going about the job. In what follows here we shall give some attention to what it means to interpret. We begin, then, with an analysis of the idea.

To interpret means to suggest meaning, to render something meaningful which before or without the process of interpreting one did not understand, or to render more meaningful something which one did not understand as well as one could. When we give an interpretation, or someone interprets for us, we are assuming that the text or the event or whatever it is that is given has a meaning that can become clear, or clearer. In assuming the possibility of interpretation we are also assuming that someone will understand or come to understand.

What we come to understand, what someone interprets to us may be very simple. The process may take only a second: 'Oh that's what you mean!' 'Ah! I see what she meant!' or it may be very complex. A group of teachers takes three years to interpret a subject to their students, who may then say, 'I now begin to understand!'

2 WHEN THE QUESTION, 'WHAT DOES IT MEAN?' ARISES

What does it (a text, an action, or an event) mean?' arises when we do not understand it. There is a certain unclarity, ambiguity, obscurity or doubt about it. So we are puzzled or perhaps baffled, or we just draw a blank. I remember as a boy reading in one of my textbooks of a 'mephitic pond.' I did not know what that meant. It was no use guessing. I was ignorant of the meaning of the word 'mephitic.' So I looked it up in a dictionary and then I understood. That was a relatively simple case of a process of interpretation, finding out the meaning of one term which then illuminated the meaning of the phrase and then of the sentence. It is not always that simple. It may not help me to understand it if I look up a word in a dictionary when that word features in a technical explanation. To understand the explanation one has to know the subject, expose oneself to the discipline.

Everyone who learns a new discipline has to learn a new vocabulary, and will then begin to understand the literature of that discipline. That is true whether it is physics, biology, sociology, law or theology. To understand the literature we have to master the vocabulary. It takes time, expenditure of effort and a degree of intelligent and sustained interest to grasp such meanings. The professional is often not able to interpret adequately to the layman the meanings which he, the professional, understands. So he does the best he can to bridge the gap, by providing as adequate an understanding as he may under the circumstances. Simplification may be misleading, especially if it leads to reductionism. To be simply expressed is not always to be adequately expressed.

Sometimes the question arises when we know the meaning of the words but are unsure of the intention of the writer and speaker. We are in doubt as to how they are to be taken. Such doubt may be present whether the words are literal or metaphorical. If I take the words in one way they mean one thing. If I take them in another way they mean something very different. So the way I take them will influence my understanding and also what I will do as a consequence of that understanding. Difference in understanding a person's actions can lead to quite different relationships with that person. We have stressed earlier the primary importance of theory to life and to action.

Problems arise with a written text when we feel a distance from it. We may no longer be able to agree with the sentiments it expresses. Even though we understand very well what *they* meant by it, *we* can no longer make that meaning our own. There is a Victorian hymn which runs:

> The rich man in his castle,
> The poor man at his gate.
> God made them high and lowly,
> And ordered their estate.

It is not hard to understand what *they* meant by that. They meant that a person's position in society is part of the order of things divinely appointed and is not to be changed. We understand them but we cannot accept their point of view. We may feel estranged and hostile to that meaning. What they affirmed we feel we have to deny. What they denied we feel we must affirm. There is a gap between them and us. In such a case as this we feel we cannot close the gap because the content of their belief is opposed to ours. We know what they meant but we reject it. We cannot make their meaning our own.

3 WHAT INTERPRETATION MEANS

There are several meanings the term *interpretation* carries.

(1) It may simply mean to translate from one language to another.

(2) To interpret may mean to render meaningful. It results in illuminating that which one did not originally understand. That can happen when one translates from one language to another. It happens also when one makes an explanation which clarifies what was previously obscure. Now it is obvious that a writing, or a speech, may still need interpreting after it has been translated. One example of this is the case of writings which come to us from times and cultures very remote from our own. After the interpretation that is translation they demand the interpretation that is explanation.

(3) We speak of interpretation in another sense. An author or a composer may express himself in a play or a musical composition. For a group of actors to interpret a play well or for an orchestra to interpret a symphony well they will have to do justice (as we say) to the intention of the composer. This will demand technical skill./ That is fundamental. So the London Symphony Orchestra will do better in rendering Brahms than will the West Bridgford School Orchestra because they have much more technical skill. But that skill will have to serve the expression of the composer, so as to present his composition well. A creative interpretation will be possible because the music allows of it, because of the technical skill of the performers, and because of the imagination (within proper limits) of the conductor. Since he will be experienced, his imagination will be a disciplined imagination. In this case the material is non-verbal. But something similar must be said when the subject matter is verbal. Three demands of a similar kind to those of an orchestra can be made: first technical skill, in the case of the New Testament for example, knowledge of Greek and of the contemporary culture

and history; secondly, a sympathy with the author, and a desire to understand him; thirdly, a disciplined imagination to render the meaning so understood through the skills present, in an appropriate way.

(4) We must now pursue our question, 'What does it mean to interpret?' in another direction. Interpretation provides an answer to the question, 'How am I to understand reality?' The term 'reality' is a convenient term for different areas of human interest. Sociology interprets society — the social reality. It uses models and looks at society from different perspectives. Physical Science interprets natural reality. It constructs theories and puts questions to nature. Philosophers interpret human experience and analyse human expression. Artists, for example musicians, interpret, i.e. render a musical composition, presenting it to us for appreciation. A doctor interprets the symptoms. A court interprets the evidence. Historians interpret the deposits of the past. In each of these cases the interpreter takes an attitude to and attempts to make meaningful some area of human experience or of non-human reality.

Take, for example, the question, 'What does it mean to be human?' Faced with a question as important and as wide-ranging as this, there is need to frame and then to address quite fundamental questions, to decide whether evidence is appropriate or whether our answer is a priori, to decide what would count as evidence, how the evidence is to be obtained and how assessed, what methods are to be employed in the interpretation of the evidence.

People differ with respect to what they judge to be the appropriate methods as to what are vital clues, even if they may be agreed as to the limits of the subject matter, and of an approach. So there emerge, even within one particular discipline, alternative perspectives, rival theories, differing approaches to and accounts of the evidence. Different interpretations reflect differing experiences of the world. Different interpretations lead us to see reality in different ways.

With the emergence of rival theories we have a problem of interpretation at one remove so to speak. How shall we assess the rival explanations? How shall we interpret the interpretations?

Needless to say, such questions arise within specific contexts within sociology, physics, history and philosophy. Of course such questions also arise in theology. Our point is that they do so on different levels. One has to reckon not only with the question about the written text. There are other more complex questions of interpretation: (1) What was the written text interpreting, and how can we (the contemporary interpreters) understand that? We have to find our way through the many divergent interpretations of Christian teaching. We have to deal with the many different interpretations of one particular teaching. This leads us to another level of questioning: (2) How are we to interpret the interpretations, based as many of them are (or at least claiming to be based), on the text of Scripture? So arises a third kind of question: (3) How shall we, modern interpreters understand our contemporary situations in the light of our Christian faith? How shall we do what the biblical writers were doing, bearing witness to and giving an intelligible account of our Christian faith?

A note of warning needs to be sounded. We shall oversimplify if we say that we are to be as untheoretical as possible. There is no virtue whatsoever in being over-simple. Nor is there is any virtue whatsoever in trying to be non-theoretical. What could be more important than theory, and a recognition of its importance? The reader ought to give his own responsible answer to this highly important question. We should remind ourselves of the primacy of theory in all the significant areas of human life and activity, not the least in matters religious. It is through theory that we achieve understanding. It is by theoretical construction that we interpret. Without theory we could not begin to understand. It is on the basis of theory that we act. As our theory is different so our decisions, our activity, our life, our destiny will be different. Read a little book which proposes seven answers to the question 'What is human nature?'[2] and you will readily see that the different theoretical answers to the question will lead you in quite different practical directions.

In what follows we shall try to show how the problem of interpretation relates to the subject matter of Christian faith. These several definitions will enable us to do so with some degree of clarity.

'To translate' means to render a meaning expressed in one language into another. The ideas expressed in one form (say in German or in Greek, the one who expressed them intending to convey a meaning), are not understood in the form in which they were expressed, say by an Englishman who can speak a little French. If he is going to understand them, someone will have to render them into a *linguistic* form he can understand. Someone will have to act as a translator who, if he does his work well, will produce an intelligible, i.e. meaningful, English version of the original words. Words in one particular language structure will be put in words in another language structure.

Let us now suppose that an original foreign speaker was either very incoherent or very obscure or was talking, in his language of course, about something with which we were not familiar, say nuclear physics or higher mathematics. Then it might happen that even if what he said *were* translated into our language, and we heard the sounds or read the sentences, we would still not be able to understand. In such a case there would have to be a further process, to enable us to understand. If when it had been translated it was still obscure, a further effort at rendering it meaningful would have to be made. This would involve something additional to translating words from one language into words from another.

4 Their Understanding and Ours

Take the case where there is a feeling of distance between us and the text when there is a gap between them and us. The cultural climate has changed and we can no longer understand their form of expression so as to make it our own, even if we might wish to affirm the content, the substance of what they were saying. We cannot say what they wanted to say in the way they were saying it. When the cultural climate changes we can no longer simply transmit their meaning without changing their form of expression. The form in which they expressed their ideas may lead people of another culture to mistake the message they are trying to convey.

Say one thing in one way and it makes contact and produces a favourable response. Say it in another way and it scandalises and evokes resistance. It is thus important sometimes to distinguish between the form and the content of what someone says.

People resist the Christian message of God's love in Jesus Christ because they feel that they are being asked to believe, in connection with the essential message, things they cannot believe. People reject the Christian message because they cannot believe in miracles, in supernatural beings acting upon human beings, in God becoming a cause like any other historical and natural cause. The message of God's love for man and of the gift of forgiveness and freedom in Jesus Christ thus does not really get a hearing. How in interpreting the Bible shall we be able to bridge the gap between the present and the past? That is the Christian's problem in trying to interpret the meaning of Jesus Christ for today, and the documents which contain the past witness to Jesus Christ — the Bible. Today's is a context in which thought is secular, scientific, historical, post-Enlightenment and analytical. The Bible is a book written long before the developments which have brought us to where we are today. In short we are modern readers dealing with an ancient book.

How is it possible to get at the real message of the New Testament and not to stumble at the form in which that message is expressed?

We should distinguish between two possible meanings of the term 'understand.' For there is a difference between understanding what the writer means or meant, and the appropriation of this meaning for ourselves. We may well grasp what the writer said but have no desire to take it on board for ourselves. I may know what the writer means, even if the process in some cases is an arduous one and requiring historical imagination and knowledge. But I may not accept the meanings which I have come to grasp. On the other hand, I may find it possible to take as my own the meaning which I understand the writer to be conveying, but find I have to abandon the framework within which he had presented that meaning. But then I shall have to make clearly the distinction between the form of expression, which I may have to reject, and the content, which I may be able to appropriate.

For example I am in a different world when I read the myths of ancient Babylon, or the miracle stories from the Middle Ages, than when I read the *New Scientist*. In the former cases, I seem to be in a strange world. I shall need to make a real effort to understand their world, the sort of effort I do not need to make if I read a modern textbook of science or of sociology. Where the writings have a message, I shall have to discern it from within the form in which they expressed it. Our difficulty is that such writings have come out of a different cultural context, from people who held a different worldview from ours. There are difficulties which do not present themselves when we read a modern author, whose worldview we share. Orwell's *1984* makes an immediate impact. But Paul's Galatians and Milton's *Paradise Lost* are a different matter. In these cases you have to be aware of their tradition, their patterns of thought and get behind the form of expression to the meaning they attempt to convey.

Failure to understand therefore may be due to many causes. It may be due to one's lack of capacity. This may be because of lack of intelligence, lack of training. It may be due to prejudice. Some of us simply lack certain competencies and skills. There may be also a lack of clarity, or ambiguity in the material itself.

For an example we may refer to a passage in the New Testament itself, where the writer is complaining about the letters of Paul. 'There are some things in them hard to understand, which the ignorant and unstable twist to their own destruction, as they do the other Scriptures.'[3] Here the difficulty of attaining a correct understanding is twofold. The materials are genuinely difficult. Hence they require a serious and unprejudiced approach. But if ignorant and prejudiced people try to interpret them then the results are disastrous.

5 AMBIGUITY AND INTENTION

In the case where sentences are ambiguous it is a common experience that the words one person speaks are intended in a way different from the way another person hears them. Take, for instance, the following quite simple sentences:

(1)   I'm inviting some friends around.
(2)   It's going to rain this afternoon.
(3)   Father is sewing and mother needs dough.

You hear rather than read (3), since only when spoken and heard are three of the words ambiguous.

How should we take (1)? Is it an invitation for everyone else to leave the house, or for mother to buy some cake or for cash to buy something to drink? What does (2) mean? That I shall not be planting the roses I had promised to do? An expression of relief therefore? In both cases there is more than the sentence says.

In the aural case (3) where there are deliberate puns, the particular interest or inclination of the hearer will colour, if not determine, the way he understands what he hears. So there is no guarantee that what the speaker meant by what he said will be the meaning that will be heard. The process of communication is fraught with all manner of difficulties.

Between the origin of the message and its receipt there are many different ways in which the meaning of the message can be channelled.

Take case (3) again. The words were spoken, so the sounds heard conveyed an ambiguous message. How can father be 'sowing' if he's in the house? Doesn't he 'sow' in the garden? And mother doesn't seem to be very active, just sitting in the chair. So write the message down. What do the words look like? They could read, (3a) Father is sowing and mother needs dough? or they could read, (3b) Father is sewing and mother kneads dough. 'Oh!' you say, 'He's sewing.' Now I understand. But when you have figured out the intended words, you will still have to ask, 'Why did whoever said it say it? What were they trying to tell me? Their parents are active? They are poor and have to make ends meet? What kind of situation have the words come out of? What do they point me to? I have to make further inquiries.' If there is ambiguity you ask for clarification.

Interpretation here means clearing up the ambiguity. Interpretation articulates what was before unclear, inarticulate. You can then grasp what the writer or speaker intended to say. The obscurity is removed. The meaning is clarified. The process of making something plain may simply lead us to clarify the nature of the ambiguity. It may not remove it. This is a very important function of interpretation. Any interpreter worth his salt will, when it is appropriate to do so, make clear that there are alternative meanings and (when this is the case) set out the options available. Interpretation may sometimes simply indicate an ambiguity. It may come as a great insight that such an alternative meaning is possible. A successful process of interpretation may not result in providing one meaning and one meaning only. It may produce an indecisive and debatable position, whether with regard to grammar, history or theology. With regard to the New Testament we cannot always define beyond doubt the significance of the genitive case or of the present tense, or in some cases even the *exact* meaning of the word. Even if we know the precise meaning or a word or phrase in the other language, we may find that there is no equivalent in the language we are translating into.

We cannot always make the historical judgment we would like to make from the evidence we have. We cannot always hold that a particular passage unequivocally supports one doctrinal position over another. It is the responsibility of the interpreter in any case to make clear what problems still remain when the word or passage has been duly considered.

When we are in doubt concerning the meaning of what someone has written or has said, sometimes we can check the original meaning and sometimes we cannot. 'What do you mean by that?' we may ask of the speaker. But if he keeps quiet and refuses to open up, we shall have to interpret his meaning as best we can. Even if he is physically available, he may still keep his secret. But there may be other ways and means of finding out what he means. We can consider his interests, his modes of conversation, his personality. We consider them and interpret what he said in relation to them. Is it a joke, or was he grimly serious? What has he done and said before in similar situations? Does he like to shock people? Is he egocentric?

A case in point is the obscurity, ambiguity or unclarity of a passage in translation. The Bible has been translated more than any other book and some translations are better than others. It is not the case however that the best translations are the most widely used. So let us suppose we find obscurity in the English version we are reading. What help can we get in arriving at a good interpretation? The language of the New Testament is Greek. In reading and interpreting the New Testament, a person without a knowledge of Greek will always be an amateur. But if you do not know Greek you will have to do the best you can. It very often hinders rather than helps to look the word up in an English dictionary. Indeed it could produce bizarre results. 'To justify,' for example, has a technical meaning with regard to setting type for the printer. The dictionary may give many meanings for the English term, but that would only complicate the matter. You would then have to decide between them and that could be extremely arbitrary.

You could compare translations and set the different words and phrases side by side. But again there is the problem of adjudicating between them. That might be very arbitrary. With regard to the New Testament, if you can't read Greek you don't have the reference point for assessing the fidelity of the translations you are comparing. Suffice it to say that word studies have limited value. One has to immerse oneself in the thought of the writer, consider his purposes and his particular style, take note of the particular circumstances, be aware of the thought pattern of the time, and of the author's in particular. Then there is the question of the precise meaning, and perhaps the distinctive use, of the Greek words, phrases and grammar. And that is only the beginning.

So the point that we can sometimes check the original meaning of what has been said does have application to the English version of the New Testament we are reading. But it is not always a simple process to 'check the meaning' if we really do want to have the most satisfactory interpretation possible We then have to see whether in certain passages we can 'check the meaning' of the Greek text.

Now we must return to an earlier and very important distinction. Giving an interpretation means saying what the writer intended. It also means to provide a relevant contemporary and fitting meaning of what the writer wrote.

6 BEING FAITHFUL TO THE TEXT

Since the Scriptures are in some sense fundamental for the Christian theologian, how is he to be faithful to them in constructing theology? What does it mean for him to claim that what he says is in accordance with the Scriptures?

Is he simply to repeat what the Scriptures say? But that would not be to interpret. To repeat is not to bring us any closer to understanding, but only restates our problem, when we have difficulties with the text. But of course the theologian does not begin from scratch. He does not start on his own. He stands within a tradition of interpretation to which he is indebted both positively and negatively. He affirms and he criticises what that tradition says. If he is at all constructive he follows and he departs from the guidance it gives him.

The writer lived a long time ago. Is the temporal gap between him and us important or not? It may be. Time separates. I may be able to understand *his* meaning, and without any difficulty make it *my* meaning, whether I agree or disagree with it. But suppose his circumstances are very different from mine and what he said was closely related to his very different circumstances? Suppose indeed that what he took for granted can no longer be taken for granted since his culture no longer exists. How shall I interpret what he meant so that it has meaning for me? His words may well have a *different* meaning for me than they had for him. If that is the case, can we speak about being faithful to *his* meaning? How shall we know whether we are 'taking' his words correctly in our different situation? Note that the situation is different from one in which we want to know what the writer meant and could not (for various reasons) get him to pronounce on it (e.g. he was silent or he was dead). We are now asking whether there is a relation between his meaning and ours such that we may say that our meaning is a faithful interpretation of his.

'Faithful' here may mean: (1) that there is some common meaning or intention which we can specify between his meaning and ours; (2) that a generalization can be made to cover both meanings; (3) that our meaning is a possible derivative from his, that he may well have meant and understood what we understand by it if he were in our circumstances. In each case we have considered all the evidence available, historical, linguistic, literary, and theological. (4) that we in our time share the intention which the biblical writer and in particular the writer of the New Testament shared and that we attempt to execute it in our context. The task is to interpret the revelation of God in Jesus Christ which takes place here and now. This involves presenting its meaning for us and its application to the situations which we now encounter. The continuity of the task is thus rooted in the continuity of God's revelation in the past with his revelation in the present. This involves moving beyond strict 'biblical' theology to constructive or systematic theology.

Langdon Gilkey addresses himself to the question 'how the theologian is 'faithful' to the scriptural source and how he or she shows a continuity with the spirit of major elements of tradition.'[4] He writes,

> Does this mean the theologian copies or repeats the
> words, the categories, the propositions of Scripture
> and tradition; that he or she makes a précis of
> Scripture or writes a commentary on accepted dogma?
> If copying or repeating is futile because anachronistic,
> what is it that the theologian "draws" from this source
> and this resource?[5]

He explains that the Christian tradition has a set of central
symbols, through which it interprets the meaning of beliefs, values
and goals.

> In the Christian tradition these symbols find their
> normative expression, and for theology their source, in
> the Scriptures, since their primary reference is to the
> events of revelation to which the Scriptures witness. It
> is these symbols that are reinterpreted in various ways
> in tradition; and it is they that the theologian must
> reinterpret, re-present, in a manner intelligible to us
> and yet "appropriate" or faithful to their sense in their
> original locus.[6]

The symbols to which Gilkey refers are such as the following:
God as Lord, as judge, as electing, choosing, covenanting; God as
giver of the Law, God as redeemer, God as faithful; the covenant,
the elected people, the Messiah, the New Age to come. These
symbols familiar in the Old Testament reappear in a new pattern
in the New Testament where they are centred around Jesus Christ.
In turn, new symbols emerge: incarnation, atonement, resurrection,
second advent.

He then explains the task of theology in reference to these
symbols.

> "Biblical theology" is the attempt to give a unified
> account of these symbols as they appear in the Old
> and New Testaments; historical theology is the story
> of these symbols as they have been reinterpreted in the
> tradition. Theology as a whole, then, concerns itself

with these symbols and with their power to illumine our existence. The awesome and risky task of "constructive" or "systematic" theology is to provide or propose a unified *contemporary* understanding of that same complex of symbols, an understanding that is (a) faithful to their original sense in Scripture and tradition, (b) adequate to our own general experience, and (c) intelligible in our time.[7]

Doctrine does not simply repeat or summarize the Scripture. For one thing, it uses language not found in Scripture. For another thing it is selective. How then does doctrine, theology, interpret Scripture? The task of systematic theology is to present the meaning for today of God's revelation in Jesus Christ. In doing so it uses language which the Bible does not use. The Christian Church has done that from the beginning. Such theology is constructive in that it does for us today what the writers of the New Testament were doing in their time: interpreting the Gospel of Jesus Christ. What we are in our turn interpreting in expounding the New Testament writings is itself a series of interpretations of this fundamental event. That event is Jesus Christ. As history proceeds each particular church community reflects upon the meaning of Jesus Christ for itself, and relates that meaning to the special circumstances of its own history. It will also take account of, and select from, the long history of Christian tradition that which it finds amenable and suggestive for its doctrinal construction.

So what does it mean for a doctrine or a theology to be in harmony with, to be faithful to Scripture? Let us look at alternative answers to the question:

(1) repeating the original words of Scripture;
(2) repeating the original meaning of Scripture;
(3) making a direct application (where possible) of the original meaning of Scripture;
(4) making an indirect application of the original meaning of Scripture;

(5) providing meaning not contradicted by passages of Scripture, where there are such passages as treat of the same subject;

(6) providing meaning not contradicted by Scripture, for the reason that Scripture does not speak about the same subject;

(7) doing today in our way what the writers of Scripture did in their way, namely to interpret the meaning of God's action in Jesus Christ as we have experienced it, and in meaningful contemporary language, addressing men and women who live in our world and in no other.

The right place to begin is with the last of these suggestions (7). We shall understand Scripture only if we know the reality they were proclaiming, the revelation of God's love in Jesus Christ and the faith which has responded to it. That happens now and the light from that continuing event illuminates the whole of life in *our* world: a very complex world. It is our task to show now how that event, that experience, casts light on our problems for instance on our self-understanding or our understanding of our social relationships and on what we have learnt about it from the psychologist and the sociologist. How does the Gospel illuminate our world in which barbarity and oppression, affluence and abject poverty, hatred between human beings and totally inadequate social and political measures to cope with world problematic etc. etc., are so evident? It is this world of advanced scientific and technological knowledge that has made our outlook so different from ancient peoples, in which we understand and present the Gospel of Jesus Christ as best we can. It is in this world that we address ourselves ever anew to the questions of humanity, Who is God? What is man? Why is there evil? Can there be hope? Who am I?

We shall as we do so construct our answers in different ways. Sometimes Scripture language will seem appropriate. At other times the language of Scripture will be very remote from the problems with which we wrestle. That is only to be expected. They did not live in our scientific, bureaucratic, technological and international world. But that to which they witness is that to which we witness. We are bound together in a common witness and in a common task.

To attempt to fulfil this task will obviously take us beyond the text of Scripture. It will involve us in construction of language and ideas, in the use of words and concepts from secular and non-theological spheres. But in being faithful to Jesus Christ, we are in our turn and in our way being faithful to the Bible.

7 HOW THE NEW TESTAMENT USES THE HEBREW SCRIPTURES

In the New Testament itself we can observe the intention to interpret the 'Scriptures,' 'the writings.' The authors of the New Testament maintain by so doing that God's revelation in their present is in continuity with his revelation in the past. They interpret Jesus Christ by selecting and using passages from the Hebrew Scriptures.

In doing so, New Testament writers took great liberties with the writings they use, so as to achieve their objective. We feel that on occasions they took unwarrantable liberties we ourselves would never consider taking with the writings of the New Testament. If we followed some of their examples we would produce results not subject to any sort of control. Let us take an example and draw some conclusions from it.

Paul argued that those who spend their whole time in the preaching of the Gospel ought to receive support from the church so that they do not have to engage in work to support themselves over and above their preaching and leadership tasks. The book of the law said that when an ox is treading out the grain, no muzzle is to be put on it. It is perfectly clear that the law book meant literally what it said. 'You shall not muzzle an ox when it treads out the grain.'[8] There is nothing obscure here which needs clarification. Jews knew very well what 'muzzling' was, could identify an ox when they encountered one, and needed no explanation to acquaint them with the process of 'treading out the grain.' They could very well act upon this law, having no doubt about its meaning. But suppose we take it out of its original setting and give it quite a different meaning? Is that a proper thing to do? Paul gives it a quite different setting, a quite different meaning, and then even claims that it was written so to be applied! 'Is it for oxen that God is concerned? Does he not speak entirely for our sake? It was written for our sake. . . .'[9] Here Paul not only alters its meaning but goes on to claim that the meaning he gives it is the one it ought to have.

8 Can We Follow the Example of the New Testament?

But here we must object. It is one thing to make an allegorical interpretation of the text in full awareness that one is giving the original passage a quite different meaning, a meaning which may be most appropriate in the new situation, but not as an interpretation of a particular passage.

The original meaning of the passage Paul quotes is quite straightforward. The allegorical meaning Paul derives from it is not. 'Oxen are to be treated well,' he interprets to mean, 'Apostles are to be treated well, supplied with funds for their activity.' Then he adds: 'That is the meaning of the original passage.' It *was* not. Paul has given it a meaning suited to his case, and then made a remarkable (and indefensible) claim about that new meaning, namely that that *is* now its proper meaning.

If we reset a passage it is inevitable that its meaning will change, since no two historical circumstances are identical But we cannot claim that the meaning we then give it is its 'real' meaning. What we may claim is that the original meaning may be clearly stated, and that another meaning which is given to the passage is an appropriate meaning.

The New Testament employs the Old in a great variety of ways. A clear distinction is often made between a *typological* and an *allegorical* interpretation.[10] But there are many other ways they use in appropriating Old Testament passages: *paraenesis* i.e. hortatory, fulfilments of prophecy, proofs from the precise language of the passage quoted, 'situation similarities.'[11] Nor can we always put the particular cases clearly into one category rather than another. The particular instances of interpretation overlap the classes. What is certain is that Christians took the Hebrew Scriptures very seriously indeed and found meanings within it which helped them to understand and apply their Christian faith. They reinterpreted the Old Testament by referring its symbols to Jesus Christ and to the church.

But we may not permit ourselves to do with the biblical texts what the New Testament writers did with the Old Testament text. They frequently ignored its original meaning and context, put the passage in a quite new setting and gave it a quite different meaning, and were little if at all concerned whether they were doing justice or violence to that original meaning.

To achieve historical understanding we must respect cardinal rules of historical interpretation: (1) Consider the original context. (2) Ask how the originator and the original hearers or readers would have understood the passage. (3) Be aware of the historical distance between an ancient text and the modern interpreter.

We cannot in every instance accept the meanings, the intentions, the directives to action of the biblical writer and make them ours. We cannot just reset the text, thinking that merely to repeat is to ensure that it is unquestionably acceptable. Sometimes we readily agree with Scripture, give it an immediate application and interpret it positively. Sometimes we simply ignore it. Sometimes we reject the ideas and sentiments of a passage or of a book. Sometimes we do not know what to make of it. Am I never to call someone a fool or use some equivalent term?[12] Are homosexuals to be put to death?[13] Are we to curse our enemies in good heart?[14]

When it is a question of what to do, and when we cannot avoid acting, if we are looking for guidance from the Bible, we will have to make up our minds whether there is anything relevant there, whether what seems to be is indeed relevant, whether we shall just have to make our own decisions without direct guidance from Scripture.

9 OFFENSIVE PASSAGES

We have already spoken of the selective way in which Christians use the Bible in church and as individuals.[15] Christians cannot find an edifying meaning in every passage of Scripture. We will simply have to say that there are some passages which do not speak to us. There are other passages whose meaning we have to resist. There are passages whose meaning is quite secular or quite at odds with the message of God's saving love in Jesus Christ. There are passages which we can readily understand as expressions of real human emotions and aspirations, frustrations and disappointments but which we cannot connect in any direct way with the distinctive revelation of God.

If one rejects the allegorical method of interpretation, and if one does not welcome an historical approach to the Scriptures, one may then be in the irrational and untenable position of having to affirm as true whatever the Scripture proposition says or of having to acknowledge all the directives of Scripture as binding, having their source in the divine.

We should not be so attached to a dogma about Scripture that we overlook something that is very plain. Let us take some examples, bearing in mind what is implicit by a high theory of biblical inspiration. The first is the story of Elisha's instigation of Jehu's revolution.[16] A blood-letting is initiated by Elisha, the prophet of the Lord, who gives one of the sons of the prophets a flask of oil and instructs him to go and to anoint Jehu, by that symbolic act proclaiming him king of Israel. The young prophet is then to get away and disappear. The prophet Elisha in this way caused a bloodbath. Jehu took the message, rode furiously to Jezreel, shot Joham through with bow and arrow; pursued and shot Ahaziah through. He then ordered Jezebel's slaves to pitch her out of the upstairs window, blood spattering over the walls and the horses, the meanwhile Jehu eating and drinking, while the wild dogs devour most of Jezebel's remains. Jehu then sent messages to the guardians of the seventy sons of Ahab demanding of them that they kill their charges. This was duly done and the seventy heads of the seventy kings were put in seventy baskets and sent to Jehu in Jezreel. The next move was to obliterate any who had any connection with Ahab. This Jehu duly performed. The word of the Lord was being performed. Jehu next set out for Samaria and encountered kinsmen of Ahaziah, king of Judah en route. He captured forty-two of them and massacred them 'at the pit of Biheked.' At Samaria other butcherings took place, including the very last of the line of Ahab.

He then played his bizarre trick on the Baal prophets. He announced a grand Baal festival, gathered all the Baal worshippers together, brought out all the ceremonial dress and went in to the house of Baal, to all appearances to worship Baal. Jehu offered the burnt offering and then set his soldiers on the assembled multitude, slaying, destroying, burning, until neither temple nor worshipper was left. 'And the Lord said to Jehu (among other things), You have done well.'

The second is an excerpt from the Song of Solomon.[17]

How fair and pleasant you are;
O loved one, delectable maiden.
You are stately as a palm tree,
and your breasts are like its clusters.
I say I will climb the palm tree
and lay hold of its branches.
Oh, may your breasts be like clusters of the vine,
And the scent of your breath like apples,
And your kisses like the best wine
that goes down smoothly,
gliding over lips and teeth.
I am my beloved's,
and his desire is for me.
Come, my beloved,

let us go forth into the fields,
and lodge in the villages;
Let us go out early to the vineyards
and see whether the vines have budded,
whether the grape blossoms have opened
and the pomegranates are in bloom.
There I will give you my love.
The mandrakes give forth fragrance,
and over our doors are all choice fruits,
new as well as old, which I have laid up for you, O my
beloved.

The third is an instruction from the apostle Paul:

As in all the churches of the saints, the women should
keep silence in the churches. For they are not
permitted to speak, but should be subordinate . . . For
it is shameful for a woman to speak in church.[18]

The fourth is an ancient law:

If a man lies with a male as with a woman, both of
them have committed an abomination; they shall be
put to death, their blood is upon them.[19]

What then are our responses to these passages? We are simply
revolted by the treachery, butchery and deception of Jehu,
prompted by the prophet Elisha. It outrages our moral sense and
we recoil from it all. It is grossly immoral. We say that because we
would make the same judgment about such acts whatever the
circumstances. There is simply no defending such atrocity and
perversity.

We find the poetry of the Song of Solomon a sensuous and
beautiful expression of the love of man for woman, far removed
from Victorian prudery, or contemporarty crudeness and vulgarity.
It is a charming example of the Hebrew joy of the body and of
the springtime. To allegorize it is to spoil it. It is to change it into
something foreign.

We just outright reject the advice about women and the law about the homosexual.

We need make no further comment about the Pauline instruction!

So when we put together our responses to four rather different passages, we find ourselves having to reckon with our own honesty in view of a traditional dogma about the spirituality and inspiration of all parts of Scripture. We find we have to revise such a view of inspiration. It cannot be right. Our practice is directly opposed to such a theory. Any theory which requires us to take attitudes which in practice we do not and cannot take is radically wrong.

A 'flat' theory of the inspiration of the Bible also leads to other intractable problems. Two particular corollaries follow from the claim that Scripture is the inspired word of God throughout.

The first is that, since all is inspired (= was inspired by God), any passage taken from any place in Scripture could be set beside any other passage. Passages are selected, correlated, reset. They seem to be about the same topic and so are arranged to present a doctrine. The appropriateness of the arrangement spoke for itself, and so a minimum of explanation was required. In this way the Bible was self-interpreting. Here you find a little. There you find a little. Put it all together and you have 'Bible Doctrine', the teaching of the Bible. You can now claim, 'The Bible says. . . .' There is here no consistent regard for the interests of the writer, the circumstances under which he wrote, the style, the form, the understanding of the first readers, or the general and specific historical situations prevailing at the time. It was enough that one put this 'truth' alongside that 'truth' and continued until a biblical doctrine emerged. Since the doctrine so arrived at was drawn directly from the Bible, was expressed in the actual words of the Bible, the claim was then made that the authority of the Bible attached to the doctrine drawn from it. The doctrine had divine authority because it had its source in the Bible, which was the divine authority. So the doctrine of sin, of judgment, of immortality, of rewards and punishments, of grace or whatever it was, placed a divine demand upon one's belief. Since the doctrine was true and of divine authority, it must be believed. Assent became an obligation. Refusal to assent was a sin.

The second corollary was that the meaning of the passages and of the doctrine was unchanging. What is true on one occasion is true on another occasion. All that is needed is that the words of the Bible be repeated and arranged to reveal that eternal truth. There was no understanding that the same words repeated in a different time and place might mean something quite different from their original meaning or that the resulting doctrinal system may have little relationship to the original intentions of the Scriptural writers, or that the construction might be artificial.

The fundamental fault of both of these corollaries, as indeed of the theory of inspiration from which they derive, is that they lack all historical sense. Before you may engage in correlation and comparison, you have, in the first instance, to take the context of the writer into account and see what he said within the framework of his own writing and thought. Setting passages of Scripture side by side without due regard for proper historical method is bound to lead to distortion and to error.

There are other implications of the traditional doctrine of inspiration. It led to the belief that the Bible is a unity, and this meant that there could be no diverse and contradictory doctrinal viewpoints in the Bible. Moreover, 'the patterns of thought of the biblical writers were essentially like our own so that their language and concepts could be taken at face value.' What they assumed, and very naively, was that the only real problem of interpretation was to establish the literal meaning of the text. 'Few theologians dreamed that it required an act of historical imagination just to reconstruct the intention of the author.'[20]

10 THE BIBLE MEDIATES GOD

Nothing in what we have now said implies that it is unprofitable to ask for a summary of the teaching of the biblical writers on a particular topic, provided that choice of topic is appropriate. To do so will reveal a great variety of approach and understanding, and will then lead to the question about the unity of the biblical revelation. That can only be a valuable step in the right direction providing, as it may, a corrective to the naive, unhistorical and misleading approach we have just summarised.

A satisfactory contemporary understanding of the Bible will recognize two quite fundamental facts:

(1) The Bible is an historical document.
(2) The Bible mediates the Word of God addressed to us in the present.

These claims imply that God speaks to us now through an ancient book, whose words need interpreting. Because this book is an ancient book, we must be ready for an earnest and protracted confrontation. While we approach this book with our traditions and our questions, we must also respect the text in its distance, its difference, its distinctiveness from us. We shall let the texts confront us. There will be a two-way traffic. We question them and they question us. At the point of confrontation we achieve understanding. We wrestle both with what they meant and with what they could possibly mean for us. It is a kind of conversation, the sort of encounter between two parties from different worlds. We bring our concerns and our questions to the text which we allow to speak in its own right. So we learn from the text. We have not simply repeated the words in the same form as we found them. Nor, conversely, have we simply imposed our meaning on the text and claimed it was theirs. We have confronted the text and been confronted by it. It is in this confrontation that the importance of the Bible consists. We have to be ready in reading the text to have our pre-understanding and our traditions re-shaped. In this process of understanding God may reveal himself to us. That calls for a response.

11 A DIALOGUE WITH THE PAST

The problem of interpretation involves us in examining our attitudes to the past. We may disown it, attempt to transmit it unchanged, or seek to appropriate it. If we are to achieve honesty and authenticity we shall seek dialogue with it.

What is true of the interpretation of the Bible is also true of the doctrinal heritage. There is a past and there is a present. The old doctrine, if simply repeated in a new context, becomes stultified and otiose. 'Time makes ancient good uncouth.' Nor can we simply ignore or disown the traditions. That would be irresponsible. A heritage is living if it enters into present life and thought. It is meaningful as it has living importance and is not simply formal. A doctrine is formal if it does not have a vital and significant place in the life and thought of the community professing to hold it. Doctrines that were once living can become formal. We should be aware that what we inherit we need to assess critically.

> Interpretation then is a dialogue between past and present which allows both parties to have their say. The process of such a dialogue aims not only at the interpretation of the past on the part of the present, but also the interpretation of the present on the part of the past. The interpreter interprets the text, but only insofar as the text is permitted to interpret the interpreter and the interpreter's world. In order for these movements to occur, the distance between past and present must be recognized rather than abrogated by too hastily collapsing the past into the present (the danger of existential interpretation) or collapsing the present into the past (the danger of all varieties of orthodoxy). Perhaps the most important contribution to the recognition of this salutary distance between past and present is made by the methods of historical criticism.[21]

12 FORM AND CONTENT

To collapse the present into the past leads us to the illusion that we in fact believe what we do not believe. It leads us to overlook in the text those elements which need our best critical judgment. What then are necessary conditions for an adequate understanding of the New Testament?[22]

We believe that illness has natural causes. When we meet with cases of epilepsy, skin disease, stomach ailments, etc., we act on the well-grounded belief that some natural cause is responsible and that there are natural, i.e. non-supernatural, methods for treating such disorders. So we depend upon the findings of modern medical science and when in need consult the doctor and follow his advice. We do not believe that demons cause disease. We would have little idea what it would mean for a superhuman being to 'cause' sickness or death. We would have to speak of hormone deficiency, viruses, bacteria, etc. It is superfluous to speak of something over and above these.

But when we read the Gospels we are in a world in which the commonly accepted belief was that supernatural beings, demons, were the cause of illness and that a cure was effected by 'casting out demons.' So we have a problem of interpreting those passages which specifically and unequivocally state such matters. Our world is not peopled with supernatural beings in conflict with one another. To refer to such 'causes' provides for us no explanation of what happens in the world in which we live our lives. We cannot abandon our firmly established belief about cause and effect when we consider the literature of the Bible. To do so would involve us in holding contradictory beliefs at the same time. That would be a kind of self-deception, and self-deception can be communal! So how shall we understand the stories in which non-natural agencies, i.e. the divine or the demonic, angels or gods, feature as cause, either of sickness, health, victory or defeat in battle and in other spheres of history? Then how shall we understand the stories that assume a universe conceived with no understanding of its vastness or complexity, and a totally inadequate comprehension of the relative position of the earth and the relative motions of planets in the universe. How can we conceive ascension as a movement from earth to heaven 'above', God dwelling in the heavens, Second Advent as a coming back from 'above'?

The answer to our question is that we shall begin where they began, with the conviction that God has decisively revealed himself in Jesus Christ, and that this revelation represents a victory over evil, and sets in motion within human history forces which lead to human fulfilment. None other and none less than God is at work within the world with the coming of Jesus, and that revelation continues and is contemporary. Human beings for their part participate in the new life Jesus Christ has made possible. That is the great miracle: that all events of one's personal history, and of human history are given meaning by the change of understanding and the freedom which Jesus Christ has brought. Gospels then are witness, testimony to that event, as they portray Jesus as the man living for God and setting in motion in human history new forces and opening up new possibilities for us.

As the interpreter approaches this body of texts he does not have an empty head. There is no way of interpreting without having some ideas before approaching the text. There is no such thing as 'presuppositionless exegesis.'

The interpreter of the text must know the historical conditions of the text. He must also know the language[23] of the text he is interpreting and how that language is being used. That language is historically conditioned. For The New Testament this means knowing that the Greek of the New Testament is being used in a particular way. When for example, the New Testament used the word 'spirit,' the language is Greek (*pneuma*) but the background is Hebrew. One must ask about that Semitic background to arrive at a sympathetic understanding of this idea. To understand language one must understand culture and be alert to cultural differences.

The continuing task of systematic theology is, in part, to interpret earlier symbols. There is no one way of doing this. Different theologians will perform the task in different ways.[24] We interpret their symbols in our terms so as to make them meaningful for ourselves and our contemporary hearers. We shall not be satisfied with earlier frameworks since we discern them to be inadequate or distorting.

To take examples: Augustine's teaching about sin and Anselm's teaching about atonement are attempts to present the biblical understanding. But the assumptions they made when they approached and represented the biblical materials, the models which were important to them, are questionable for us. We have learned in the last century and a half a great deal about the social and psychological make-up of human beings. We must take into our account that between one person and another historical and social ties are quite basic. A person is what he is because of other persons who have gone before. To take this 'historicity of the human' seriously will lead us to re-express those older teachings, about original sin and about atonement for example. The language of demons and of the biological transmission of sin will not seem for us the appropriate way to talk of sin. Nor will the notion of the satisfaction of the aggrieved lord of the manor seem the right model for presenting the doctrine of atonement. Both are non-historical, and since we have come to think historically, neither of them is in harmony with some of our most deeply held convictions about what it means to be a person. It is the continuing task of the church to find acceptable ways of interpreting the central symbols of the Christian faith.

To take another example, this time from Paul. He, an erstwhile 'Pharisee of the Pharisees,' wrestled with the problem of how to express theologically the implications of his experience in Jesus Christ. He inherited the legal terminology of Judaism. But legal terminology is not the only way and not necessarily the best way of expressing the experience of the Christian.

But if we use the language of law outside the realm of law, outside the realm of the court, we are very likely to go astray. If we use legal concepts to portray personal experience we will, if we are not very careful, find ourselves in error. If we use the language of law about God's relation to man, we shall find we are up against its limits very quickly if we have not already gone on to a false path. How can we adequately speak of forgiveness in the language of law or of justice? 'Forgiveness of sins is not a juridical concept. It does not mean the remission of punishment. If that were so, man's plight would be as bad as ever. Rather, forgiveness conveys freedom from sin, which hitherto had held man in bondage.'[25] The experience of such freedom cannot be expressed adequately in legal terms. Such terms easily tend to distort.

We should therefore be concerned to replace any way of expression, however familiar, which represents a distortion of the meaning that lies behind the form. If you are going to distort the meaning of the experience of divine forgiveness by using legal terms, then the legal terms will have to be supplemented or replaced. The form must *now* be comprehensible, adequate. It must treat of the experience of the believer and represent it without distortion.

In both of the examples we have now considered, the expression of faith in Jesus Christ through the miracle stories of the Gospels and through the legal terminology of the Pauline literature, what comes to expression is a conviction, based upon experience, of the relationship between God and man, of man's situation before God.

The modern interpreter is able to understand the earlier expression because he has access to and awareness of the same reality which they did and which they were attempting to express. That is the act of faith which makes Christian theology possible. The God who revealed himself in Jesus Christ in the first century continues through Jesus Christ to reveal himself in the present. So the interpreter has a point of contact with what he is interpreting, a life-relation to the subject-matter. He can thus understand it and put the form in which it is expressed into its proper perspective.[26]

13 SUMMARY STATEMENT

Interpretation, in different instances, has different goals.

(1) The aim of the interpreter may be to discover what happened. He may, in pursuing this aim search for, discover, assess the value of various pieces of evidence

and various kinds of evidence. The process will involve making judgments both as to the value and as to the meaning of the evidence. Did it or did it not happen, at that time and in that way? Is this or is that the best available interpretation of what took place. Here the process of interpretation includes that of reconstruction. Sometimes the interpreter may be surer than at other times. Historical reconstruction is always relative.

(2) The aim of the interpreter may be to make the best possible judgment as to the most satisfactory text of a document. The word 'criticism' is roughly the same in meaning as 'interpretation' when it is used of the process by which the most probably correct reading is established. Such 'textual criticism' as is involved in making this kind of judgment can be a rather complex process.

(3) The aim of the interpreter may be to say what the writer meant by what he said or wrote.

(4) The aim of the interpreter may be to say what the word spoken or written in the past can now mean. He here is trying to bridge the gap between the past and the present. When he has provided his interpretation, he hopes that the old sayings or writings will come alive again. But then, as time passes and new understanding and fresh knowledge comes into being, his interpretations (if they are significant enough) will have in their turn to be interpreted. It is by this continuing chain of interpretation that the past continues to exercise an influence over the present and the gap is bridged. There must always be a 'new hermeneutic' to keep the past alive. There must be constant attempts at systematic statement of the meaning of faith.

In interpreting the Bible, the interpreter is dealing with words grammar, historical occasions, events and settings and limited understandings shaped by particular cultures in the past, very different approaches and presentations, even of theological understandings. It is literature of many kinds.

But we must go a step further. In interpreting the Bible the Christian interpreter is dealing with the revelation of God. The believer confesses that here one encounters the living God. Through these words God encounters him. He finds that God comes to him, speaks to him, becomes a reality in his experience. Hence the Bible is not simply a book to be studied as literature. What the Christian interpreter reckons with is that the reality of God has become known and is becoming known through Scripture. It is the same God known through Jesus Christ to those who in the New Testament witnessed to their faith. So the interpreter presupposes that the reality revealed to him is the same reality revealed to them. On that basis he has the fundamental prerequisite for the understanding of Scripture.

Chapter XI Notes

[1] Robert M. Grant, *A Short History of the Interpretation of the Bible,* p. 153.

[2] L. Stephenson, *Seven Theories of Human Nature.*

[3] II Peter 3:16.

[4] Langdon Gilkey, *Message and Existence,* p. 55.

[5] *Ibid.*

[6] *Ibid.,* p. 56.

[7] *Ibid.,* p. 57.

[8] Deuteronomy 25:4.

[9] I Corinthians 9:9-10.

[10] We have discussed this distinction above. See Chapter X: 1-3

[11] James Barr lists seven kinds of situation. They are as follows:

(a) explicit types, e.g. Moses and Christ.

(b) real allegory, e.g. the muzzled ox.

(c) paraenesis, e.g. Balaam, Sarah.

(d) fulfilment from prophecies cited.

(e) proofs from linguistic details, e.g. 'seeds.'

(f) situation similarities in style and language e.g. the Magnificat.

(g) situation similarities in action.

Cf. *Old and New in Interpretation,* p. 115.

[12] Matthew 5:22.

[13] Leviticus 18:22, 29; 20:13.

[14] Cf. especially Psalm 109. Should we, for example, dedicate this Psalm to those whose doctrine differs from ours?

[15] See I. 4 above.

[16] II Kings 9, 10.

[17] Song of Solomon 7:6-13.

[18] I Cor. 14:33-35.

[19] Leviticus 20:13.

[20] Van A. Harvey, *The Historian and the Believer,* p. 20.

[21] Theodore W. Jennings Jr., *Introduction to Theology,* pp. 127-128.

[22] This is the question to which Rudolf Bultmann returned over and over again. Cf. his essay, 'Is Exegesis without Presuppositions Possible?' in Bultmann, 1960, pp. 289-296 (written in 1957).

[23]Knowing the language in the case of the New Testament means having mastered Greek grammar and being sensitive to how the language is being used, being aware of style, for example.

[24]Kelsey's book is a survey of five different ways in which it has been done by writers in our century.

[25]Rudolf Bultmann, 'New Testament and Mythology,' in Bartsch, *Kerygma and Myth,* p. 32.

[26]For a more extended summary of these issues and related problems, see the excellent treatment in Van Harvey, *The Historian and the Believer.* Apropos the point made in our text, cf. pp. 24-33.

Index of Biblical Passages

Index of Names

BIBLIOGRAPHY

Althaus, Paul. *The Theology of Martin Luther.* Philadelphia: Fortress Press, 1966.

Anderson, Bernhard. *Understanding the Old Testament.* Englewood Cliffs, N.J.: Prentice Hall Inc., 1957.

Augustine. *On Christian Doctrine*, III, 22-23. Translated by D.W. Robertson, Jr., Indianopolis: Bobbs-Merrill, 1978.

Augustine. *Quaestiones Evangeliorum*, II. Quoted in Dodd, 1967. p. 13.

Baillie, John. *The Idea of Revelation in Recent Thought.* London: Oxford University Press. New York: Columbia University Press, 1956.

Baillie, John. *The Idea of Revelation in Recent Thought.* New York: Columbia Press/London: Oxford University Press, 1956.

Barnabas, The Epistle of in Lightfoot, J.B. *The Apostolic Fathers.* London: Macmillan and Co. 1883. pp. 405-482.

Barr, James. *Fundamentalism.* London: S.C.M. Press, 1977.

Barr, James. *Old and New in Interpretation.* London: S.C.M. Press, 1982.

Barth, Karl. *Church Dogmatics, I/2, II/2.* Edinburgh: T. & T. Clark. 1956, 1957.

Bartsch, Hans-Werner. (Translated and edited by H. W. Barker and R. Fuller). *Kerygma and Myth*, Vol. II, London: S. P. C.K., 1972.

Beckett, Samuel. *En Attendant Godot*, London: George Harrap and Co. Ltd., 1966.

Berger, Peter. *Invitation to Sociology.* Harmondsworth: Penguin Books, 1978.

Bonhoeffer, D. *The Cost of Discipleship.* London: SCM. Press, 1959.

Boyle, Patrick. 'Evidence for the Book', *Focus*, Vol. 1, No. 1, Grantham: Stanborough Press, no date (1981).

Braaten, Carl. *History and Hermeneutics*. Philadelphia: The Westminster Press, 1966.

Bultmann, Rudolf. 'New Testament and Mythology,' in Hans-Werner Bartsch, *Kerygma and Myth, Volume 1*. Translated by Reginald H. Fuller, London: S.P.C.K., 1972.

Bultmann, Rudolf. *Existence and Faith*. Edited by Schubert Ogden. New York, Living Age Books, 1960.

Buttrick, George Arthur. *The Interpreter's Dictionary of the Bible*, Article: 'Scripture, Authority of', Vol. IV, New York and Nashville: Abingdon Press, 1962.

Catholic Dictionary of Theology. (Edited by H. Francis Davis and others). London: Thomas Nelson and Son Ltd., 1962. Articles, 'Bible, Use of in Theology', 'Tradition.'

Chalmers, A.F. *What is This Thing Called Science?* Milton Keynes: The Open University Press, 1980.

Clogg, F. Bertram. *Introduction to the New Testament*. London: University of London Press, 1952.

Dodd, C.H. *The Authority of the Bible*. Glasgow: Collins, 1960.

Dodd, C.H. *The Epistle of Paul to the Romans*. London: Hodder and Stoughton, 1932.

Dodd, C.H. *The Parables of the Kingdom*. London and Glasgow: Collins, Fontana Books, 1967.

Donovan, Peter. *Religious Language*. London: Sheldon Press, 1976.

Driver, Tom. *Christ in a Changing World*. London: S. C. M. Press, 1981.

Dugmore, C. W. *The Interpretation of the Bible*, Dale, R. W. quoted in Albert Peel, *The Bible and The People*. London: S. P. C. K, 1944.

Ebeling, Gerhard. *The Word of God and Tradition* Translated by S. H. Hooke, Philadelphia: Fortress Press, 1968.

Edwards, Paul. (editor), T*he Encyclopaedia of Philosophy*, Vol. 1, New York: The Macmillan Company and The Free Press, 1967.

Evans, C. *Is Holy Scripture Christian?* London: S. C. M. Press, 1971.

Farmer, H. H. 'The Bible: Its Significance and Authority' in *The Interpreter's Bible*, Vol. I, New York and Nashville: Abingdon Press, 1952.

Fox, Adam. *Meet the Greek Testament*. London: S. C. M. Press, 1952.

Froom, Le Roy E. *The Prophetic Faith of Our Fathers*, 4 volumes, Washington: Review and Herald Publishing Association, 1946-64.

Geldenhuys, J. Nowal. 'Authority and the Bible' in Carl F. H. Henry (editor), *Revelation and the Bible*. Philadelphia: Presbyterian and Reformed Publishing Company, 1958.

Gilkey, Langdon. *Message and Existence*. New York: The Seabury Press, 1980.

Gowan Donald E., *Bridge Between the Testaments*. Pittsburgh: Pickwick Press, 1980.

Grant, Robert M. *A Short History of the Interpretation of the Bible*. London: Adam and Charles Black, 1965.

Hanson, R. P. C. 'Tradition,' in Alan Richardson, *Dictionary of Christian Theology*. London: S. C. M. Press, 1969. pp. 341-343.

Harvey, Van A. *The Historian and the Believer*. New York: The Macmillan Company, 1966.

Heaton, E. W. *The Old Testament Prophets*. Harmondsworth: Penguin Books, 1969.

Hick, John. *Philosophy of Religion*. New Jersey: Prentice-Hall Inc., 1973.

Jennings Jr., Theodore. *Introduction to Theology* London: S. P. C. K., 1977.

Jeremias, Joachim. *Rediscovering the Parables*, London: S.C.M. Press, 1966.

Jowett, Benjamin. 'On the Interpretation of Scripture,' in *Essays and Reviews*, Seventh Edition, London: Longman Green, Longman and Roberts, 1861.

Kähler, Martin. *The So-called Historical Jesus and the Historic Biblical Christ*. Philadelphia: Fortress Press, 1964. (Original German edition 1896).

Kaufman, Gordon. *Systematic Theology: A Historicist Perspective*. Norfolk: Scribners, 1968.

Kelsey, David H. *The Uses of Scripture in Recent Theology.* London: S. C. M. Press, 1975.

Küng, Hans. *Infallible.* Translated by Eric Mosbacher. Glasgow: Collins, 1971.

Montague, W. P. *The Ways of Knowing.* London: George Allen and Unwin, New York: The Macmillan Company, 1925.

New Catholic Encyclopaedia, Vol. 14. Editorial Staff, Catholic University of America. New York and London: McGraw Hill Book Company, 1967. Article, 'Tradition (in Theology).'

Niebuhr, H. Richard. *The Meaning of Revelation,* New York: The Macmillan Company, 1960.

Origen, (*De Principiis*) *On First Principles.* Edited by G. W. Butterworth. London: S. P. C. K. 1936. New York: Harper and Row, 1966. *The Ante-Nicene Fathers,* Vol. IV. Grand Rapids: Eerdmans, 1956

Plato, *Timaeus* in *The Dialogues of Plato.* Volume two. Translated by B. Jowett. New York: Random House, 1937.

Rahner, Karl. *Theological Investigations, Vol.I.* Translated by Cornelius Ernst. Baltimore: Helicon Press, 1963.

Reid, J. K. S. *The Authority of Scripture.* London: Methuen, 1962.

Richardson, Alan. (Editor). *A Dictionary of Christian Theology.* London: S. C. M. Press, 1969.

Richardson, Alan. *An Introduction to the Theology of the New Testament.* London: S. C. M. Press, 1958,

Richardson, Alan. *Christian Apologetics.* London: S. C. M. Press, 1948.

Richardson, Alan. *The Bible in the Age of Science.* London: S. C. M. Press, 1968.

Robinson, H. Wheeler. *Corporate Personality in Ancient Israel.* Philadelphia: Fortress Press, 1964.

Ryle, Gilbert. *The Concept of Mind.* London: Hutchinson, 1949.

Schweitzer, A. *The Quest of the Historical Jesus.* Translated by W. Montgomery. New York: The Macmillan Company, 1964.

Smith, John E. *Experience and God.* New York: Oxford University Press, 1968.

Stacey, David. *Interpreting the Bible.* London: Sheldon Press, 1976.

Stevenson, J. *A New Eusebius.* London: S. P. C. K. 1982.

Stevenson, L. *Seven Theories of Human Nature.* Oxford: Oxford University Press, 1974.

Strauss, D. F. *The Life of Jesus Critically Considered.* Translated by George Eliot, Edited by Peter C. Hodgson, London: S. C. M. Press, 1973; Philadelphia: Fortress Press, 1972.

Tertullian, *On the Soldier's Crown* in J. Stephenson, *A New Eusebius.* pp. 182-3.

Thompson. Kenneth and Tunstall, Jeremy. (Editors). *Sociological Perspectives.* Middlesex: Penguin, 1979.

Trigg, Roger. *Reason and Commitment,* Cambridge: Cambridge University Press, 1973.

Vawter, Bruce. *Biblical Inspiration.* London: Hutchinson, 1972.

Vick, Edward W. H. *Speaking Well of God.* Nashville: Southern Publishing Association, 1979.

Vick, Edward W. H. *Jesus, the Man.* Nashville: Southern Publishing Association, 1979.

Vick, Edward W. H. *History and Christian Faith.* Nottingham: Evening Publications, 2003.

Vick, Edward W. H. *Quest, An Exploration of Some Problems in Science and Religion.* London: Epworth Press, 1975.

Von Rad, Gerhard, in Claus Westermann (ed.). English Translation by James Luther Mays. *Essays on Old Testament Interpretation.* London: S. C. M. Press, 1963. Richmond: 1963.

Vriezen, Th. C. *An Outline of Old Testament Theology.* Massachusetts: Charles T. Branford Company, 1960.

Warfield, B.B. *The Inspiration and Authority of the Bible.* Philadelphia: The Presbyterian and Reformed Publishing Co., 1948.

Wiles, Maurice, in J. Hick (editor), *The Myth of God Incarnate.* London: S. C. M. Press. 1977.

Wiles, Maurice. *The Remaking of Christian Doctrine.* London: S. C. M. Press, 1974.

Wilken, Robert L. *The Myth of Christian Beginnings.* London: S. C. M. Press, 1979.

Wright, G. Ernest. *God Who Acts.* London: S. C. M. Press, 1958.

On Christian Faith

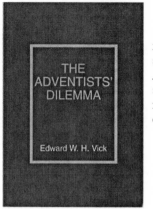

Edward W H. Vick's new monograph, *The Adventists' Dilemma*, should be required reading for any Adventist who wishes to examine seriously her or his intellectual and religious heritage relating to questions of the Second Advent.

— Michael Zbaraschuk
Spectrum Magazine

Vick gives us license to act as historians, encourages us to embrace today's scientific age, and helps us step out on a journey of discovery to verify our faith.

— Lee Harmon
The Dubious Disciple

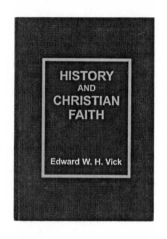

Reading Weiss was a prophetic touch to my own life at the moment.

— Joel Watts, *Unsettled Christianity*

More from Energion Publications

Personal Study

The Jesus Paradigm	$17.99
Finding My Way in Christianity	$16.99
When People Speak for God	$17.99
Holy Smoke, Unholy Fire	$14.99
Not Ashamed of the Gospel	$12.99
Evidence for the Bible	$16.99
Christianity and Secularism	$16.99
What's In A Version?	$12.99
The Messiah and His Kingdom to Come	$19.99 (B&W)

Christian Living

52 Weeks of Ordinary People – Extraordinary God	$7.99
Daily Devotions of Ordinary People – Extraordinary God	$19.99
Directed Paths	$7.99
Grief: Finding the Candle of Light	$8.99
I Want to Pray	$7.99
Soup Kitchen for the Soul	$12.99

Bible Study

Learning and Living Scripture	$12.99
To the Hebrews: A Participatory Study Guide	$9.99
Revelation: A Participatory Study Guide	$9.99
The Gospel According to St. Luke: A Participatory Study Guide	$8.99
Identifying Your Gifts and Service: Small Group Edition	$12.99
Why Four Gospels?	$11.99
Philippians: A Participatory Study Guide	$9.99
Ephesians: A Participatory Study Guide	$9.99

Theology

Christian Archy	$9.99
God's Desire for the Nations	$18.99
Ultimate Allegiance	$9.99
History and Christian Faith	$9.99
The Adventists' Dilemma	$14.99

Generous Quantity Discounts Available
Dealer Inquiries Welcome
Energion Publications — P.O. Box 841
Gonzalez, FL 32560
Website: http://energionpubs.com
Phone: (850) 525-3916

CPSIA information can be obtained
at www.ICGtesting.com
Printed in the USA
FFOW04n0805050217
31966FF